C000147687

Rob Smyth has written for
Life, *GQ Style*, *Sports Illus*
United magazine. He has w
commended at the 2009 Spo

Scott Murray has written for the *Guardian*, the *Observer*, the *Evening Standard*, *GQ*, the *Blizzard*, *FourFourTwo* and *Men's Health*. He was sports editor of the website formerly known as Guardian Unlimited, and is co-author of *Phantom of the Open*, a good book about bad golf, and *The Anatomy of Liverpool*.

And Gazza Misses the Final

Rob Smyth and Scott Murray

Constable • London

Constable & Robinson Ltd
55–56 Russell Square
London WC1B 4HP
www.constablerobinson.com

First published in the UK by Constable,
an imprint of Constable & Robinson Ltd, 2014

ISBN: 978-1-47211-103-6 (paperback)
ISBN: 978-1-47211-106-7 (ebook)

Printed and bound in the UK

1 3 5 7 9 10 8 6 4 2

Contents

Preamble

It's a scary realization for anyone who still thinks the internet is a wild new frontier, but the *Guardian* started publishing their groundbreaking live minute-by-minute football match reports during the 1998 World Cup. Sixteen years ago! Count 'em! Sixteen! That's time for five World Cups! Oh my. It's not good news, is it?

That was before the paper even had a news website – superannuated superhighway surfers may or may not recall the sports site football.guardian, part of a sprawling network that also included Guardian favourite 'Notes & Queries' and not very much in between – and sadly all of the reports from back then have, as far as we're aware, been lost to the ether. Probably no bad thing, on balance, as the medium was in its infancy and we were learning on the job. Our report of the first-round match between Scotland and Norway, for example, mainly concentrated on the ludicrous icebergs of Vaseline precariously balanced on perma-worried Scottish goalkeeper Jim Leighton's furrowed eyebrows, and is almost certainly not the witty, Seinfeldesque celebration of minutiae it was intended to be. Meanwhile, we're genuinely not sure whether anyone bothered covering the final. Don't worry, we did get a little bit better in time, honest.

But the format went on to work well at Guardian Unlimited and latterly guardian.com over the years, taking regular snapshots of big matches as they developed, priceless evidence of how things looked before goals, red cards, fistfights, rogue beachballs and countless other incidents occurred to blur the analysis. Even a match report hurriedly filed on the final whistle is viewed through the filter of the result. Turning points in the main narrative are retrospectively ascertained, and incidents that don't quite fit in are quietly ignored. (Sir Alex Ferguson loved to goad the press about the reports they had written and were ready to file at the 1999 Champions League final, before Manchester United scored two goals in injury time and hastened some wholesale rewrites.)

The great strength of live minute-by-minute reporting, by its very definition, is that no retrospective weighting can ever be applied. Things happen that may or may not prove vital, but they are what they are. It's the most honest appreciation of a match you're ever going to get. Nobody ever goes back to rewrite a live report.

So we thought: what if we applied the same process to some of the greatest games in the history of football's greatest tournament? And here we are. How unlucky were England in the 1990 semis? Did Antonio Rattin deserve to get sent off at Wembley in 1966? Just how good was that game between Italy and Brazil in 1982, exactly? And should Brazil have been so surprised that Uruguay wrested the cup from their grasp in 1950? All the answers are here.

Of course, you'll have spotted one flaw in our plan: we already know what happened. We know the final score. Well, yes. But you'll just have to trust us on this one. Sure, you'll spot a few occasions when we've used some artistic licence – we couldn't help ourselves – but the conceit remains consistent. The preambles relate to the general mood before the match, all references are contemporary, and most importantly we describe things as they occur, telling the story as it unfolds, not relaying it backwards.

The videos showed many moments we had completely forgotten or not recognized in the first place. David Platt's disallowed goal that would have put England in the 1990 final; Harald Schumacher looking for trouble with a number of France players – and even their fans – before his assault on Patrick Battiston in 1982; Brazil's legendary 1970 side mixing some of the greatest football ever seen with some of the worst during the final against Italy. You'll be surprised at the way some of these old stories will seem very new.

A caveat. A couple of matches no longer exist in their entirety. If you have your own copy on Super 8, and a good stopwatch, you might be able to prove that, though we've tried our damnedest not to be, we're a minute out here, 59 seconds off there, have mis-identified the odd player's shirt on a fuzzy film. But we've bent over backwards in the pursuit of accuracy, to ensure nothing warps the overall narrative of the matches, which we present for your leisure and pleasure, minute by minute, as they happened, unencumbered by received wisdom or retrospective thinking. And anyway, the bottom line is, it's supposed to be a bit of fun. We hope you enjoy reading it as much as we enjoyed writing it. In fact, we hope you enjoy it more: we've been bent forward squinting at television sets in darkened rooms for months and our backs are killing us.

It's just like being there at the time. Sort of. If you suspend a little disbelief and let your mind wander. A bit like following games live on the internet, really.

Brazil v Uruguay

Final Pool, Estádio do Maracanã, Rio de Janeiro, Brazil,
Sunday, 16 July 1950

**Take a quick look at the early edition of today's *O Mundo*
newspaper, and it would seem there can only be one winner of
the 1950 World Cup.** Above a photograph of Brazil's *seleção*,
the national team heroes resplendent in their crisp white shirts,
runs a headline: *'Estes sao os Campeoes do Mundo!'* These are
the champions of the world!

**A presumptuous claim? Perhaps. But the form book makes a
pretty good case for jumping the gun.** Flavio Costa's team have
really grown into this World Cup. They weren't wholly convincing
in the group stage: conceding a late equalizer against Switzerland
meant they needed to beat a dangerous Yugoslavian side to
qualify for the Final Pool, and after the game the police were
forced to intervene when several members of the crowd moved
to take their frustrations out on Costa. But beat Yugoslavia they
did, even though they might have struggled to get a result had
opposing captain Rajko Mitić not missed the start after cracking
his head open on an exposed girder in the newly built Maracanã.
(Brazil took a third-minute lead against ten men, one they would
not relinquish.)

Since then, though, Brazil have put on a masterclass. They're
the bosses of this Final Pool, the four-team mini-league
that will decide the winners of the 1950 World Cup. Their
free-flowing front line of Jair, Zizinho, Ademir and Chico
has interchanged two of the best teams in the world to death:
Sweden were beaten 7–1, then Spain were tonked 6–1. Now only
Uruguay are left. Uruguay, who were effectively given a bye
in the group stage of this lopsided tournament, only needing
to beat minnows Bolivia (which they did 8–0). Uruguay, who
required a late goal against Spain to draw their first Final Pool
game 2–2, then needed two late goals to turn looming defeat
against Sweden into a 3–2 win. Uruguay, who Brazil beat 5–1
in Rio last year in the Copa America. And a draw today will
be enough for Brazil.

But it's a form book, not a form pamphlet, and there's another page to read. For Uruguay are no mugs. Their XI includes three of the best players in the world: the crafty inside forward Juan Alberto Schiaffino, the willowy winger Alcides Ghiggia and the supremely dominant box-to-box pitch-owning midfielder Obdulio Varela. All three play for Peñarol, who last year scored an average of 4.5 goals per league game. Uruguay have played Brazil three times since the aforementioned 5–1 Copa America thrashing last year, winning the first game 4–3 and narrowly losing the two others. And the way Brazil ended that 1949 Copa America bears repeating: they only needed a draw against Paraguay in their final game to finish top of the tournament league, but lost 2–1 and fell into a play-off against the same opposition. A match they admittedly went on to win 7–0, but last-minute nerves are last-minute nerves, whichever way you slice it, and it would appear Brazil are not immune.

Nevertheless, Brazil are hot favourites to lift their first World Cup this afternoon. Especially as the home crowd, usually worth an extra man, is probably going to be worth an extra two or three today. Just look at the official attendance: 173,850!

And now take a gander at the *unofficial* attendance, because a fair few Rio residents appear to have bunked in to witness history being made: 205,000 to 210,000.

Uruguayans in the audience: approx 100.

All these folk should give priceless support to Brazil. The stadium has been packed since 11 a.m. and is alive with a carnival atmosphere involving balloons, bangers and the beats of Bahia. The house band, we hear, have been rehearsing a specially commissioned samba entitled 'Brazil the Victors', which they plan to strike up on the sounding of the final whistle. And the mayor of Rio has done his bit to whip up the crowd, too: 'You, players, who in less than a few hours will be hailed as champions by millions of compatriots! You, who have no rivals in the entire hemisphere! You, who will overcome any other competitor! You, who I already salute as victors!' Blimey. No pressure, then.

Kick-off: 2.55 p.m.

Referee: George Reader (England).

Thirteen-goals-in-their-last-two-games Brazil: Barbosa, Augusto, Juvenal, Bauer, Danilo, Bigode, Friaça, Zizinho, Ademir, Jair, Chico.

Uruguay, featuring teenage debutant(!) Morán: Roque Máspoli, Matías González, Eusebio Tejera, Schubert Gambetta, Obdulio Varela, Victor Rodríguez Andrade, Alcides Ghiggia, Julio Pérez, Omar Míguez, Juan Albertio Schiaffino, Ruben Morán.

Here come the teams! There are fireworks, then more fireworks. The crowd rhythmically chant 'BRASIL! BRASIL! BRASIL!', but then they've been doing that for nigh on four hours. This is on!

And we're off, Ademir getting the match under way with a tap to Jair! And Brazil make a blistering start. The ball's knocked back to Bauer, who rolls it up the right for Zizinho. Brazil's intricate interplay is showcased from the off. Zizinho draws Schiaffino and nips the ball past him to Ademir, who attempts to return it. González intercepts, but he's hassled by Zizinho and Rodríguez Andrade is forced to get involved. He gets a toe in and concedes an early corner. Friaça takes, firing the ball straight through the area. Gambetta sweeps up, but loses possession to Chico, who nearly jinks past Gambetta down the left but loses control and runs the ball out for a goal-kick. And breathe!

2 min: Brazil could easily have racked up double figures against Sweden and especially Spain, and it looks like they're going to take up where they left off. The crowd are going bonkers; the screaming and chanting is so loud and incessant it's a wonder the walls of the Maracanã aren't caving in. Especially when you recall how the 21-gun salute at the opening ceremony three weeks ago caused lumps of still-moist concrete to rain down from the ceilings.

4 min: Varela clatters into Chico just outside the Uruguayan D. Free-kick. Jair takes it, but sends it out of play on the left. Uruguay have hardly had a kick so far.

6 min: Ghiggia has a first look at Bigode down the right. He attempts to feint past him but is held up. He tries again on the outside, but once more is stopped in his tracks. It's all a bit rough-house and the referee has a quick word with Bigode, who has been testing the limits of the laws as he tries to pin the tricky winger down. From the restart, a mistimed Bauer header gifts

Morán his first touch in this match, and indeed in international football! He shuttles it on to Varela. The Uruguayan captain, leading from the front, has his team's first serious dig at goal from the edge of the box, but Bauer mops up his own mess by charging it down.

10 min: Danilo tries to set Zizinho flying upfield but his pass from defence is cut out by Varela, who rolls the ball forward to Míguez. The striker has space to advance on the Brazilian area. Bigode comes across to cover, but he's brushed aside by Míguez. However the Uruguayan knocks the ball too far forward and the resulting shot, on the stretch, is weak and straight at Barbosa. Brazil lose possession quickly as they attempt to stream down the other end, allowing Míguez to take another lash at goal. This time it's a violent dig, and Barbosa makes a spectacular catch. A brilliant save from a goalkeeper who looks sharp despite having had little to do in the Final Pool so far.

13 min: Ademir goes on a diagonal run into the area, straightens up, and shoots. Máspoli, at full stretch, claims spectacularly.

15 min: Bauer fouls Schiaffino – there's a free-kick out on the left. Morán takes. Míguez heads down for Ghiggia, who finds Schiaffino, but the Peñarol star can only stab a shot from close range wide right. What a missed opportunity! For the first time in the match, the volume in the Maracanã takes a momentary dip, sudden sullen silence replaced by a collective sharp intake of breath.

16 min: Brazil respond brilliantly. First Friaça forces Máspoli into a split-second reaction save, then Ademir clatters the ball straight into González.

17 min: This is relentless! Varela tries to clear Uruguay's lines, but Zizinho and Jair one-two back down the pitch to set up Friaça, whose shot is blocked by Rodríguez Andrade. Pérez and Gambetta combine to hack the thing clear. Then Bauer romps down the right and welts a shot over the bar.

21 min: Uruguay looked to have calmed the storm for a couple of minutes, but Brazil spring back to life, nearly taking the lead. Jair heads down the left and draws Varela across. He combines with Chico, who digs out a cross that's met by a thumping header from Ademir. The crowd are already celebrating when Máspoli arcs his back and tips over the bar for a corner. From the resulting setpiece there's a minor stramash in the box, but neither Ademir nor Bauer can guide it goalwards and Schiaffino clears.

25 min: Pérez tries to relieve the intensity for Uruguay by launching an attack, but he's divested of the ball by Bigode, who finds Jair. Ademir takes up possession in the middle of the park and drifts to the right, skipping past González and then Tejera. He passes to Chico who cracks a rising shot that shaves the crossbar. After a fairly balanced opening period, this is total Brazilian domination now! A goal for the home side seems inevitable.

27 min: Obdulio is being obdurate. First he charges down a shot from Danilo, then he cuts out a pass from the same player meant for Jair. Uruguay are able to zip upfield through Schiaffino, who slips a ball past Augusto to release the debutant Morán into the area! He's one on one with Barbosa, who tries to smother at his feet but can't get down quickly enough. The goal's gaping, but Morán puts the ball over the bar! What an opportunity to open the scoring, the second major miss for the visitors despite all the pressure they've had to soak up. The crowd are audibly taken aback by that.

28 min: O TAPA DE OBDULIO!!! URUGUAY'S CAPTAIN THROWS HANDS!!! Bigode has been tussling with Ghiggia down the right, and struggling to contain him, it has to be said. He's nudging the willowy winger in the back. Varela and Jair join in the tussle as the ball flies out for a throw. Varela takes a step towards Bigode and reaches to pat his opponent on the head, as he often does in matches. This time, however, he gives Bigode a little cuff round the ear! Bigode – the literal translation is Moustache – bristles at this. He's shaken at Varela's slap, as are the crowd. The referee demands the two players embrace, which they reluctantly do. Varela struts off talking loudly to himself, pulling at the front of his light-blue shirt with his fist, every inch the victor of that little spat. You sense he thinks he's put down some sort of marker and that the defender won't be so quick to foul Ghiggia again. Imagine being in Bigode's boots just there, with Varela – a man with biblical willpower and a face made of granite – approaching you, arm cocked, ready to clip you round the lug. Imagine the chill that would shoot down your spine.

29 min: Schiaffino and Danilo scrap and wrestle for the ball in the middle of the park. The decision's given to the home team. Varela arrives on the scene and throws the ball away, with words for both referee and the nearby Bigode, who appears to be the target of precision psychological terrorism. Varela's given a stern talking-to by English ref George Reader for his trouble.

32 min: Pérez slides a pass out right to Ghiggia, who takes on Bigode and Danilo at the same time. Bigode handles in a panic. The linesman raises his flag. Free-kick! Gambetta launches the ball into the area. Barbosa punches clear. Uruguay are knocking on the door again, a polite but firm rattle, but Brazil are looking strong enough to cope.

• • • •MAGIC MINUTES • • • • • • • •MAGIC MINUTES • • • • •

USA 1–0 England (1950, group stage)

England had finally deigned to enter a World Cup, after declining invitations to all three pre-war events. They were expected to challenge for the title, but were astonishingly lackadaisical in their preparation, only turning up in Brazil two days before their first game, and without Stanley Matthews for the first two matches to boot. They beat Chile in that opener, but things started to go badly wrong in Belo Horizonte against the unfancied Americans. One London newspaper thought the result was a misprint, and published the score as 10–1 to England. Oops! Walter Winterbottom's men were able to put him right when they were back home within the week after another defeat, this time by Spain.

GOAL!!! USA 1–0 England (Gaetjens 38). Walter Bahr is sent into space down the right, and he decides to take a potshot from 25 yards. The shot isn't accurate but turns into a cross, which is met by the diving Joe Gaetjens, who guides a header into the bottom corner past Bert Williams of Wolverhampton Wanderers! The Yanks turned up to the stadium wearing Stetsons and sucking on cigars in cowboy style, and if they can hold on to this shocking scoreline, they'll be even more big leggy when they leave it later!

34 min: Comic cuts in the Brazilian defence. For once Bigode isn't at fault; in fact he does well to stop Ghiggia down his wing. But the ball eventually finds its way into the area. Bauer hesitates when putting his foot through the ball to clear would be the wiser option. Schiaffino nips in to try to take advantage. He lays off to Míguez, but Bigode blocks, and the striker handles. The referee blows for handball, relieving the pressure on Brazil.

37 min: URUGUAY HIT THE POST! González, playing out from the back, sends Varela on his way. He rakes a pass out to Schiaffino on the left, although it's not particularly accurate and should be cleared up by Bauer. But the defender only succeeds in presenting possession to Míguez, who was sniffing around in an opportunistic capacity. The Uruguay forward takes aim from just outside the area – and sends a low shot pinging off the left-hand upright, over the desperate hand of Barbosa! Bigode is quickly on the scene to hack the rebound out of harm's way.

38 min: A glorious solo sashay by Danilo down the left culminates in a disappointing shot from the edge of the area, which Máspoli deals with easily.

39 min: Juvenal launches long in the direction of Zizinho, who presses forward. He slows, practically to a halt, as he waits for assistance. Eventually Ademir arrives and tears into the box at pace, but his control lets him down. Máspoli comes off his line to smother.

41 min: This is glorious end-to-end stuff. Gambetta slips Ghiggia away down the right, but his route inside is blocked by Bauer, who sprays the ball up the Brazilian inside-right channel for Zizinho. A pass forward for Ademir, who dances past Tejera, exchanges a one-two with Zizinho, and enters the box. He sees the whites of Máspoli's eyes, but snatches at his shot and drags the ball wide. What an opportunity spurned!

42 min: Ademir is afforded an instant opportunity to redeem himself – and he wastes it. Brazil turn on the style, Zizinho, Friaça, Bauer and Ademir triangulating down the right. Bauer finds Ademir on the edge of the box and the ball's soon whistling wide right of the target. The crowd respond with a lusty rasp of 'Brasil! Brasil! Brasil!' They'll be wondering how they haven't scored. That was their 17th attempt at goal!

43 min: Varela really needs to simmer down. Here's the good and the bad of Uruguay's combustible captain. First he battles with Jair, wresting possession from the Brazilian and setting Ghiggia into space down the right. The winger slips the ball to Pérez, but just as the pair look like unlocking Brazil down the flank, Danilo bombs across and blasts the ball into touch. Ghiggia shapes to take the throw, but Varela stomps across with a face on and demands the ball. He's complaining about the stern nature of Danilo's challenge. Now he's complaining because his team-mates spurned a good opportunity, so he's going to show them how to take a throw. He snatches the ball from Ghiggia's hands – and flings it straight down the line and out of play for a goal-kick to Brazil! After giving his charges what for, he looks a total eejit right now. Dear me.

44 min: Zizinho is teasing Tejera. He stops the ball, allows the defender to move in, then swerves past and away. The move peters out, but this isn't the first time the Uruguayan defender has been made to look like a child lost at the shops. Could this be the defining head-to-head challenge of the game?

HALF TIME: Brazil 0–0 Uruguay. And that's pretty much that for the opening 45 minutes. Nobody expected Uruguay to come here and roll over, but then nobody thought Brazil would still be goalless by this stage. Whether Uruguay's defence, solid as it has been, marshalled well by the whirlwind Varela, can hold out if Brazil take another 17 potshots at goal is a moot point. Though Brazil might want to watch what Ghiggia is up to against Bigode, who is having a nightmare, while Juvenal and Jair are doing little to help him down his flank.

And we're off again! Uruguay get the ball rolling, but it's not long before they've given up possession, allowing Zizinho to trundle towards the area with determination. His shot is dealt with fairly comfortably by Máspoli. It's another strong start by the hosts.

47 min: GOAL!!! Brazil 1–0 Uruguay (Friaça). Finally the breakthrough, and it's such a simple move. Zizinho, in the middle of the park, lays off to Ademir, who spots Friaça making a move down the inside right and sets him free with a clever reverse ball. Friaça holds off the challenge of Rodríguez Andrade, steps into the area and sends a low shot into the bottom-left corner. It's not a particularly stunning strike – the ball's bobbling about, and Máspoli should really have got a hand to the shot as it crossed his body – but it's enough to send the Maracanã into orbit. Brazil only need the draw, remember, so they're nearly there. What a time for Friaça to score his first goal for his country!

48 min: Varela is holding up the restart by arguing vociferously with referee Reader and linesman Arthur Ellis. He clearly wanted an offside flag. Or is he just playing for time, allowing the stadium to cool down a little before the game begins again? If so, it's a clever plan, for indeed a little heat has been taken out of the air as the initial crackle of the 200,000-strong celebration dies down a little. Only a little, mind; these things are all relative. The Maracanã is *bouncing*. Varela turns to Rodríguez Andrade and mouths: 'Let them shout. In five minutes the stadium will seem like a graveyard and then only one voice will be heard here: mine!!!'

49 min: Will this open the floodgates? Are Uruguay – who need to score at least twice if they're to snatch Brazil's destiny from their hands – about to go the way of Sweden and Spain? They have, up to now, played a predominantly defensive game, getting plenty of bodies in the way at the back. Now they have to come out. On the touchline, Brazil coach Flavio Costa is issuing new instructions. 'Tell Danilo to stick a bit more around the intermediate area between the centre and our box. Let's try to attract Uruguay to our half, neutralize the support Varela is giving from behind, and open up more space in their defence!' Let's see if this works, then. Varela's team-mates respond well to falling behind, or start their descent into Brazil's trap, you decide: Pérez bests Jair down the right, then finds Schiaffino in the middle, who shoots wide left of goal.

51 min: Ghiggia runs at Bigode, who with the help of Juvenal launches a pincer movement on the winger. Foul. Varela overhits the free-kick while looking for Schiaffino at the far post.

55 min: This is a decent response by the Uruguayans. Ghiggia comes off second best in a duel with Bigode for once, but his colleagues are backing him up and the attack moves into another phase. Space opens up for Míguez but his shot is hoicked well wide right of the target, sailing symbolically into a ditch behind the goal.

57 min: Despite Uruguay pushing forward with serious intent for the first time in the match, Brazil are still looking fairly comfortable and clearly fancy themselves for more goals. Ademir launches a shot out of play, then Danilo sees his long-distance strike charged down by the unyielding frame of Varela.

61 min: PENALTY SHOUT BY BRAZIL!!! They're not getting it, though. Ademir advances into the area as the noise reaches fever pitch. González comes over to challenge and knocks him down, but it's a legitimate charge, just about. One white-shirted chancer moves to place the ball, which had flown behind the goal, on the penalty spot; the referee Reader simply guffaws at his cheek. Just a corner, from which nothing happens. To be fair, that was the correct decision, even Brazilian radio commentator César Alencar agreeing that 'the play was lawful, but of great violence. Actually, shall we say that the Uruguayan defence, as soon as the Brazilian players get inside the box, are unquestionably rough. We have witnessed, from our observation position here, some moments that are not part of football. Varela has been using all possible measures against Ademir! This Uruguayan defence is incredibly tough!'

63 min: Gambetta fouls Chico on the edge of the area. Jair shoots wildly over, a directionless nonsense.

66 min: GOAL!!! Brazil 1–1 Uruguay (Schiaffino). Varela gives the ball to Ghiggia on the right. The winger has Bigode on a piece of string. He wanders inside, pauses, then ambles back to the touchline, pausing again, Bigode just about keeping up. Then he turns on the power to sashay at speed past the defender, who reacts slowly and dangles a heavy leg on the outside. Bye! That is sensational wingplay. Ghiggia crosses to the near post where Schiaffino, nipping in ahead of Juvenal, roofs a finish into the right-hand side of the net! My word, this changes the picture. As things stand, Brazil will still become world champions for the first time ever in 25 minutes. But suddenly something that looked certain is in the balance again. Losing, for the first time, appears a possibility. The crowd haven't fallen silent, but all of a sudden they are pretty damn quiet, 200,000 men and women asking themselves: how has it come to this? Varela, meanwhile, is in the centre circle once again pulling the front of his shirt with his fist, screaming to his team-mates: one last push. Suddenly, Uruguay believe they can win this! There's also a box-fresh understanding that Brazil can lose, with clear beads of cold sweat appearing on the foreheads and necks of a couple of the Brazilian players.

69 min: And maybe Brazil are starting to question themselves. Passes aren't sticking. Only now are the crowd beginning to rediscover their voice, an illustration of the shock of Schiaffino's intervention. Approximately 200,011 souls are in torment.

70 min: Corner to Uruguay, their first of the match! Nothing much happens as a result, but does that suggest a shift in momentum? The Brazilian defence certainly looks tense. Are they simply not used to this kind of pressure? They're usually a few goals to the good by this stage, after all.

71 min: Ghiggia is all over Bigode, as he has been most of the afternoon. He once again dances past his man, and whips a ball into the area for Schiaffino, whose downward header flies out of play.

75 min: Ghiggia beats Bigode yet again. This is getting old – and so is Bigode, 48, who has aged exactly 20 years since kick-off. Ghiggia's cross is headed down by Schiaffino to Morán, but Augusto is on hand to clear.

76 min: Schiaffino is causing Brazil all sorts of bother as Uruguay press for the goal that would make them immortal. He wins a corner down the left. Morán floats it in. Barbosa punches clear, albeit with no particular conviction. Varela tries to return the ball with extreme prejudice, but his effort hits his own man, Míguez.

79 min: GOL DO URUGUAY? GOL DO URUGUAY!!! Brazil 1–2 Uruguay (Ghiggia). Brazil press upfield, but the visitors hit them with a rapid counter-attack. And how! Danilo, searching for Jair ahead of him, loses the ball to Pérez, who immediately offloads to Míguez. Pérez receives the ball back, still in his own half, and fights off Jair's challenge. He one-twos with Ghiggia down the right, then returns the ball to the winger again, springing him clear of Bigode. Ghiggia drifts inside and reaches the area at full pelt. Barbosa should really come out to close him down. But with Schiaffino hovering in the middle, Juvenal leaving him as he heads over to deal with Ghiggia, the keeper clearly has the first goal in at least one of his two minds. Ghiggia spots his indecision and, with a flash of dust that suggests the universe is turning in on itself, sends a low right-footed shot bouncing towards the near post. Barbosa can't get down quickly enough, and though the keeper gets the faintest of touches, the ball bobbles under his grasping paw and into the net. There is almost total silence as Barbosa slowly picks himself up from the turf, wishing that cloud of dirt was a black hole into which he could be sucked, never to return. He can feel 400,000 eyes boring holes in him, though that was a catalogue of errors: there was no cover offered to the hapless Bigode, with Danilo caught upfield and Juvenal late to come across. The Uruguayans, cavorting in the centre circle, can be heard whooping, slapping and kissing from the stand. The World Cup is theirs now, unless Brazil score. And Brazil always score. Don't they?

79 min: The commentator on Radio Globo, Luiz Mendes, took leave of his senses when Ghiggia's goal went in. He entered into a conversation with himself, first stating 'Gol do Uruguay,' then asking himself 'Gol do Uruguay?' before responding with an affirmative but forlorn 'Gol do Uruguay.' From the almighty hush in the stadium, it's already clear that nobody in Brazil has seriously countenanced defeat. I wonder how many folk in Uruguay have seriously countenanced a Uruguayan victory? González looks as stunned by Ghiggia's strike as any of the Brazilians! Máspoli's had to give him a good shake to snap him back into focus!

80 min: But do Brazil have it in them to score? They've had 22 efforts on goal so far in this match, but have converted only one. Even worse, they've done nothing since Schiaffino equalized a quarter of an hour ago. The crowd, to their credit, recover immediately from Ghiggia's stunner to give their heroes as much support as they can muster, even if the cries now have an electric, hysterical edge. Soon, a little payback: the first Brazilian effort for 17 minutes comes courtesy of Jair, whose overly ambitious shot from nearly 40 yards (!) is blocked by Varela, surely the man of the match whatever happens now.

82 min: Another shot from Jair, romping into the area after good work by Zizinho and Chico down the left, but it whistles past the near post. Uruguay take the goal-kick, but the game is stopped as Ghiggia rolls around demanding urgent medical assistance. Referee and quack Dr Reader decides he's just malingering in order to waste time and restarts the game quickly. Good call, Doc! The embarrassed winger lifts himself up and gets on with it.

83 min: Chico is shoved over by Gambetta as they contest a high ball down the Brazilian left. Free-kick. The referee spends some time ensuring a reluctant Uruguayan wall of Gambetta and Schiaffino stays ten steps back. Jair whips the free-kick into the area. Chico meets it with a firm header, but it's straight at Máspoli. The keeper clears in an unnecessary rush. Zizinho quickly brings it back and crosses for Ademir, who hoicks wide from 12 yards.

85 min: Bigode challenges Varela, the ball clanking off the Uruguayan captain and out for a Brazil throw. Varela simply laughs in Bigode's face. Bauer shoots from distance, but Máspoli deals with it; he's clearly in one of those moods today. Brazil are throwing everything at Uruguay. There's nobody in Brazil's half apart from Barbosa! But despite the renewed pressure, this is beginning to look desperate. Ghiggia eventually relieves the burden on his defence with another run at Bigode. He shoots but his effort deflects off the defender and into the hands of Barbosa. The clock's ticking down at double speed for the hosts. Their faces betray the confusion of men who cannot fathom why something that always works suddenly isn't functioning.

86 min: Barbosa launches the ball upfield. Zizinho wins possession and feeds Ademir, who lays off to Chico on the edge of the D. He hammers a gorgeous rising shot towards the top right, but Máspoli tips round the post. Nothing comes from the corner, which sees Ademir send an aimless header out of play. The stadium announcer informs the crowd that Sweden have just beaten Spain 3–1 in the other match at Pacaembu in São Paulo. So the Spanish are bottom of the Final Pool, fourth at this World Cup, with Sweden finishing third. But can Brazil get the goal, and the draw, that would put them top?

88 min: Brazil are pinning Uruguay back, but with time a factor, panic is taking over in the final third. Friaça sends a cross into the box from the right, but neither Ademir nor Zizinho seem capable of getting the thing under control. Ademir eventually shoots, but it's a woeful effort that screws out of play on the left, out near the corner flag! That was sheer panic; he had time to take a touch and set himself, but snatched at an anxious right-foot volley instead. Brazil's heads are muddled. Zizinho has been heard to shout, 'I will dribble them all!' but this Uruguayan defence is simply too good. Rio's mayor really should have kept his trap shut.

90 min: Brazil, desperate Brazil, push Uruguay back into their own area for one last onslaught. Bigode launches the ball forward. Ademir finds Zizinho, who advances towards the area. He can't dribble them all, however: he loses control, allowing Schiaffino to clear upfield. Three Uruguayans are caught offside! This is going to come straight back at the visitors. What on earth are they all doing upfield?! From the centre circle, Juvenal restarts and returns the ball into the Uruguayan area. The immense Varela heads clear. Ademir picks up possession and feeds Friaça, but he is eased away by Gambetta. Augusto races down the right and finds Friaça. Brazil's goalscorer – who looked for 19 minutes like being today's conquering hero – falls to the ground before springing back up and forcing Gambetta to concede a corner. This is surely the last chance for Brazil to salvage their dream. Friaça sends the ball into the area . . .

90+1 min: . . . Jair goes up with Máspoli but can't get a head on it, even though he's leaning heavily on the keeper's right arm, surely a foul. The ball is loose at the left-hand post, but though Zizinho, Ademir and Danilo are close, the blue shirt of Gambetta is even closer, and as the referee blows his whistle the Uruguayan defender grabs the ball in celebration!

FULL TIME: Brazil 1–2 Uruguay. Ghiggia stares at his team-mate in slack-jawed shock, fearing a penalty has been conceded right at the death, while Rodríguez Andrade is screaming, 'What are you doing, you animal?!' But unlike Gambetta they simply aren't close enough to the ref to hear the whistle! It is indeed all over!!!

URUGUAY, VICTORS IN 1930, ARE ONCE AGAIN THE WORLD CHAMPIONS! Several of their team take turns to hug and kiss referee Reader! Perhaps they're doing so by way of apology for Varela's lip.

Several of the Brazilians, by comparison, are being helped from the pitch, limp and defeated, their energy sapped, in throes of agony. So certain were they of a win, their pain doesn't bear thinking about. FIFA bigwig Jules Rimet takes to the pitch with the trophy that bears his name – this honour was bestowed on him four years ago – but while there had been plans for a band to strike up the Brazilian national anthem and that samba 'Brazil the Victors', nobody considered that alternative arrangements should be made, just in case, like. As a result, the presentation ceremony is a complete farce. Several policemen escort Rimet on to the pitch, which is teeming with photographers, fans and journalists. Many of these folk, peelers included, are crying! Varela seeks out the FIFA president and is allowed briefly to get his hands on the trophy, but he's not permitted to raise it in front of a grieving Maracanã, and it's shoved back in its wooden box within seconds. The only concession to congratulation and celebration is a brief, firm handshake. Like Varela cares: he's out on the lash tonight, the king of Rio, the king of the world.

So this has been one of the great smash and grabs, though whether it should be such a surprise is a moot point: Uruguay are yet to lose a World Cup match, after all, and now have two triumphs on the FIFA roll of honour. Brazil, by comparison, have nothing. Someone better rework the lyrics of that samba quicksmart. Will Brazil ever get over this?

The 1930s

France 4–1 Mexico (1930, group stage)

This game, at Montevideo's Pocitos stadium, and the USA and Belgium match kicking off at the same time across the Uruguayan capital at Parque Central, were the World Cup's first-ever matches. Here's the first-ever goal, scored by Lucien Laurent, whose day job involved the construction of motorcycles and automobiles at the Peugeot factory. The goalkeeper Alexis Thépot would be injured 11 minutes after this, forcing centre-back Augustin Chantrel to play in goal, but even with ten men France were too strong, the Mexicans reportedly spooked by snowy conditions.

GOAL!!! France 1–0 Mexico (Laurent 19). Thépot launches long, the ball brought down by Chantrel and shuttled out to winger Ernest Libérati down the right. Libérati drops a hip to make ground along the wing, and pulls a cross back to the edge of the area. Laurent, racing towards the box, meets the ball first time and sends a left-footed volley whistling into the top corner. With the Americans and Belgians still scoreless, that's the first goal of this new tournament, and what a way to get the party started! It's Laurent's first for France, too. He's picked a fine time to get it.

Italy 2–1 Czechoslovakia (1934, final)

The 1934 finals in Italy were grim as hell, nothing much more than a fortnight-long fascist rally staged by Benito Mussolini. The Czechs nearly ruined the final party, Antonín Puč turning in the area to slam his side ahead with 19 minutes to play. Jiří Sobotka then hit the post, and Oldřich Nejedlý skied a shot from close range. They would eventually pay for the missed chances to wrap it up.

GOAL!!! Italy 1–1 Czechoslovakia (Orsi 81). With time running out, the veteran Raimondo Orsi breaks into the area down the right channel and sends a violently swerving and looping freak shot into the top left across diminutive keeper František Plánička. Italy are saved! Behind the goal, Italy coach Vittorio Pozzo, who has been hanging around in an attempt to put off Plánička, leaps around like a man possessed, while the crowd wave white hankies and chant for Il Duce (English translation: The Fat Galoot). The favourites will surely go on to win against the broken-hearted Czechs now.

France 1–3 Italy (1938, quarter-final)

Italy were the reigning world champions, and expected to beat hosts France at Yves du Manoir in Colombes, Paris. They made doubly sure of going into the match with an advantage by dressing in an away outfit of all black, a deliberately provocative move sanctioned by Benito Mussolini to antagonize the thousands in the crowd opposed to fascism. Grim times – and what was about to happen to France goalkeeper Laurent Di Lorto wouldn't lift the mood.

GOAL!!! France 0–1 Italy (Colaussi 9). The Italian striker Gino Colaussi glides down the inside-left channel and loops a shot towards the top left. It's a tame effort and should be gathered by Di Lorto, but the keeper suddenly develops severe dyspraxia, bump-set-and-spiking the ball into his own net volleyball style. He then chases after it like a drunk puppy and honks his beak on the right-hand post. It's straight out of the silent-movie textbook, as smooth and perfectly timed as Keaton, Chaplin or Lloyd. Di Lorto, who executed the own goal and nose bash in one hectic sweep, could only have looked more ridiculous if he had somehow managed to get his head stuck in a cooking pan or found himself hanging off the face of a clock.

Chile v Italy

Group 2, Estadio Nacional, Santiago, Chile,
Saturday, 2 June 1962

22 May 1960, 3.11 p.m: The most powerful earthquake ever recorded, registering 9.5 on the Richter scale, hits Valdivia in southern Chile. The quake triggers landslides, tsunamis and floods, and even sets off a volcano in the Andes. Up to 6,000 people are killed, while two million Chileans, from a total population of six million, are left homeless in biting winter conditions.

May 1962: Italian journalists Antonio Ghiredelli and Corrado Pizzinelli arrive in the country ahead of the upcoming World Cup. They send home dispatches that paint a picture of Santiago as a giant slum, a poverty-stricken hellhole. They also denounce the local female population as loose slatterns. Upon publication in Italy, and word getting back to Chile, the pair insist their reports have been buggered around by sensationalists working at their paper back in Rome. But the damage has been done. And after an Argentinian journalist, minding his own business in a bar, is mistaken for one of the lippy Italians and given a bloody good hiding, the poor sod, Ghiredelli and Pizzinelli decide to flee the country for their own safety.

June 1962: Stuck in Chile, forced to deal with the consequences of the actions of these two clowns and having drawn the hosts in Group 2, are Carlo Mattrel, Mario David, Enzo Robotti, Paride Tumburus, Francesco Janich, Sandro Salvadore, Bruno Mora, Humberto Maschio, José Altafini, Giorgio Ferrini and Giampaolo Menichelli.

The hosts, who are not best pleased at their country's reputation having been traduced in the face of tragedy: Misael Escuti, Luis Eyzaguirre, Sergio Navarro, Carlos Contreras, Raúl Sánchez, Eladio Rojas, Jaime Ramírez, Jorge Toro, Honorino Landa, Alberto Fouilloux, Leonel Sánchez.

Kick-off: It probably will. Especially as the hosts can effectively put the Italians out if they win this game. The match starts at 3 p.m.

Referee: Ken Aston (England).

Feelings: Running high.

The teams have taken to the pitch. Time to swap pennants. And bodily fluids, it would seem, with several of the Italian side claiming that they've been doused in spit by the Chileans.

And we're off! The hosts get the ball rolling. Five passes later . . .

13 seconds: . . . oof! It's the first wild lunge of the game! Ramírez looks to scamper down the right touchline but is forced to put on the brakes to avoid Robotti, who comes to meet him at uncompromising speed. Ramírez is able to dance round the challenge and keep possession.

32 seconds: Ooyah! The first foul of the game! Chile play it back down the other wing, as Mora hassles Contreras off the ball and looks to break upfield. Navarro is having none of it, and cynically clips Mora's ankles as he skitters up the touchline. Rojas has a little swipe as well, just to make sure. Mora's chin nearly hits the floor at full tilt, but he somehow manages to stay upright and continues running upfield waving a dismissive, disgusted hand in the air. The tone, one would humbly suggest, has been set. Do you think we can get through another 89 minutes and 28 seconds without this one going the shape of a badly rolled and undercooked pizza?

4 min: This is a decent start by Italy. Tumburus, by the centre spot, slides a pass down the left channel to release Altafini, who drops a shoulder to pass the covering Raúl Sánchez and enters the area, fizzing a low shot towards the bottom left. Escuti smothers.

4 min and a bit: Eyzaguirre cuts in from a deep position on the right and makes ground upfield. His progress is abruptly, cynically and illegally checked. A common-or-garden free-kick, but animosity crackles as Chile prepare to take it. Rojas places the ball. Maschio questions the positioning. Rojas shoves Maschio in the chest. Referee Aston places the ball a couple of yards back up the pitch. All the while, Fouilloux stands statue still, piercing eyes fixed upfield, staring out whichever Italian's attention he can grab. Doesn't matter who. Rojas takes a preposterous 20-yard run-up and whacks the ball towards the penalty area. He's surely not trying to score, the free-kick's nearly 40 yards out. He's just after walloping someone in the face, isn't he? Tumburus clears. And then the inevitable occurs . . .

5 min: IT'S ON!!! BRAWL TIME!!! We've not been going long and yet this has been coming. And what a beautifully choreographed piece of thuggery this is! Leonel Sánchez is meandering near the centre circle. Ferrini, malevolence on his mind, shoves Toro out of the way so he can reach the back of Sánchez's legs. Wheech! He hacks away with such excitable glee that he falls to the floor before Sánchez. Sánchez untangles himself and, while still prone, takes a wild swipe at his assailant's legs. Meantime Toro comes in and blooters the loose ball off Ferrini's back, then stumbles over the Italian clumsily. This gives Ferrini, still prone, the chance to sweep his studs across Toro's ankles. They spring up. Toro turns with a view to belting Ferrini in the mushki. He can't get within arm's reach, though, as Ferrini sticks up a knee to protect his personal space and his teeth, then dukes up. The referee steps in, boxing style, to usher Ferrini away. Sánchez, still in the thick of the brouhaha, falls to the floor after being shoved in the chest by the Italian captain, Mora. In fact, on second viewing, it's a nonchalant rabbit-punch straight in the kisser from Maschio! He walked over gently, considered Sánchez from the side and then, when he was sure the referee's attention was elsewhere, landed a straight-arm punch on him! Sánchez goes down in bizarre slow motion, almost like it took a few seconds for the pain to reach his brain, but he was nailed all right. It all calms down soon enough – give or take a pitch invasion of photographers – but for a second that looked like breaking into a 22-man brawl. The initial tangle between Ferrini, Leonel Sánchez and Toro also briefly threatened to break into an interpretive dance piece, but let's not confuse the issue. The referee takes no action whatsoever. Let's hope the players don't take advantage of that largesse!

7 min: FERRINI SENT OFF!!! The players take advantage of that largesse. Ferrini has a wild, retaliatory hack at a pair of legs, this time the ones dangling from Landa's trunk, again near the centre circle. That's a textbook boot up the trousers in the music-hall style! This time Aston puts his foot down. Or, to be more accurate, throws his arm around Ferrini, marches him away from the rest of the players and points to the dugout.

He's been sent off! While Aston is sending Ferrini off, Leonel Sánchez sneaks up behind Maschio and connects with a cracking revenge left-hander before fleeing the scene. Maschio staggers a few yards, hands over his face, and then collapses to his knees.

8 min: Ferrini's not going off. He's point-blank refusing to do one!

9 min: The Italians are incensed. Their captain Mora is arguing passionately with Aston, getting right up in the official's grille. He's having to fight two battles at once, as well, because he's fending off several of the Italian's team-mates, all of whom wish to discuss the matter with Aston in the full and frank style. Why he's bothering to stop them is anyone's guess, because there's no danger of this situation escalating – as it's simply not possible to escalate it any further. The pitch is flooded with photographers, officials and folk from the benches, all of whom have something to say. This is unreal! Several stramashes are taking place in different areas of the pitch, each starring a few wildly flailing players, officials and irate folk in suits. It's like a Bruegel painting brought to life by Cecil B. DeMille, with the entire cast ripped to the tits on PCP.

10 min: THE BOBBIES ARRIVE MOB-HANDED! Several peelers have been called on to the field and are attempting to lead Ferrini away. He's not having a bar of it. Salvadore is in the heart of the melee, trying to extricate his friend from the grip of two stern-looking state apparatchiks.

11 min: What appears to be the entire Santiago constabulary start to march Ferrini off the pitch. Mora has a go at persuading the officials to unhand his midfielder, but he's unceremoniously bundled out of the way. If this wasn't farcical enough, the kops throw some Keystone shapes: they're leading the player off in the wrong direction! They're forced to take a massive U-turn and haul the poor bugger back from whence he came, then down the other end of the park! It's a small wonder they didn't drive off in a collapsing Ford Model T, with Ferrini on the back seat at the apex of a human pyramid.

12 min: The military manoeuvres fizzle out relatively quickly. Ferrini is gone. Aston has a word with his linesman on the far side. Mora, Altafini and Menichelli mill around, pattering away in the ref's ear. They're not happy about this at all. Thing is, Ferrini's thuggish challenge was wholly preposterous. What was Aston expected to do?

14 min: Mora is still having to place himself between his teammates and the referee. Aston mimes the universal gesture for Calm Down Sonny, then points to the centre of the pitch, where he wishes Chile to restart the game. Oh, this game's going to restart all right.

15 min: We're up and running again! A whole 59 seconds elapse before Maschio leaves a little calling card on Ramírez's shin. Nothing major, just enough for the Chilean forward to require a minute's worth of treatment. That's an 'innocent kick', according to Italian television commentator Nando Martellini, developing some new concepts live on Canale 5 back home.

16 min: Italy are really pushing their luck at the moment. The referee's patience, never mind Chile's, is a shoo-in to snap.

19 min: Just about every challenge is an agricultural lunge now. It's not even news any more. Both sides have totally lost their heads. There are a couple of hot-blooded ligament-bothering swipes that are, happily, so badly mistimed they miss their intended target. Tumburus, chasing back after a long ball down the left, lifts a boot to hook it out of play and is an inch away from taking Landa's face off. I'm not sure whether that's a superb defensive clearance or assault with intent to maim.

21 min: It's easy to forget how well Italy had started. Now their play is utterly disjointed, totally aimless. Chile are enjoying the lion's share of possession, but doing very little with it.

22 min: Leonel Sánchez, approaching the left-hand corner flag, has his feet swiped from under him by David, rushing in from the middle. Sánchez gets up and hops around in pain, his left foot dangling in mid-air like a dog with a splinter in its paw. David wanders up to the stricken player, ostensibly to apologize, and gives him a playful cuff round the left ear with just a little bit of menace, but not so much that Sánchez can be sure it was a deliberate attack. Very sly. Fouilloux turns up to shove David lightly in the chest. Then the situation suddenly cools. It's nothing short of amazing how this scene has failed to end up in a large cloud of dust with boots and fists sticking out of it.

Sánchez decides to concentrate on the free-kick instead, which he floats harmlessly into Mattrel's arms at the near post.

23 min: Rojas drops a shoulder in midfield and has a rake from the best part of 35 yards. It's always going wide left and Mattrel had it covered, but it was a decent enough effort. Chile, for all their possession, really have to turn this up a notch. Cranking their central heating down might help in that regard.

24 min: Mora chases a ball down the inside-right channel and enters the box. Contreras is over to cover, but he's not in total control and Mora is justified in going for the loose ball. Escuti is out to smother and takes a clatter from Mora's boot for his trouble. For once, the collision is totally accidental, and to his credit Mora springs up and immediately apologizes to the keeper, putting a friendly arm around his shoulder. His apology is accepted, as it is by Chilean captain Navarro, who races in with troublemaking intent but quickly realizes there's no problem here, and play restarts. A genuinely sporting moment, which is lovely to see, albeit highly incongruous in the context of what's gone before.

25 min: Normal service is quickly resumed up the other end. Fouilloux sashays into the Italy area from the left, and is dispossessed by Janich, who jets in for landing with both sets of studs showing. That's just a ludicrous challenge. No foul, though! The ball flies loose near the corner flag, where it's picked up by David. Now he's flipped into the sky and the aggressor is Fouilloux, who had left the last theatre of war and instantly launched himself into a new dispute with a slide tackle that disregards reason. Free-kick.

26 min: Fouilloux certainly is on one at the moment. As Robotti clears up a Chilean attack down the left, the striker flies in from stage right with another extra-special slider. If he connects, Robotti's bones are surely flying into the air then cascading back down to earth in a cartoon pile accompanied by xylophone sound effects. But he misses. It's like Billy Wright going to the wrong fire in pursuit of Ferenc Puskás at Wembley in 1953, only this time Billy's wearing knuckledusters and twirling a flick-knife.

27 min: David bundles Leonel Sánchez to the floor down the left, then stands over him gesticulating in the stereotypical style.

Ay ay ay ay ay. The crowd respond to the assault as if this were a pantomime, which it sort of is.

29 min: Robotti is about to embark on a sortie down the left, but Contreras, charging out from the back, leaves his foot in. Foul. Mora, powered by steam coming from his ears, sails over to ask Aston if he really thinks that sort of carry-on is acceptable. The crowd give it plenty. The volume in the stadium hasn't always been the loudest, it should be noted, with extreme tension winning out. As Canale 5's Martellini mentions, there's 'a lot of electricity in this match . . . the climate is very heavy. There has been hostile propaganda against our players!' Yes, good point, though in fairness, who started flinging the insults about?

32 min: Landa goes on a magnificent high-speed slalom down the middle of the park. It's Garrincha-esque. He's gently nudged off the ball by Janich. Free-kick. Leonel Sánchez dinks it into the area, but it's headed clear with ease. What a waste of a promising position.

33 min: Eyzaguirre is sent down the right wing and fires a low cross into the centre. With several red shirts lurking, David manages to intercept and Italy hack clear. Chile are beginning to carve out some half-chances. Mora looks to relieve the pressure by taking Italy on an attack of their own up the right, but he's professionally felled by Fouilloux, who chainsaws his ankles.

34 min: Leonel Sánchez finds space down the left and fires a gorgeous ball along the corridor of uncertainty. If Fouilloux was a yard further ahead, he'd have had a simple tap-in from six yards, but the cross sails straight through the area and away from danger.

35 min: A chance for Italy! And it's probably the best of the match so far. Menichelli wins a throw near the left-hand corner flag. He finds Mora with his back to goal. Mora turns and, from the left-hand edge of the area, whips an inswinging ball on to the head of Altafini. The striker's slap-bang in the middle of the area, seven yards out, and unmarked. He really should score, but flashes a header wide right. The stadium falls silent in fear and shock, before 66,057 fans blow their cheeks out in relief.

38 min: Chile respond by pinning Italy back in their own area, but the Azzurri are holding firm. There's nothing going on in the area. Chile resort to hopeful long balls and equally aimless long shots. In other news, it's become quite sunny.

41 min: But here come dark clouds! **WHAT A LEFT HOOK!!!** Leonel Sánchez is trying to wriggle round the outside of David near the left-hand corner flag, but the route to the penalty area is cut off and he's forced to turn back. As he does so, he falls over, his legs covering the ball. David decides to see if matter can pass through matter by thrashing his boot twice at Sánchez's shins, in a wholly disingenuous attempt to release the ball. Sánchez springs up, plants his right foot on the turf, and with much venom pivots his body to throw a southpaw hay-maker. He connects cleanly with David's jaw. David falls to the floor on his back, spark out. You can get too pious about stuff like this, so let us just say that's the best left hook you'll ever see on a football pitch! Pow! Right in the kisser! Straight to the moon!

42 min: A melee. Many people have much to say. Sánchez, having hopped around to draw attention to the fact he was kicked in the first place, somehow escapes censure, which is beyond extraor-dinary. This really should be ten against ten. Or possibly ten against nine. Or even . . . actually, let's not even go there, we'd have to abandon the match.

44 min: After all that, it's a free-kick to Chile, down by the corner flag. Rojas sends it whooshing straight into the arms of the ever-relaxed Mattrel.

45 min: Tumburus slices an awful shot from distance so far wide right that Mora is able to pick up possession down the wing and win a corner. The setpiece is wasted.

45+1 min: DING! DING! ROUND TWO! The referee really should have sent Leonel Sánchez off for that punch. And so, with a grim inevitability, David takes justice into his own hands. The ball is bouncing in the general environs of Sánchez down the Italian right. David ignores the orb and instead launches at the southpaw with a head-high karate kick. He connects cleanly, boot on neck. Ooyah! Oof! As David Coleman says on the BBC: 'He bought that right in the face! That was one of the most cold-blooded and lethal tackles I think I've ever seen!' David is immediately sent packing. Rather gloriously, he has the chutzpah to throw the internationally recognized shape of What? Me? as the referee orders him off.

45+3 min: Sánchez is still getting treatment. Mora goes across to show some human concern. Rojas is reasonably responsive to a player who, despite losing the plot once or twice himself, has done more than most in his attempts to keep a lid on this.

45+5 min: Sánchez, up on his feet but tottering around gingerly, is helped off. Aston spots something suspicious deep in the Italian half. He wanders upfield – and, sure enough, his instincts were right! He checks the number on the back of an Italian shirt – and it's David! He's crept back on to the field and was lining up, ready for the restart of play! Aston ushers him off the field for the second time with a heavy sigh, perhaps reflecting on how much easier his life would have been had he taken up a career in childminding. Or minesweeping.

45+6 min: The game finally restarts and Rojas goes on a skilful slalom down the centre of the field. He's eventually bundled over just in front of the Italian D. Toro takes a quick free-kick, sliding in Ramírez down the inside left, but Italy are wise to it and crowd the striker out.

45+7 min: Maschio loses it a wee bit. He's brought down by Navarro as he diddles down the right. Free-kick. Rojas, dropping back to defend the setpiece, sends the ball a few yards back upfield as he runs past. Maschio chases it, sliding in viciously to hook it out for a throw. Play hasn't even restarted yet! He really needs a cooling flannel on the noggin.

45+8 min: Italy are wasting time, with a view to regrouping at the interval, which can't be long in coming, all those stoppages or not. They ping it around at the back, then Salvadore turns and fizzes an awful backpass wide left of goal. Mattrel can't stop it going out for the most needless of corners.

HALF TIME: Chile 0–0 Italy. Leonel Sánchez's corner is easily cleared, then Toro, coming back at Italy, hesitates on the edge of the area and misses a chance to shoot. And that's that for the half. No goals, is the quickest and most tactful way to sum that one up. But Italy are in trouble. They're two men light and can't afford to lose if they want to stay in this tournament.

And we're off again! Italy restart the bout, and quickly lose the ball. Maschio reclaims and sets Menichelli and Mora scampering upfield. They reach the edge of the area before the move breaks down. Have Italy decided that the best form of defence is attack?

47 min: No, they've decided the best form of defence is *physical attack*. Mora entertains himself with a sly kick in the back of Navarro. That might have been a good old-fashioned boot up the arse, but it's hard to tell in the bright sun whether toecap connected with ringpiece. Mattrel's staring into the yellow menace and he claims a deep Leonel Sánchez cross from the left with élan.

49 min: Landa and Toro so nearly one-two their way through the thick blue line on the edge of the Italian area, but their intricate play doesn't quite come off. Toro is scythed to the floor by Maschio, just to the right of the D. Leonel Sánchez takes a long run up, but pea-rolls the free-kick straight to whoever wants it in the wall. That was dismal. The ball's reclaimed and Navarro has a dig from distance. It's on target for the bottom right but easily smothered by Mattrel.

53 min: Italy are already trying it on with a view to running down the clock. Mattrel and Salvadore faff around at the back, tapping it to each other until Landa jogs up and forces the keeper to pick the ball up and get a wriggle on.

54 min: Maschio plays a little basketball as he prepares to take a throw. He'd have stopped and whistled four verses of 'Sweet Georgia Brown' if the referee had let him, but Aston runs over and taps his watch theatrically.

55 min: Toro, drifting right to left, evades two reckless sliding challenges before firing a shot just over the bar from 20 yards. Chile are getting closer, step by careful step. Mattrel takes an age to retrieve the ball. The crowd do their pantomime duty. In the next phase of play, Landa, perhaps getting a tad frustrated that the scoreline is still goalless, chases a ball he's never going to get down the inside right and leaves a foot in on Salvadore, who was shielding his keeper as he came out to collect. There's a bit of chat about this, a lively back-and-forth.

56 min: Salvadore decides to sit on the turf and roll around for a while, eating up another minute or so.

58 min: A rare moment of attacking creativity from Italy as Mora tries to make ground along the right by flicking the ball over his own head and spinning away. It's a fine trick but Navarro is waiting for him a couple of steps upfield.

59 min: The ever-busy Toro is brought down 30 yards from goal by Janich. Leonel Sánchez sends the free-kick rising towards the top left, an unerring heatseeker. But Mattrel is its equal, and tips the ball round at full stretch. Italy deal with the resulting corner without fuss.

63 min: It's been fairly quiet in terms of nonsense since the restart, but things may just be heating up again. First Mora – the peacemaker in the first half, remember – hacks at Navarro and Raúl Sánchez in quick succession as he goes on a sortie down the right, then Eyzaguirre pointlessly runs into Maschio on the other wing, before trotting away waving his arms dismissively.

64 min: So much for Mora of the United Nations. He takes a full-blown rake down Contreras's calves as the two tangle down the right. He'd already won the free-kick, for goodness sake. Aston, showcasing what appears to be his signature move, does absolutely nothing. Although he then makes a small show of ordering Maschio to hurry up with the setpiece, a strange diktat seeing the player's nowhere near the ball and clearly not going to be taking it anyway. It's fair to say Mr Aston's head has gone too, if in a different way to the constantly sparring players.

66 min: ITALY HAVE THE BALL IN THE NET!!! But it won't count. Altafini ghosts past Navarro, tight on the right touchline, drifts inside, past two other Chileans and sticks the ball away from a tight angle. But the whistle's long gone, the ball having marginally drifted out of play. That was a close call and it'd be lovely to see another angle of that. Still, Italy shouldn't feel too hard done by, as the covering players, Raúl Sánchez and Landa, had stopped competing, and Escuti didn't even pay lip service to making a save. Mora isn't happy with the decision, though, and engages the referee in appropriate discourse.

67 min: Mora exchanges passes with Altafini down the left and cuts inside as he approaches the box. Contreras bundles him over, then stamps on the prone Italian captain's leg for good measure. This didn't start well and it isn't going to end well.

71 min: Italy win a corner down the right but nothing comes from it. They've rarely threatened since Altafini missed that header in the first half. It looks like they've settled for the point that would at least keep them in this competition, understandable in the circumstances.

74 min: FINALLY, A GOAL!!! Chile 1–0 Italy (Ramírez). So much for holding on for that point. Toro bustles down the left and is clattered by Robotti. Maschio arrives on the scene to throw a little snide kick into the mix. The karmic payback is instant. Navarro swings a free-kick into the Italian area. Mattrel comes off his line to punch clear but it's a weak effort, the ball dropping towards Ramírez, eight yards out, level with the right-hand post. He sends a looping header towards the top right and, despite two blue shirts defending the line, it creeps in. The instant snap and crackle of celebration pops many an eardrum. The pitch is flooded by photographers again, who finally have a few smiling faces to snap instead of the usual sour phizogs.

75 min: Mora and Altafini hold up the restart, as they're complaining to Aston about goodness knows what.

76 min: ANOTHER GOAL FOR CHILE!!! BUT IT'S DISALLOWED. What a lovely sweeping move this was. Ramírez, to the right of the centre circle, rolls the ball inside to Rojas, who romps upfield and sets Landa into the area, free down the inside right. He half-rounds Mattrel on the outside before slotting home, helped by the keeper's hands flapping back like the shutters on the window of a haunted house. The pitch fills with over-excitable snappers, but they quickly U-turn when it's clear Landa was some way offside.

77 min: Italy are rocking here. Landa nearly breaks clear down the left but is forced to check back. Toro picks up possession, drops a shoulder to get into the box and fires a shot towards the bottom-left corner. Mattrell parries brilliantly.

78 min: Well, this game has opened up, all of a sudden! Altafini feeds Maschio down the right. Maschio swings a long ball into the area, which Altafini meets, eight yards out. But his header is weak and straight at Escuti. On another day, Altafini could have had two goals. Perhaps another day for the Milan striker, another big match.

* * * *MAGIC MINUTES* * * * * * * *MAGIC MINUTES* * * *

Brazil 3–1 Czechoslovakia (1962, final)

Pele had been injured in Brazil's second game of the tournament – coincidentally against Czechoslovakia – so it was all down to Garrincha. He didn't disappoint, with two goals in both the quarter-final and semi against England and hosts Chile. He failed to work much magic in this match, though, which would be remembered for the biggest-ever individual howler in a final . . .

GOAL!!! Brazil 3–1 Czechoslovakia (Vava 78). If Garrincha has been Brazil's man of the tournament, then short, bald Viliam Schrojf has been Czechoslovakia's. He made save after save as his team upset Hungary in the quarters and then Yugoslavia in the semis, but his form has deserted him at the death. He's already been beaten at the near post when Amarildo quickly cancelled out Josef Masopust's opener, robbing the Czechs of all momentum. And now he's come out to claim a looping Djalma Santos cross from the right, but immediately drops it as he turns back and tees it up for Vava to slap into the empty net from six yards. That's a second World Cup for Brazil, Vava having scored in both finals, but what a tragedy for the Slovan Bratislava stopper.

79 min: FOOTBALL AS SCRIPTED BY D. H. LAWRENCE!
Mora is wandering with the ball near the centre circle. Toro gives chase and rugby tackles the Italian to the ground – then refuses to let go! Aston is forced to bend down and prise them apart, as though the pair were wrestling naked for cash in a barn. This is beyond pathetic. Toro finally gets up and presents the very picture of innocence, while Mora has to be stopped from attempting to spark a Hegelian dialectic using only his hands. He's livid – real after-last-orders let-me-at-him stuff. There's a lot of pushing and shoving, before Aston finally tries to calm Mora down. He doesn't meet his targets: Mora stomps off waving his hands around in Mediterranean fashion. Toro should

probably have seen red as the aggressor and there's a case for Mora going too.

80 min: Toro goes on the most basic but brilliant of runs, straight down the middle of the pitch. Sheer determination and presence allow him to retain possession, and he whistles a low shot inches wide right of goal. That snippet of football was superlative sport, nearly as good as the all-in wrestling.

82 min: Salvadore is bundled off the ball in the middle of the Chilean half. Mora decides what the hell, and goes for goal straight from the free-kick. He's nearly 40 yards out! The ball bounces out of play harmlessly wide right of goal, an effort rewarded with ironic cheers from the home support. 'A long distance free-kick is all we've got left,' sighs our man from Canale 5.

85 min: Fouilloux is in acres down the left. He curls a ball into the middle for Landa, who is clear in the box, but he lets the ball clank around under his feet and can only dig out a shot that flies straight towards Mattrel. Somehow, Italy are still in this match.

88 min: GOAL!!! Chile 2–0 Italy (Toro). Scrub that. This is all over and Italy are going home, the inevitable outcome since events of 80 minutes past. The prize wrestler Toro ends the bout with one almighty blow, lashing a shot into the bottom right from 25 yards. A gorgeous goal, totally out of keeping with the general aesthetic.

90 min: Mora goes in late on Eyzaguirre, meeting his dangling leg, the full-back having long dispatched the ball. He follows up by throwing hands. Eyzaguirre doesn't seem that interested in engaging in unarmed combat, no doubt influenced by the scoreline. Altafini comes in to separate the two and ends up laying hands on referee Aston, which doesn't go down too well. The official, clearly long tired of the whole affair, tetchily throws the ball to the floor so the free-kick can be taken. The sooner that's done, the sooner we can all go home.

FULL TIME: Chile 2, Italy 0, Dignity -783. The last act of the match sees Salvadore, thoroughly razzed off, jump in on Landa with little interest in connecting with the ball. Aston once again positions himself to stop World War Three breaking out and then, utterly bored, takes the opportunity to blow for full time. As Mora rushes up to get in the ref's grille, ostentatiously applauding in the sarcastic style, there's one last majestic piece of childish nonsense. Maschio offers his hand to Landa; as the two are shaking hands, Maschio crumps his other fist on to Landa's jaw! Snide as hell, but set your morals aside and there's something quite special about that, so cold and calculating and cynical. Contreras rushes in to assist his friend, who aims a kick at Maschio, but the Argentina-born Italian takes up a boxing stance, sticks up his dukes in the old-fashioned I'm-prepared-to-go-ten-rounds fashion, and he's left well alone. Aston trudges off the field in a straight line, the shortest route, head slightly bowed. He's away, washing his hands of the bedlam continuing behind him and leaving everyone else to sweep up a mess that, let's face it, was partly of his own making.

So the hosts are guaranteed a place in the quarter-finals. Italy, on the other hand, are almost certainly going home. Perhaps, given all that's gone down on and off the field, that's just as well. And anyway, there's always next time. 1966 can't pan out any worse, can it?

The 1950s

Hungary 4–2 Uruguay (1954, semi-final)

The holders versus the favourites. Hungary's Golden Team had gone two up through Czibor and Hidegkuti, but Uruguay had still to lose a World Cup match (they hadn't played in 1934 and 1938) and Juan Eduardo Hohberg scored twice to force extra time. Then, just after the start of the second period . . .

107 min: URUGUAY HIT THE POST! Hohberg nearly grabs his hat-trick by taking down a loose ball 25 yards from goal and, despite the close attendance of two cherry-red shirts, crashes a low drive off the left-hand post with the stretching Grosics beaten. The ball rebounds into the middle of the area, then hacks clear. So close to the final, and yet so far because . . .

GOAL!!! Hungary 3–2 Uruguay (Kocsis 109) . . . in their next attack, Hungary score what is surely the decisive goal! Budai makes good down the right and whips a cross to the near post, where Kocsis rises imperiously to plant an unstoppable header into the top corner! That's his tenth goal of this tournament! Hungary are on the verge of their second final! And are Uruguay about to be beaten for the first time ever in the World Cup?

Hungary 2–3 West Germany (1954, final)

The Golden Team had beaten the Germans 8–3 in the group stage, were unbeaten in four years and were surely a shoo-in to lift the Jules Rimet Trophy. When they went 2–0 up in the first eight minutes through Puskás and Czibor, it seemed a formality. But the Germans hit back twice in the following 11 minutes, Morlock and Rahn scoring, and the score remained tied until they reached the business end . . .

GOAL!!! Hungary 2–3 West Germany (Rahn 85). What a sweet finish this is! Rahn latches on to a poor Lantos clearing header, just to the right of the D. He takes a touch inside with his right and lashes a left-footed stinger into the bottom left! If 1950 wasn't a big enough shock, wait for this!

87 min: PUSKAS SCORES! BUT IT WON'T COUNT! József Tóth slides a ball down the inside left to release Puskás, who steals a march on Ottmar Walter and, leaning backwards on the left-hand corner of the six-yard box, slides the ball through the advancing Toni Turek and into the net. Hungary celebrate but the Germans (save Turek, who is face down on the wet turf in despair) appeal to the linesman. And the Welsh flag-waver Mervyn Griffiths sticks his flag up! Despair for the Golden Team, whose legacy is on the verge of being forever tarnished!

USSR 0–2 Brazil (1958, group stage)

The winner of this game would advance to the quarter-finals. Neither team had wholly impressed in their first two matches, though the Soviets were favourites, their methodical, scientific, new-fangled approach expected to be too much for a Brazilian side throwing two young reserves into the team. Problem for the Russians was, those reserves were Pelé and Garrincha.

And we're off! And within a minute, Garrincha sends Boris Kuznetsov and Viktor Tsarev, both of the famous Dynamo Moscow, spinning round like children. He teases them as he enters the area down the right, making space to hammer a shot off the right-hand post. It's a wonder the goalframe is still standing. A minute later, Pelé rattles the woodwork too! And then: **GOAL!!! USSR 0–1 Brazil (Vava 3).** Didi, in the middle of the Soviet half, flicks a sliderule pass down the inside-left channel to take out Valentin Ivanov and release Vava past Konstantin Krizhevsky. Vava's the one who batters home, but it's Garrincha and Pelé who have scrambled the USSR's collective noggin and made this possible! What an opening salvo!

Wales 2–1 Hungary (1958, group stage play-off)

A winner-takes-all decider to see who would advance to the quarter-finals to play Brazil. Hungary's team had been severely weakened in the wake of the 1956 revolution – no Puskás, Kocsis or Czibor – and politics played a further role in colouring the mood of this game. The leader of that uprising, Imre Nagy, had been executed by the Soviets 24 hours earlier. The mood in the crowd was sombre, but one moment proved incongruously glorious . . .

GOAL!!! Wales 1–1 Hungary (Allchurch 55). Derrick Sullivan, on the edge of the centre circle, rolls a ball forward to John Charles, his back to goal, just to the right of the D. The Juve giant flicks a high first-time pass to his right, over three Hungarian defenders. It drops to Ivor Allchurch, on the edge of the area, to the left of the D. Sándor Mátrai isn't close enough to the striker, who meets the dropping ball with a sugar-sweet left-foot volley that's set outside the right-hand post but curls back into the top right at high speed. Unstoppable brilliance, and all the great Grosics can do is turn to watch it fly into the net. This is as stunning a strike as has ever been scored in the World Cup! And the Welsh dream is alive again!

Sweden 2–5 Brazil (1958, final)

The hosts versus the favourites. After his introduction against the USSR, the 17-year-old Pelé had been the star of the tournament, with the winner in the quarter-final against Wales and a hat-trick in the semi against France. Could he do it again in the final? Yes.

. . . . .MAGIC MINUTES . . . . .MAGIC MINUTES . . . . .

GOAL!!! Sweden 1–3 Brazil (Pelé 55). The nerve to do this on the biggest stage of all. And to do it as a teenager. Pelé's already hit a post from 20 yards and now he's scored the greatest goal in a World Cup final to date. Twelve yards from goal, level with the right-hand post, he chests down a high Nilton Santos cross to pass Parling, then flips the ball over the head of Gustavsson. As the ball drops towards the penalty spot, only Pelé's anywhere near it. Parling and Gustavsson have been so totally discombobulated that they are running in opposite directions. Pelé dispatches the falling ball into the bottom corner with elan. That's preposterous. And that's the World Cup for Brazil. At last.

England v Argentina

Quarter-final, Empire Stadium, Wembley, London, England, Saturday, 23 July 1966

England's World Cup report card reads: so far, so-so. They topped their group without conceding a goal but without ever hitting the highs – and often struggling to hit the mediums. They will have to improve today against an Argentina side who plenty feel are the best left in the competition now that Brazil have gone. They are such a good side that it beggars belief that this is their first appearance in the knockout stages since 1930. They are, as the man from *The Times* said this morning, 'a fiendishly clever side'. They can also be plain fiendish – as they showed in that vaguely disgusting group game against West Germany, after which the entire team were formally cautioned by FIFA. Not that England are particularly innocent themselves: Nobby Stiles was also rebuked by FIFA after that appalling tackle on France's Jacques Simon and has been the subject of a bit of a witch-hunt since, with suggestions that senior members of the FA asked Alf Ramsey to drop him.

There has been a bit of a moody atmosphere in the build-up to this game, a fear and suspicion of the unknown on both sides. Argentina weren't best pleased at not being allowed to train at Wembley yesterday afternoon – because stadium officials wanted to prepare for last night's dog meeting! England are understandably apprehensive about South American sides: they struggled to a 0–0 draw against Uruguay in the group stage and were beaten by both Argentina (1–0) and Brazil (a 5–1 humiliation) in a tournament to celebrate the fiftieth anniversary of the Brazil Football Confederation two years ago. But they did beat Argentina at the last World Cup in Chile, a happy memory for the two Bobbys, Charlton and Moore, and Ray Wilson.

The prize for the winners is . . . actually nobody really knows what it is, beyond a semi-final. They will play either Portugal or North Korea on Monday at Goodison Park or Tuesday at Wembley. That will be decided when the World Cup organizing committee meets after the game.

Team news: Stiles starts! That's a significant show of faith from Alf Ramsey, not to mention two fingers to the rest of the world. Jimmy Greaves is injured, his leg gashed open against France, and it's Geoff Hurst rather than George Eastham who will replace him. Young Alan Ball also comes in for Ian Callaghan. Ramsey has tried Callaghan, Terry Paine and John Connelly in the group stages, but now it seems he will revert to the wingerless side that was such a triumph during last December's 2–0 win in Spain. Argentina make just one change: Albrecht, who returns from suspension in place of Calics. Albrecht was sent off (and limped off) after kneeing Weber in the groin against West Germany.
Kick-off: 3 p.m.
Referee: Rudolf Kreitlein (West Germany).
England: Banks; Cohen, Jack Charlton, Moore, Wilson; Stiles, Bobby Charlton, Peters; Ball, Hurst, Hunt.
Argentina: Roma; Ferreiro, Perfumo, Albrecht, Marzolini; Rattin, Solari, González; Onega, Artime, Más.
A quick word about the title sequence on the BBC. It's in keeping with the sinister mood surrounding this match. Once the pompous Eurovision fanfare is out of the way, a highly uptight flute, xylophone and brass number rattles out of the telly, before the camera zooms in on a black-and-white globe that wouldn't have looked out of place in *Dr Strangelove*. It's the sort of package that would trail one of Lew Grade's action thrillers over on ATV. You half expect Roger Moore to heave into view and boot the globe into next week before driving off with the trophy in an open-top car. A highly insistent theme ends in a welter of drums. WORLD CUP '66!!! Gulp. Are they trying to scare the entire country to death? Isn't the sight of the statu-esque Antonio Rattin enough?
It's a sweltering day at the Empire Stadium. The two captains, Bobby Moore and the imperious Rattin, two of the world's best players, cheerfully swap pennants in the centre circle.
1 min: Argentina kick off from right to left, in blue-and-white stripes. England are in white. The crowd are in lively mood: there are hearty boos when Solari commits the first foul of the match within ten seconds, an obstruction on Peters. They've obviously read the scaremongering notices in this morning's *Times*.

2 min: An early half-chance for the new boy Geoff Hurst. Banks's long kick is allowed to bounce by Perfumo. Hurst chases it into the box, where it bounces again, and eventually he stabs it instinctively wide of the near post under pressure from Perfumo and Ferreiro. At least it seemed he stabbed it wide; a corner has been given. This is a huge day for Hurst. He notched 40 goals last season for West Ham but this is a big step up: just his sixth cap for England and his first at a World Cup.

3 min: BOBBY CHARLTON HITS THE POST FROM THE CORNER! Charlton drove the corner hard and low from the left, and it smacked off the outside of the post. Ferreiro actually allowed it to go past him and got lucky, although the keeper Roma probably had it covered.

4 min: This is a fantastic start from England. Stiles wins the ball smartly infield and pushes it forward to Hunt. He lays it back to Charlton, who hammers a very sharp pass into Hurst, 30 yards out. Hurst's control is excellent and he switches the ball on to his left foot before swerving an awkward low shot that is fumbled behind by Roma, diving low to his right. From the corner, England win another – their fourth already – after Bobby Charlton's shot from the edge of the area is deflected wide right. Roma plucks that setpiece from the air to give the visitors some respite.

6 min: England should have had a penalty there. Peters's cross from the left was headed up in the air, first by Perfumo and then by the under-pressure Hurst. Ball collected it just inside the box and went over spectacularly after a tackle from Rattin. England appealed for a penalty, the referee said no and the crowd launched into another furious round of booing. As they did so, Rattin fled the scene with comic brazenness, loping upfield as if nothing had happened. We haven't seen a replay so it's hard to be certain, although it did seem like Rattin took Ball's right leg. Ball stayed down for almost a minute.

7 min: Wilson sends in a high, hanging cross from the left. Hurst goes for it – and then goes flying after colliding with Albrecht. That seemed a fair enough shoulder challenge, if a little on the zestful side, although the crowd don't agree: the boo is their default setting at the moment. It's a pretty febrile atmosphere in Wembley . . .

8 min: . . . and this isn't going to help. Ferreiro is down. In what might not be deemed a surprising development, Stiles was involved. After play was stopped, Ferreiro seemed to go in a fraction late on Stiles. Then the camera cut to the referee and by the time it returned to Ferreiro he was on his back, with Stiles surrounded by Argentina players. Stiles walks away and motions for Ferreiro to get up. A few more Argentina players follow Stiles and Ball steps in to make peace.

10 min: Solari, in full flight, is hacked down 30 yards from the England goal by Stiles. He hitches the left leg of his shorts right up to show a bit of thigh, or more specifically the brand-new graze on it. He's not happy. Good luck with keeping a lid on this.

14 min: Jimmy Hill, the BBC co-commentator, is not impressed with the continuous jeering. 'I hope this is not going to develop into a booing and hooraying session by the crowd because it's quite childish and apart from that it's very unjustified at the moment.' Hill is actually keeping score of the fouls by each side – seven by England, four by Argentina, since you ask – which tells you all you need to know about expectations of this match. Has such a card ever been kept except in the boxing ring?

17 min: The captain and half-back Rattin is controlling the game with his usual serene authority in midfield. He never, ever breaks into a sprint – he just lopes around the field playing little passes here and there, taking the temperature and dictating the tempo. He is currently slowing the game down to suit Argentina's needs. When they keep the ball for 30 seconds, waiting for an opening, the crowd express their displeasure – not with boos this time but with some slow handclapping. What a pantomime this is!

19 min: These are dangerous signs for England. Another patient move from Argentina ends with a deep cross from González on the left that is headed to the edge of the area by Jack Charlton. Más meets it with a technically superb volley, wrapping his foot around the ball even though his body is facing towards the corner flag. The ball bounces fractionally wide of the near post with Banks scrambling desperately across his line. In fact, he must have got a touch because the referee has given a corner.

21 min: A good spot from the BBC's Kenneth Wolstenholme, who notices that Argentina's keeper Roma is actually wearing gloves. That's unusual to say the least, especially in dry, sunny weather.

23 min: Rattin contemptuously ignores a tackle from Bobby Charlton, who has a second go by hooking his leg around Rattin's. Charlton goes flying and the ref's given the foul to England. That's a bit strange: Charlton fell over but only because he tripped over Rattin in the process of fouling him. Solari has his name taken for complaining.

27 min: Argentina are stealthily taking control of the match with their patient, almost hypnotic passing. The crowd are getting a little restless. Argentina haven't silenced the crowd but they've done the next best thing: they have got them grumbling. The boos have largely been replaced by groans. The match is, as Wolstenholme says, a bit of a 'tactical battle'.

28 min: The crowd break into applause after hearing the score from Goodison Park: apparently it is North Korea 3–0 Portugal! That is astonishing. North Korea's fairytale continues. Hang on, apparently it is now 3–1, but even so: if England win this they could be meeting North Korea in the semi-final on Tuesday or Wednesday. There is not a soul in the country who would have predicted that two weeks ago.

29 min: That was a good chance for Hunt. Stiles was tripped by Onega 40 yards from goal. Jack Charlton charged on to the ball and mishit a ridiculously ambitious shot that was deflected into the path of Hunt, just inside the box. He reacted smartly, getting away a shot on the turn before defenders converged, but it was straight at Roma.

33 min: Rattin is cautioned after cynically trying to leg up Bobby Charlton, who burst past him. Charlton stayed on his feet and ran within 25 yards of the goal before hitting a low left-footed shot that Roma comfortably saved. The referee allowed play to continue and took Rattin's name afterwards with the game still going on.

34 min: Rattin commits another foul, this time on Hurst. It was harmless enough, but it came so soon after the foul on Charlton as to invite trouble. The crowd chant 'OFF! OFF! OFF!' and there is obvious concern on Rattin's face as the referee runs over. Rattin puts his arms out to signal his innocence and looks extremely thankful when the referee waves him away.

35 min: Stiles touches the resulting free-kick to Moore, who plays a crisp pass into Hurst on the edge of the area. Hurst is fouled by Perfumo, prompting another minor skirmish. Rattin, towering over the little bald man in black, seems to want to be the world's first player-referee. Yakking away, he's pushing his luck here; he'd do well to keep a low profile well away from this overly fussy ref. England take the freekick quickly, with Charlton dragging his shot wide.

36 min: Before the goal-kick is taken another player is cautioned, presumably for talking to the referee. **AND NOW RATTIN HAS BEEN SENT OFF!** This is a sensation! The goal-kick was taken out to the left, and then suddenly the camera cut to the referee pointing Rattin off the pitch! The entire team surround the referee, with Perfumo trying to drag his arm. Rattin stands still, hands on hips, a picture of astonishment!

37 min: Now the whole team might be going off! Artime has run over to talk to the coach, Juan Carlos Lorenzo, and now most of the players are chatting to the Argentina party on the touchline. This is bedlam. Rattin is waving his hands around to protest confusion and innocence, and in fairness we have no idea what he was sent off for, although presumably it must have been something he said.

38 min: The match has come to a standstill. There are loud chants of 'ENGLAND!' Ken Aston, the referee liaison officer and the bloke who failed to keep the lid on the Battle of Santiago, has come to the touchline to talk to the referee and the posse of Argentines. He is talking to Rattin, who still hasn't left the field – but most of the other players have. The match could be over!

39 min: Rattin is having a long, animated discussion with Aston, with both men surrounded by the officials and the Argentina party. The gist of Rattin's body language is: I DIN'T DO NUFFIN! Aston tries to lead Rattin from the field; Rattin flinches his shoulder then pulls his arm away. This is ridiculous. There are still some suggestions that Argentina won't continue unless Rattin's sending off is overturned.

40 min: The referee is walking back on to the field with the ball and a few Argentina players are following him. They seem to have reluctantly accepted the decision, although there are still a few more by the touchline. Jimmy Hill, on the BBC, says Rattin must have been dismissed for 'violence of the tongue'. There might be some violence of the fist in a minute the way this is going. As much as anything, it seems the referee had had enough of Rattin's attempts to become the world's first player-referee. Although technically speaking there's nothing in the laws that says you can send a player from the field because he's boring the bejesus out of you.

41 min: Now the Argentina players are walking back over to the touchline. Rattin is still on the pitch. 'I think they've got everybody on the field except the prime minster,' says Kenneth Wolstenholme. The crowd are now chanting 'Why are we waiting?' And it almost kicked off then! Rattin was talking to Aston, whereupon a suited Eric Morecambe lookalike got involved, prompting Rattin to wave his hands aggressively. Perhaps he doesn't like Eric's paper-bag joke or the way he treats Ern. He certainly doesn't like it when Eric tries to usher him in the direction of the tunnel, recoiling with extreme displeasure. It looks like he now has a police escort to leave the field.

42 min: There are three Argentina players on the field, which is enough for Bobby Moore: he's trying to restart the game! Rattin is still in front of the Royal Box arguing the toss with Eric and Aston in forceful style.

43 min: Play has finally restarted, 7 minutes 57 seconds after Rattin was sent off. Hurst gets things going again with a free-kick in the centre circle. Eh? Wasn't it a goal-kick to Argentina? If not, then at least a drop ball. This is high farce. Have you ever seen anything like this? That hasn't been scripted by Brian Rix?

44 min: Here we go again! Hurst kicks Ferreiro, who rolls over quite ridiculously – at least five times, violently fitting on the turf like a dead animal being cattle-prodded. The Argentina players charge towards the referee, asking for another dismissal. It was certainly not worthy of that, even though it was a poor tackle. Speaking of poor tackle, that's where Ferreiro claims he's been hit.

45+1 min: Rattin is only now making his way to the dressing room, watching the game continue as he makes his slow exit. As he leaves the stage, he runs his fingers over the corner flag, a small Union Jack with a World Cup logo on it, a touching moment of existential contemplation.

45+2 min: This could turn into a fight any minute. Más shields the ball from Moore, who impatiently shoves him to the floor. Más's momentum takes him into the legs of the referee, who tumbles over to prompt the biggest cheer of the afternoon! Solari waves contemptuously at the referee, telling him to get up (!), and then Ferreiro gives Moore a light slap round the cheek. Moore walks away innocently, with a look on his face that says, 'How can you reason with these people?' But it was his shove that started it. Jimmy Hill disagrees. 'Bobby Moore stopped as he was going into the tackle knowing the player was going to throw himself down, and actually he caught him out beautifully: the player threw himself down without getting touched.' The video, it's fair to say, challenges Hill's interpretation ever so slightly. Okay, it makes him look vaguely like a jingoistic ass. In fact, the video caught him out beautifully.

45+3 min: 'Without any doubt, this game must win the Variety Show of the Year Award,' says Wolstenholme. 'As if it really mattered, the score is still 0–0.' Rattin is finally disappearing down the tunnel, boos ringing in his ears.

45+6 min: What an ugly half of football. Argentina will probably be blamed but it takes two to tango and all that. And, as Jimmy Hill points out, there have been 14 fouls by England and 12 by Argentina. It has been a stop-stop first half.

HALF TIME: England 0–0 Argentina. After 52 minutes, at least two of which contained some football, it's time for everyone to cool off.

46 min: England begin the second half, kicking from right to left.

48 min: Here we go again (again): Cohen has a couple of hacks at Más, the second sending him spinning over the touchline like a boxer sent over the ropes. Artime runs to exchange unpleasantries with Cohen and the referee gets in between them.

49 min: GREAT SAVE BY ROMA! That's more like it. England moved the ball around patiently – Argentina-style, in fact – before Moore pushed it wide to the overlapping Wilson on the left. His deep chipped cross was chested down by Hurst at the far post. Marzolini tried to clear the ball with a wild swipe of his right foot but made a total mess of it, inadvertently kneeing it back to Hurst with his left and falling over in slapstick style. Hurst hammered a snapshot towards the near post from 12 yards and Roma flew to his left to push it behind for a corner. Roma runs over to his far post, pulls both his socks up and then gets ready for the setpiece.

50 min: The corner is drilled towards the six-yard line. Jack Charlton attacks it and is sent flying by Albrecht, who ran across him and barged him to the floor at speed. That was a cynical, dangerous and – provided nobody is seriously hurt – hilarious challenge, and it sparks another major to-do. Charlton, face down, is dragged forward by one of the Argentinian players – who slyly stamps on his arm as well – and rolls over a little exaggeratedly. The keeper Roma is also down: he claimed the corner and then fell backwards over Charlton, landing awkwardly as a result. The Argentina players seem to think it was a dangerous challenge from Charlton but he only made contact with Roma because he had been clattered by Albrecht. The two physios are on, and there's another full and frank exchange of views between the teams. This is all highly unedifying – but, let's be honest, also very funny.

55 min: Ball plays the ball off to Charlton and then, approximately four minutes later, is whacked up in the air by González. That's an appalling tackle. There is no flow to this game, never mind any ebb, because of the constant breaks in play. The players on both sides are so sidetracked by the enmity that they've almost forgotten the purpose of the game: to score goals.

56 min: Jimmy Hill says that England need to attack more down the flanks and he has a point. God forbid, Alf Ramsey might even have to bring on a winger.

58 min: Can somebody do something please? This is dreadful.

61 min: It seems the Fairytale of Goodison Park is over: it's now Portugal 4–3 North Korea. That's probably bad news for England if they get through this match.

63 min: It sounds impossible but this game is getting worse.

At the moment neither side looks like scoring. If the game is level after 90 minutes we will go to an extra period of 30 minutes, and if they are still level after that we will decide the match on the toss of a coin.

65 min: WHAT A CHANCE FOR MAS! Argentina so nearly take the lead on the counter-attack. Perfumo, just short of the centre circle, plays the pass of the tournament to put Más through on goal. He drove it 50 yards with the outside of the right foot, between Cohen and Jack Charlton and with enough late swerve to take it into Más's path once it had beaten Charlton. Banks started to come out and then went back, realizing he was in no-man's-land. Más's first touch took him too far to the left when he should have gone straight on, and with his second he dragged his shot wide of the near post with Banks scrambling towards his line and diving to his right. Banks was in a diabolical position then, which is maybe why Más went left to try to make the angle to score at the near post. Either way, he made a mess of a great chance. But what a sweet spray from Perfumo!

69 min: The ten men of Argentina are the better team at the moment, keeping the ball with an ease that should alarm England.

72 min: Jimmy Hill again criticizes England's lack of width and crosses. It's true that they have not played at all well here – but then they didn't play well in the three group games when they did have a winger.

73 min: Argentina keep the ball to the sound of more slow hand-clapping. Stiles has had enough and wins the ball back. A few seconds later, Peters's volley from 20 yards hits a defender and Charlton's follow-up from a prohibitive angle and distance on the left is comfortably saved by Roma.

78 min: GOAL! England 1–0 Argentina (Hurst). England are ahead out of nothing! They have Ferreiro to thank: he ineptly booted a free-kick near the corner flag straight out of play and seconds later England scored. Wilson threw it to Ball, took the return pass and then played it down the left wing to Peters. He curled over a fine cross to the near post, where Hurst got away from the defence to flick an accomplished header across Roma and into the far corner. Argentina appeal for offside, although it's impossible to tell from the angle of the replays. Even Gordon

Banks has charged 80 yards to celebrate. Who needs James Greaves? Hurst has scored on his first World Cup appearance and England are 12 minutes away from the semi-final! Peters celebrates this news with childlike glee: a roly-poly! How sweet! Speaking of innocent wonder, a little boy runs on to the pitch to join in the party – and is promptly cuffed round the lug by Más, who has the heat on. What a rotter!

79 min: This is hilarious: while Banks was celebrating, Argentina kicked off and booted the ball into the empty net! The referee had not blown his whistle so it won't count, and now there's a brief stand-off between Onega and Bobby Charlton. Banks runs forward to intervene, which is a dangerous tactic as Argentina might just kick-off and score again. There are a lot of grown men, on both sides, playing silly buggers today. Argentina restart properly and boot it long again. Banks, still incensed at Argentina's cheek, fumbles and is forced to rush from the area to batter the ball clear. Keeping calm is just not possible in this cauldron.

81 min: A bit of space for Bobby Charlton down the right, but with Hunt demanding the ball in the middle, he opts to lash an overly optimistic effort over the bar from a tight angle. What a waste of a chance to wrap this up. 'We want two!' the crowd yap.

84 min: England are comfortably defending their 1–0 lead. It's now 354 minutes in this tournament without conceding a goal. Argentina are playing with much more urgency but still no real penetration.

85 min: Ball clips Ferreiro, who drops to the floor with a yelp so loud it drowns out the tumult from the stands, 'Rule Britannia' and all. No foul. The Argentinian stays on his knees awhile, perhaps to pray.

87 min: England are closing this down without fuss. They've been impressive in containing Argentina since taking the lead. Bobby Charlton drags a weak shot wide left from distance. He flops his arms about like a rag doll in a mix of frustration and exhaustion.

FULL TIME: England 1–0 Argentina. There's just enough time for Bobby Charlton to be upended as he romps down the left, sent bouncing on his arse as though he's stepped on a banana skin. And that's it! To a huge roof-bothering roar, the referee blows his whistle for the 985th time today. Here's something else that isn't happening for the first time: the pitch is flooded with hectic types, and perhaps the most hectic of all is Alf Ramsey, who physically stops Cohen from swapping shirts with González. The Argentinian simply saunters off and makes the exchange with Wilson instead. Referee Kreitlein is shuttled out of harm's way by a police escort, with a few Argentinians fancying a word. Everyone's lost the plot totally. Let's hope Alf calms down before he gives his post-match interview or he might say something he'll regret!

England v West Germany

*Final, Empire Stadium, Wembley, London, England,
Saturday, 30 July 1966*

**You've got to hand it to World Cup finalists England: they've
come an awfully long way awfully quickly.** SIXTEEN YEARS!
That's the time since their first appearance at a World Cup, a
sojourn to Brazil that ended in abject humiliation, Joe Gaetjens,
the USA, all that. TWELVE YEARS! The time since Hungary
inflicted a record 7–1 defeat on England, a result that came hot
on the heels of the infamous 6–3 Wembley evisceration. THREE
YEARS! The time since Alf Ramsey took charge, losing his
first match 5–2 in France to spin out of Euro 64, and his second
upon being *thoroughly outplayed at home by Scotland*. Let those
last six words hang, proud sons of Albion.

**But never mind all that; England have come a long way since the
start of this tournament a mere NINETEEN DAYS ago.** Going into
this World Cup, it was clear that Ramsey had turned England
into a compact, competitive team, capable of beating anyone on
their day. And, of course, the manager had long predicted that
England would emerge triumphant at their own party. But while
this was a land of hope, there was little expectation of glory. 'All
the indications are, as a national prestige booster, the World
Cup is going to be a resounding flop' screamed the front page
of the *Observer* just before this tournament began. 'Let's not
talk too much about England winning the World Cup,' added
the *Mirror*, 'because we ought to be more worried about whether
they are going to qualify from their group. Oh for a Tom Finney
on the wing!' And in the *People*, England's star striker in the
1962 World Cup, Gerry Hitchens, confidently predicted West
Germany would be beaten in the final – by Italy.

**But while the Italians were sent home early doors to face a rotten-
vegetable frenzy, England *did* qualify from their group, then
battled past Argentina, before Bobby Charlton spectacularly
brushed aside Portugal, a team many had fingered as eventual
winners.** England have made history already, simply by reaching
the final tie, and exceeded expectations while doing so. Now

they're one match away from immortality, though there's a sense that even if West Germany's up-and-coming team beat the English for the first time in history, the nation will remember Alf's lads fondly anyway. 'Even if Bobby Moore and his men just fail at this last touch,' notes the Special Correspondent from *The Times*, 'they have done magnificently even to reach the final in a tough, uncompromising field, a feat many of us thought beyond their capabilities.'

As for the other lot? Here's the jaunty pre-match view of a journalist from Düsseldorf, in the press box at Wembley, talking to some chap from the *Observer* newspaper: 'I know that if we win some of our people are going to say we have beaten the world. I hate that. I will not have beaten the world. Eleven German footballers will have won a cup and I will be glad to see it. But I am not saying I have beaten anybody. Of these eleven players, how many at home would I have in my apartment for coffee or beer? Maybe two of them.' We're sure if England win, the press will keep a similarly level-headed perspective over the years to come. **Not all reporters have maintained their equilibrium, mind.** The German tabloid *Bild Zeitung* have described British sports writers, many of whom are still obsessed with a war that ended over two decades ago, as 'chaps who write their copy in steel helmets and gas masks'. They quoted one English report that suggested the USSR had, in their semi-final defeat to the Germans, displayed 'the spirit of Stalingrad'. There's no need for it, so we promise there will be no military metaphors in this minute-by-minute report, and assure German readers that the Fourth Estate in England are bound to have finally got this out of their system by 1996 at the very latest.

Anyway, the teams! And sure enough, there's no Jimmy Greaves. Some have expressed surprise at Greavsie's omission, though in truth it's been expected. 'It is far too late surely to experiment,' argued Eric Todd in the *Guardian* this morning, and the conservatively minded Ramsey was never going to get the lab coat on and pipettes out at this stage.

Kick-off: 3 p.m. If, like poor old Greavsie, you have little interest in the game, BBC2 are showing *The Great Dan Patch*, a 1949 movie about a man, a fast horse, the horse's trainer's daughter, his love for the fast horse and his love for the trainer's daughter. There's a romantic triangle for you. Hopefully it'll have a happier ending than Ramsey–Greaves–Hurst; more heartache might push the Spurs striker over the edge.

Referee: Gottfried Dienst (Switzerland).

England: Gordon Banks, George Cohen, Jack Charlton, Bobby Moore, Ray Wilson, Nobby Stiles, Alan Ball, Bobby Charlton, Martin Peters, Geoff Hurst, Roger Hunt.

West Germany, very much as expected: Hans Tilkowski, Horst-Dieter Höttges, Willi Schulz, Wolfgang Weber, Karl-Heinz Schnellinger, Franz Beckenbauer, Wolfgang Overath, Helmut Haller, Uwe Seeler, Siegfried Held, Lothar Emmerich.

And the teams are out! England, ever the gracious hosts, are in their away strip of red shirts and white shorts, while the Germans are in crisp white shirts with black trim and black shorts. Pandemonium in Wembley as the players take to the field. A lot of nervous jogging and trotting by both sets of players. The coolest man appears to be the youngest, Alan Ball, who ambles out from the tunnel at his own speed. The Queen takes to the Royal Box in time for the national anthem, the lyrics of which promise her the moon on a stick. She's wearing an ostentatious hat, which matches her handbag. What's in the bag? Programme and pie, we'd imagine. Perchance some baccy. Next to her is FIFA president Stanley Rous, presumably holding Her Majesty's Bovril. Then the German anthem, like the British one before it, is met with a silent and thorough respect that speaks volumes for the sixties football fan. No need to be opening old sores 21 years down the line; there's hope for us all yet. Then, as the last notes drone out, a roar of anticipatory noise. Bedlam, bedlam, bedlam. What an atmosphere!

The captains exchange trinkets. Seeler gives Moore a lovely shiny tapered pennant with his football association's futuristic pointy logo on it, and receives in return a hunk of wood. It's either a doorstop, bookend or trivet. Not sure who's got the best deal there – it's an aesthetic/practicality toss-up. The teams are doing their stretches. Jack Charlton is milling around, picking his nails nervously, trying to kid on like he doesn't care. Speaking of kids, his wife Pat is expected to give birth any time now, so he can be

forgiven for looking like a bag of nerves. As a result Pat is watching the game at home in Leeds rather than quaffing champagne
with the other wives. Going into labour in the stands wouldn't
be the best thing, not least because there will be approximately
96,000 people already moaning and in extreme pain. It's been
raining, by the way, but it's stopped in time for kick-off.

**Now then, we need seven goals today if the 1966 tournament
isn't to be statistically the most defensive World Cup of all time.
Let's get to work, then. And we're off!** Germany get the ball
rolling, Overath hoicking it out of touch down the right immediately. The only way is up.

1 min: Hurst and Bobby Charlton exchange passes down the left.
The ball's fed inside to Stiles, who attempts a daisy-cutter from
distance. It drags along the soft turf and is easily blocked.

2 min: Peters now attempts to guide something goalwards from
the edge of the D, but can only screw wide, the ball always
too high to control with confidence. Germany stream upfield
through Emmerich, who slides a pass into Held, just inside the
England area, in space. He's got far more time than he thinks
and turns a weak shot well wide right of the goal. That could
have been a dream start for West Germany.

3 min: Emmerich slips Held away down the left. Held reaches
the corner flag and digs a cross out, but Jack Charlton is on hand
in the middle to hoof clear with extreme prejudice.

5 min: Germany stream upfield, Held down the left passing
infield to Emmerich, who from 20 yards slices a slapstick effort
out for a throw on the right. The crowd deliver their verdict with
a rasping yay. Everyone's a critic these days.

7 min: Seeler busies himself upfield, making good from the
centre circle and having a long-range wallop himself. The ball
balloons off Wilson and out for a corner on the right, the ball
bouncing along the sort of parabola that would please Barnes
Wallac . . . no, we made a promise, didn't we? Haller takes but
it's headed clear by Jack Charlton with no fuss.

8 min: Utter bedlam in the German area. Stiles swings a ball
into the box from the right for Hunt. Tilkowski comes out to
punch clear, though not very effectively. Charlton takes up possession on the left and swings another in. The keeper biffs out

again, this time under intense pressure from Hurst, who clatters him. Cohen heads the clearance back into the area from the right. Overath is in the business of calming things down when the referee blows for a foul on the keeper, who has remained on the floor. Moore steps in to lash the ball, loose to the left of the D, into the net, simply for the purposes of crowd-pleasing. And by the sound of the amused roar, the crowd have indeed been pleasured.

9 min: Charlton races forward. He slides the ball out left to Peters, who takes two rangy strides towards the box and unleashes a shot towards the bottom right. Tilkowski is right behind it, and at full length palms away from danger. A fine shot and magnificent save. And this is a lovely, open, end-to-end affair.

10 min: OH DEAR! SO MUCH FOR ENGLAND'S STAUNCH DEFENCE! England 0–1 West Germany (Haller). Ball breaks down the left and drifts inside, finding Peters down the inside right, who drags a shot from 25 yards wide left of goal. So close to an opener, but it's the Germans who make the breakthrough. Held, with time down the inside left, pitching-wedges a diagonal ball in the general direction of Haller, lurking in the right-hand side of the England box. Wilson rises to clear with a header but his timing is all over the shop, and he only succeeds in cushioning it down to the German winger. Haller takes a touch with his right as he turns and bumbles a shot into the bottom left, past Banks, who was unsighted by Jack Charlton. A run, a punch, a leap and a modest wave to someone in the crowd. Haller considers a grin but then decides it's time to get back to work.

13 min: Stiles is given a stern talking-to by the referee for giving Haller's ankles too much attention in the midfield. Stiles doesn't seem willing to engage in the philosophical debate, responding to the ref's thesis with a couple of effs, not the sort of antithesis likely to lead us to any satisfactory higher truth. Play's waved on.

18 min: GOAL!!! England 1–1 West Germany (Hurst). Well, this came out of nothing! Bobby Charlton evades Beckenbauer in the centre and slides the ball out left to Moore, who has his ankles clumsily clipped by Overath. Moore jumps to his feet and doesn't bother making an MGM-sized song-and-dance production of taking the setpiece, simply looking up and clipping it into the area, having spotted Hurst ludicrously unmarked on the penalty spot. The ball's perfection itself and the in-form Hurst is unchallenged as he adroitly guides the gently dropping ball into the left-hand side of the net. Tilkowski stands on his line, his jaw hanging loose in disbelief, pointing into the space Hurst has just taken advantage of and looking around at his defenders as if to say 'aw . . . *c'mon*'. Hurst leaps on the spot in celebration, nearly shearing off his own nipples with his knees. Jimmy who?

19 min: Schnellinger and Seeler tackle each other in the centre circle. Now it's the Germans' time to look a wee bit flustered.

20 min: Peters makes a lung-bursting run from a deep-lying position. He's got the German defence backtracking, with all sorts of space opening up. What he doesn't have is the ball. He's waiting for Ball to rake it in from the left but the pass comes too late. Germany were all over the place there.

21 min: Peters is robbed by Overath in the centre circle and responds with a petulant shove on the German midfielder. Now now. The referee takes his name. Peters half-turns to show his number in the stroppy schoolboy style. The ref plays his part by wagging his finger three times. Naughty, naughty boy.

22 min: England move upfield, Bobby Charlton's incomplete one-two with Ball down the inside-left breaks to Cohen, who screws wildly wide left of goal, the sort of shot that would have eventually come back round to him if only everyone had left it.

23 min: The sun's out!

28 min: Bobby Charlton and Beckenbauer are never far away from each other. The England man drops a shoulder and slides past the great young German hope, in the imperious style of Alfredo di Stefano. He teases a delicious ball into the centre for Hunt. Weber is forced to hoick the ball out for a corner on the right just as Hunt looked like ghosting in to strike. The corner is an egregious disgrace, Ball wafting his delivery straight into the arms of Tilkowski.

32 min: A couple of minutes of attritional nonsense, then the game suddenly springs to life! Cohen hits a high diagonal ball into the German area from deep on the right. It's met by Hurst, level with the left-hand post, 12 yards out. He sends a majestic header towards the bottom left, but it's saved brilliantly by Tilkowski, slithering across his line. Ball is first to the rebound, spinning through 180 degrees to send the ball across the face of the six-yard area from the left, but there are no red shirts in the danger area and Overath clears for a throw on the right. Germany mop up from the restart.

34 min: Incredibly sloppy play by Weber, just in front of his own area down the right. He tries to slip the ball past Hunt but only batters it into the striker. The ball breaks to Peters, who attempts a delicate chip goalwards, but gets it all wrong, allowing Tilkowski to claim.

37 min: And with that, England's ring-rustiness shows. Held enters the England box down the left but is turned back by Cohen and dispossessed by Stiles. So far, so good. Stiles gives it to Ball, who then puts Cohen in all sorts of bother with a lazy backpass. Cohen, who was starting to move upfield and was wrong-footed by the pass, turns round with the weary resignation of a man who was about to leave work only to be told he'd be needed for a double shift. At that precise moment in time, Cohen was the personification of the phrase "Fuck*sake*". But Cohen recovers and holds off Held just as it looks like he'll break clear down the left. And then takes one touch too many, allowing Held to burst into the box! Jack Charlton, almost certainly fuming, comes sliding in to concede the corner, planting Held into a bed of photographers behind the goal as he does so.

38 min: From the setpiece, the ball drops to Overath on the edge of the area. He creams a rising left-footed shot goalwards. Banks parries wonderfully, then smothers Emmerich's snapshot on the turn at the left-hand post.

41 min: Hurst lifts an aimless ball back into the England midfield. Emmerich beats Jack Charlton to the bouncing ball, just to the left of the centre circle, and makes off down the channel. He'll be in on goal if he evades Moore but the England captain slides across to make a brilliant last-ditch tackle.

42 min: Wilson loops a speculative header down the inside right. Weber rises, mistimes his leap and nuts a weak clearance to Hunt on the left. The striker takes a thrash at goal with his left peg from a tightish angle, but Tilkowski batters his rising shot down and Höttges is on hand to mop up.

43 min: Bobby Charlton shapes to shoot down the inside left but instead slides a diagonal pass into the centre for Peters. For a second, he looks to have time to shoot but Weber comes sliding in to clear. Germany go up the other end through Seeler, who sashays through the midfield and sends a heatseeker towards the top right. Banks is forced to tip spectacularly over. The corner comes to naught.

44 min: Höttges shoots from 30 yards down the right. Come along, some respect for Banks, and indeed goalkeepers everywhere, please.

HALF TIME: England 1–1 West Germany. This could so easily be three apiece. A magnificent half of football. Good luck splitting these two sides because the margins are paper thin.

Amid torrential rain, we're off again! And England are immediately on the attack through Bobby Charlton, who breaks into the box down the right-hand channel. He looks to pull the trigger but Schulz bundles him to the floor. The crowd scream for a penalty but there's no reaction from Charlton, who taps hands with the German centre-back as he picks himself up and trots back upfield.

49 min: A scrappy start to the half for the West Germans. Cohen, Stiles and Ball have all taken turns to romp into space down the right, but their cutbacks are inaccurate and easily dealt with.

53 min: Ball clips a cross in from the right. Peters, always stretching, pokes a header wide right.

56 min: There's not much of an atmosphere, give or take a few smatterings of 'England! England!' Come along, Wembley, World Cup final going on over here.

59 min: Walley Barnes, the colour guy on the BBC, has been filling in dead air time by explaining the concepts of energy conservation. Very green. Both teams appear to be willing to take their chances at the business end of this game.

62 min: From a German corner on the left, the ball breaks to Beckenbauer on the edge of the area. He drops a shoulder and nudges the ball to the left, but drags a lame effort right of the target. He's been pretty successful in blunting Bobby Charlton but is diminished as an attacking force as a result, a pale shadow of the goal threat he was against Switzerland, Uruguay and the USSR.

64 min: With this perhaps in mind, Beckenbauer takes a crack at a free-kick from 35 yards. That is astonishingly unrealistic.

65 min: Hurst chests down a long Moore pass on the edge of the area. Peters hoicks over the bar. This half must start soon. The crowd entertain themselves by singing 'Oh my, what a referee' over some perceived slight when Jack Charlton was penalized for handball a while back. In truth, they've little to complain about, and if they're not careful they'll put the official in a mood to give them nothing.

68 min: Hunt is bowled over down the left. Moore sails a free-kick to the far post, where Jackie Charlton rushes in to face the ball wide right of the target.

70 min: 'When the reds go marching in' chant the crowd, no doubt in celebration of the Labour Party's current parliamentary majority of 96 seats. And perhaps they're also trying to get England going again. It's all a wee bit flat. From his trademark position on the left, Wilson – Ray, not Harold – crosses towards Hunt, who is gently nudged out of the way by the shoulder of Schulz. Crafty, but not a foul. No pen.

73 min: Ball slides the ball to the left for Moore, who swings a cross back to the far post where Hurst heads down. Bobby Charlton is looking to latch on to the knockdown but Tilkowski comes out to claim. Beckenbauer had nipped in between to guard his keeper and clatters into him, sending Charlton flying into the net as he does so. No foul, though there's a suggestion of obstruction. An indirect free-kick, six yards out by the right-hand post, would have been interesting.

77 min: Ball bursts down the right after a Hunt knockdown. He hammers a shot towards the bottom right, forcing Tilkowski to turn round his post. Corner. From which . . .

78 min: GOAL!!! England 2–1 West Germany (Peters). Ball floats in the corner. Schulz heads clear but only to Hurst on the edge of the box. Hurst shoots under some pressure but only manages a weak effort, which is dribbling towards the left-hand side of the goal. But Höttges slices a woeful clearance up into the air, the ball dropping into the heart of the German box, eight yards out. Peters, rushing in, meets the ball sweetly with his right and slams it into the middle of the goal! England, having waited 103 YEARS since inventing the game, are now 12 MINUTES from becoming the champions of the world! As Peters runs back upfield, arms waving wildly, he's joined by Hurst and Hunt in celebration. But he doesn't lose himself in the moment too much. As he waits for the game to restart, he stretches out his fingers as far as they will go, talking to himself, cognitive techniques to help him snap back to reality and get on with finishing the job in hand.

79 min: Ball makes his way into acres of space down the left. Near the corner flag, Höttges comes flying in from behind, a ludicrous scythe of malign intent totally out of keeping with anything we've seen in this match. How he doesn't have his name taken is a fair question, for players have been sent off during this tournament for far less. Just ask poor old Antonio Rattin. Perhaps the referee is taking into account that Höttges has just made the mistake that's likely to cost his country the World Cup.

81 min: Chances are coming thick and fast now. Peters slides Bobby Charlton into the area down the left but he shanks it way off target. Schnellinger, drifting inside from the left, batters a shot straight at Banks. Hurst cuts in from the right and blooters a shot from 20 yards wide left and high. 'We want three' chant the crowd. Some folk are never happy.

84 min: Stiles snaps too energetically at Held's feet down the inside left. Foul. Emmerich floats the ball into the area. Weber eyebrows a header wide right of goal. A mild panic seems to be setting in. England can't keep giving away free-kicks.

86 min: HUNT SPURNS A CHANCE TO WRAP IT UP! Moore takes control of the ball in the area, dribbles out to the left, then finds Peters up the wing, who in turn shuttles the ball forward to Ball. The young midfielder takes a touch back towards his area, then whips a ball upfield to release Hunt down the channel. Suddenly, England are three on one, with Bobby Charlton and Hurst in the middle! Hunt's ball inside is dreadful, though, lacking the pace to reach Charlton before the covering Overath arrives to hassle the England midfielder. Charlton screws a lacklustre shot wide right, then gives Hunt a look. Hunt should probably have dropped a shoulder and gone on the outside of the only covering defender, Schulz, taking a shot himself. But he lacked both pace and confidence. Will England rue this?

87 min: Emmerich sends a pea-roller towards Banks.

88 min: Overath lumbers down the inside-left channel, using up every last drop of energy. He drops a shoulder past an equally tired Peters to cut inside and unleashes a fizzer just wide right of goal. Whistles are ringing around an anxious Wembley. England are hanging on.

89 min: HEARTBREAK FOR ENGLAND!!! England 2–2 West Germany (Weber)! Schulz heads forward deep into England territory. Seeler is mounted by Jack Charlton, who heads clear. A needless panic by Charlton and that's a free-kick, 30 yards out, just to the left of goal. Emmerich blasts the free-kick straight at, and through, the wall. The ball comes off Cohen and falls to Held, who from the left-hand corner of the six-yard box blasts goalwards. The shot's going towards Banks but hits the back of Schnellinger and deflects to the right, drifting slowly through an anarchic melee. The ball somehow evades both Wilson and Seeler, but Weber is sliding in at the right-hand post and lifts the ball over the despairing arms of Banks. What a farce! Only the young Beckenbauer seems to have the energy to celebrate for Germany. Banks is claiming handball but his head must be as cluttered as the England area was. You can tell he doesn't really believe it. And England don't really believe it. Because . . .

FULL TIME: England 2–2 West Germany . . . the second they restart the game, the referee blows his whistle for full time. They came *that* close! Stiles boots the ball upfield in impotent rage. We go again for another 30 minutes. Something decisive will have to happen in extra time or we're all here again on Tuesday for a replay.

Germany get extra time under way. A strange sense of anti-climax at the moment. England are understandably deflated, the Germans seemingly too knackered to be elated. It's all fairly understandable.

92 min: Schnellinger sprays a lovely crossfield ball from the left to Seeler on the right-hand edge of the England area, but he slips on the sodden turf and Moore is able to lash free. He finds Ball, who goes on a slalom down the middle of the park and sends a rising shot straight at Tilkowski. The keeper palms over the bar. The corner's wasted.

94 min: BOBBY CHARLTON HITS THE POST! Ball swings one in from the right. Peters and Hurst make a nuisance of themselves on the edge of the area. The ball's laid back to Bobby Charlton, who sends a low shot crashing – admittedly not at the highest speed – off the base of the right-hand post. Tilkowski wasn't far away from reaching it. The ball rebounds back into the keeper's startled face and away from danger! That was slapstick at its finest. How on earth did that stay out? England will curse that goalframe if they lose this final.

95 min: Unperturbed, they keep pressing Germany back. Hunt cuts in from the left and fires a shot across goal and wide of the target.

96 min: Overath robs Ball and sends Seeler away down the right. He sprays a ball to the opposite wing for Emmerich, who slides a diagonal ball into the box for Held. The striker takes a tired touch – earlier you'd have fancied him to turn and shoot from ten yards – and England are able to mop up without too much fuss. The German fans try to gee up their team with some metronomic horn parping.

99 min: The sun's out again. Held powers down the inside-left channel to the byline, past a half-arsed challenge from a leggy Jack Charlton, who is possibly also worried about giving away a penalty. Held whips a dangerous ball through the six-yard area, but only Seeler's in the centre and it flies over his head, with Banks kidding on he's under complete control. Hunt goes down the other end and whips a fairly aimless cross-cum-shot into the side-netting.

101 min: GOAL!!! EXCEPT IT ISN'T!!! BUT NEVER MIND THAT, BECAUSE IT'S GOING TO COUNT!!! England 3–2 West Germany (Hurst). Conducting the match from the centre circle, Stiles sprays a lovely pass down the right for Ball to race on to. He's got a jump on Höttges, who races over to cover but is never getting there in a million years. Ball connects first time, cutting back an arcing cross into the heart of the area. The ball takes one bounce just before it reaches Hurst. The striker, ten yards out with his back to goal, just to the right of the penalty spot and ahead of his marker Schulz, brings the rising ball down with the side of his foot and turns to his left. As the ball bobbles towards the right of the goal, Hurst swivels and unleashes a powerful rising shot towards Tilkowski. The ball rockets up over the keeper's head and off the underside of the crossbar, before bouncing down on the line and back into the centre. Hunt, who really should be following it in, turns instead to celebrate, both arms aloft. Weber steps in to head over the bar for what he imagines will be a corner. For a couple of seconds, it appears a corner's what it'll be. Hurst's shoulders slump, his hands resting on his knees. But they're soon in the air in celebration: the referee quickly consults his linesman and points to the centre circle. The home crowd erupt and Wembley's twin towers are launched into space!

102 min: The Germans were surrounding the linesman after that decision, screaming in his phizog. You can't really blame them. On the other hand, that goal had been coming. England have been excellent since the restart. 'We want four' chant the home support. Some people are never happy.

104 min: Space for Emmerich down the left. His sliderule diagonal ball into the middle nearly finds Held rushing through, but Cohen slides in to guide the ball away from immediate danger. He looks to have conceded a corner, but Banks scrambles across to save, the ball sticking to his fingertips. Every little helps and England aren't in the mood to give anything away.

EXTRA TIME, HALF TIME: England 3–2 West Germany. One of the more expansive moves of the match. Haller sprays a long ball down the right for Held, who knocks a pass along the front of the England area. Emmerich takes control and welts a shot towards the far-right corner. High and wide. Banks would have had it covered unless Emmerich found the postage stamp. And that's it for the first half of extra time.

England get the ball rolling again. They soon lose possession. But West Germany, drenched in water, look short of energy. Overath and Emmerich combine down the left but the latter doesn't have the power to engage Stiles in combat.

107 min: Beckenbauer shows good feet to dance past Bobby Charlton in the middle of the park, but having gone on a 40-yard run, he's kaput by the time it comes to shooting and his effort bobbles through to Banks.

108 min: Hurst cuts in from the right and, looking for the first-ever hat-trick in a World Cup final, shoots from the edge of the area. Bereft of juice, it's never getting past the keeper.

110 min: Hunt has a chance to free the overlapping Wilson down the left but opts to go for gold instead. His attempt to dance into the area is brought to an unceremonious end when Schulz sticks in a shoulder and sends him crashing to the turf. The striker's decision-making hasn't been all that in this extra period.

111 min: Stiles on the wing shanks the ball straight out of play. It's not just Germany who are running on empty.

113 min: Held drifts in from the left and from the best part of 30 yards scores two rugby points. Unfortunately, rugby points are not recognized as currency by the FIFA mandarins. Refusing to give up, Held's soon back at England, breaking clear down the inside left and shooting inches wide, a powerful shot that Banks probably didn't have covered, but he's handled the ball en route and play's pulled back. Hearts in mouths for England.

115 min: Corner for Germany as Held crosses deep from the left, forcing Wilson to twist in mid-air and head out on the right. The setpiece is rolled back to Beckenbauer, whose long crossfield ball is too clever by half and intercepted. England swish upfield and this is better by Hunt, who moves inside from the left and sends a rasping drive flying just wide of the right-hand post.

116 min: Held, who has been nothing short of magnificent, powers down the left and fires a low cross into the area, but Overath miscontrols, the ball shooting out of play for a goal-kick.

118 min: It's attack versus defence now. 'This is Held,' says the BBC commentator Kenneth Wolstenholme, though his received pronunciation sounds suspiciously like 'This is hell.' Which, of course, for England fans it is. Germany aren't going to dash the cup from England's lips at the death again, are they? It doesn't look like it, Haller sending a cross from the left whistling straight down Banks's gizzard.

119 min: This is more like it from Germany, though. Schulz, deep on the right, sends a diagonal ball into the area for Haller to head down into the path of Seeler. Moore has allowed the little German to nip in front of him, but the ball's whizzing through the air too quickly and Seeler is forced to scamper towards the corner flag after it. He pulls the ball back to Schulz, who crosses deep again. Cohen calmly heads behind for a corner. He looks calm, anyway.

120 min: Haller sprints to the corner flag and takes. He whips the ball in. Banks punches clear. The ball lands 30 yards upfield at the feet of Hunt, who rather brilliantly rotates through 180 degrees, drops a shoulder and leaves Schulz, sliding in, for dead. That's as good a piece of skill as we've seen all afternoon. Unfortunately, his attempt to release Ball down the right with a raking crossfield pass is abysmal, trickling along the ground and easily intercepted in the centre circle by Höttges. The ball's sprayed right to Schulz, who curls a desperate last cross into the area. Moore chests down, and . . .

120+1 min: THE GOAL THAT MAKES IT CERTAIN – ENGLAND ARE THE WORLD CHAMPIONS!!! England 4–2 West Germany (Hurst) . . . launches an exhausted but brilliant pinpoint pass down the left channel for Hurst. Who's clear! The striker looks like he's wading through treacle on the heavy, cut-up pitch but he makes it to the area and, a millisecond before Overath completes a futile pursuit, lashes an unstoppable shot into the top left! 'That's it,' says the ITV commentator Hugh Johns. 'That. Is. It.' I wonder what Wolstenholme's saying over on the BBC?

IT'S ALL OVER! England 4–2 West Germany. Hurst barely has the energy to jog round in a small semi-circle but he's got to support Ball, who races up to congratulate him. And it's the final act of the game! The Wembley pitch floods with well-wishers. England, just as Alf Ramsey said they would, have won the World Cup!

As England troop up the stadium's famous 39 steps to the Royal Box, Ramsey shakes each of his players warmly by the hand. And here's something: he's smiling. Aw, bless. Moore lifts the trophy. Three irate peelers have to batter a path back down to the pitch for the team, so many folk are leaning into the stairwell hoping to slap the new world champions on the back. And now Stiles has started skipping around in the sort of big-leggy fashion that suggests he might have seriously chafed his inner thighs. In fairness, he has put in quite a shift.

TRAFFIC UPDATE: Roads in the West End of London have ground to a halt, with thousands of punters milling around Trafalgar Square and Piccadilly Circus. 'It's like VE night, election night and New Year's Eve all rolled into one,' says an Automobile Association spokesman in his steel helmet and gas mask.

England v Brazil

*Group 3, Estadio Jalisco, Guadalajara, Mexico, Sunday,
7 June 1970*

The world champions have been through the mill of late. Their
pre-tournament jaunt to Colombia and Ecuador didn't quite go
to plan, with Bobby Moore accused of stealing a bracelet from
the Green Fire jewellery shop in Bogotá, and being thrown in the
clink for four days. When the team returned to Mexico, a tired
and emotional Jeff Astle staggered off the plane having gone
to great lengths to keep himself fully hydrated at high altitude,
his mid-air refuelling methods causing a stink in the press. Sir
Alf Ramsey put up the backs of the entire Mexican press corps
by replying to a journalist welcoming England 'with open arms'
with a bitter laugh of 'you must be joking'. The resulting anti-
English feeling, whipped up in the local papers – one trenchant
rag has called Ramsey's men 'a team of thieves and drunks' – has
led to an orchestra of Mexican fans hanging around outside the
team hotel every night performing moonlit sonatas on whistle,
horn and car engine. And then there's the heat. Oy, the heat.

It's been touching 98 degrees at times in Guadalajara. To put
that into perspective, the US Army go indoors for their own
safety whenever the mercury nudges 85. Most of England's
players lost ten pounds in weight during their opening game, a
workaday 1–0 win over Romania. 'I was better off in jail' was
Moore's tinder-dry assessment of that one. But at least the game
kicked off at four in the afternoon. Today's match kicks off at
midday, with the sun at its best, doing its worst.

**High noon, though. What a deliciously symbolic time to kick
off.** For this, more than any other game in this tournament,
promises to be a proper shoot-out, between the two teams most
likely to lift the trophy. England don't always get the credit
they deserve internationally: many have questioned whether
such a pragmatic side are valid world-champion material, while
you don't have to look very far to find someone from South
America who'll allege that England's home win four years ago
was an authority-sanctioned inevitability. Both sides will almost

certainly qualify whatever happens today, but England need a good performance here, for no other reason than to ensure 1966 isn't marked down for ever in some quarters as a strange fluke at best, a dubious aberration at worst. But ignore the knockers. The Brazilian players – coming off the back of a resounding 4–1 victory over Czechoslovakia, which saw Pelé attempt to score from the halfway line – know quality when they see it. 'Nothing will be simple against England,' says Jairzinho, while Gerson, who'll miss this one through injury, adds: 'England will be more difficult than Czechoslovakia. Their defence will not be so naive.' **But let the record state that Brazil haven't had it all their own way during the run-up to these finals either.** Less than two years ago, the team was a complete shambles. During 1968, they lost games against West Germany, Czechoslovakia, Mexico (twice) and Paraguay. In order to placate the press, they gave the manager's job to the journalist who had been most critical of the team since their shambolic defence in 1966. João Saldanha embarked on a stunning qualification campaign in which Brazil won all of their matches, scoring 23 goals while letting in only two. However, all was still not quite right. Off the field, Saldanha tried to get rid of Pelé, accusing the player of going blind in one eye! He refused to play Dario, the striker beloved of Brazilian military dictator Emilio Medici, declaring, 'I don't choose the president's ministry and he can't choose my front line.' When his predecessor as coach, Dorival Yustrich, made some mild criticisms of him in the press, Saldanha went after him to discuss the matter in depth, toting a loaded gun. The Brazilian FA took the opportunity to sack him – 'I am not an ice cube to be dissolved!' was his measured response – and replaced him with 1958 hero Mario Zagallo. Brazil look the finished article now but what a journey they've been forced to take.

Kick-off: Midday in Mexico, 7 p.m. back home.

Referee: Abraham Klein (Israel).

Brazil: Félix, Carlos Alberto, Everaldo, Clodoaldo, Brito, Piazza, Jairzinho, Paulo César, Tostão, Pelé, Rivelino.

England: Gordon Banks, Tommy Wright, Terry Cooper, Alan Mullery, Brian Labone, Bobby Moore, Francis Lee, Alan Ball, Bobby Charlton, Geoff Hurst, Martin Peters.

So, then, the 1966 winners versus the 1958 and 1962 champions and tournament favourites, a proper summit meeting, and not just because of the altitude. Pre-match prediction, anyone? Oh look, here's Alan Ball: 'We'll beat these.'

Fashion watch: England are in all white, wearing a special 'tropical' kit, which is basically the same shirt but with a lot of small holes in it, and tennis sweatbands on their wrists. Brazil are in their famous 1950-shunning yellow, green and cobalt blue.

A rare old atmosphere in Guadalajara. Let's see if the crowd can keep this up in the searing heat. I hope they're wearing hats and have doused themselves liberally with lotion. The players of both sides, meanwhile, are noticeably not bothering to warm up. No need. A couple of stretches, a juggle of the ball and that's their lot. And we're off! England get the ball rolling.

2 min: A fairly confident start by the champions, who ping it around hoping Brazil chase the ball and knacker themselves out. Brazil don't bother chasing. But there's a cost to this energy preservation. England put together a gorgeous move. Labone strokes a pass down the right. Charlton pings it inside for Mullery, who knocks a pass forward to Hurst on the edge of the D. The 1966 hat-trick hero lays off first time to the onrushing Peters, who aims for the bottom right from 25 yards. Félix gathers, which is never a given for a keeper infamous for clownish mishaps.

3 min: Mullery comes straight through the back of Pelé. The crowd whistle their displeasure. Then jeer in the pantomime fashion when Moore skies a pass out of play on the left.

4 min: It's been all England so far! Mullery is looking dominant in the centre of the park. He sends Wright away down the right. He skins Everaldo. Corner. England opt to faff about. Eventually Pelé gets fed up and steps in, nicking off with the ball and pinging a couple of triangles down the Brazil left. The crowd roar in delight at this pretty way of playing out of trouble. It'll never catch on.

7 min: England look to be in the mood for this. Wright is stuck on the right-hand touchline, 30 yards out. He sends a cross into the box and it nearly lands in the top-left corner. Félix is never getting to that! He's come off his line to collect but totally misjudges it. He sticks out a pathetic arm and falls backwards in impotent panic. Luckily for the keeper, the ball sails just wide left of goal. In fairness to Félix, it must be hard to move around in those outsized shoes. At least his whirling bow tie will keep him cool in this heat.

10 min: BRAZIL FINALLY DO SOMETHING . . . AND IT LEADS TO THE SAVE OF THE CENTURY!!! Lee has a dig from miles out wide on the right. The highly ambitious shot goes straight down Félix's throat. Even accounting for altitude and this keeper's slapstick style, that's just rude. Brazil, perhaps piqued at his cheek, flood up the other end with extreme prejudice. Félix throws out to Carlos Alberto down the right. He fires an astonishing, physics-defying pass up the wing that swerves right and then left – *in mid-air* – before bending to the right again, around Cooper and to the feet of Jairzinho. He burns past Cooper, reaches the touchline and loops a cross to the far post. Pelé, ten yards out, rises ten yards into the air, beating Wright all ends up. He bangs a header down, sending the ball bouncing up off the turf three yards from goal. It's heading into the bottom-left portion of the net, a nailed-on goal. But somehow Banks digs it out! He'd already positioned himself well in anticipation of the header by shuffling along the line to his right. Now he takes another step before diving down, arching his back and spinning around in one motion, corkscrewing his body, the human form as fusilli pasta. A strong right hand scoops the ball upwards, just before it's going to cross the line, and sends it over the bar. That defied all physics! Eh? The ball lands behind the goal and takes a massive break to the right. Jim Laker would have been proud of the spin on that! Tostão stands with his head in his hands for a second, before applauding in a mix of frustration and acknowledgement. The resulting corner is wasted, but that's not really the point.

13 min: Rivelino executes one of the great Ludicrous Dives, running behind Moore and falling to the ground on his knees, before letting his nipples hit the turf also. That had all the elegance of a toddler tripping over a kerbstone while running to meet the ice-cream van. He has the good grace to pick himself up and look slightly ashamed.

15 min: Lee attempts to make ground down the right wing. Everaldo gets in his way and takes a knee in the swingers for his trouble. Lee really is a belligerent wee bugger – that looked deliberate. Brazil's Man with Bucket comes on and sponges down Everaldo's Special Place.

19 min: Brazil are beginning to enjoy more of the play, after a slow start. Jairzinho, who has the beating of Cooper, breaks clear down the right, but his low pull back is missed by all. England break upfield through Charlton, who, from deep inside his own half, skips over a preposterous lunge by Clodoaldo, strides down the right, evades another mistimed lunge by Rivelino, cuts inside, and balloons a shot from 30 yards over the bar and out of the stadium. A fabulous run, albeit one that ended in high farce.

22 min: Jairzinho looks to pester Cooper down the right again but Moore steps across to snatch the ball away. He calmly strokes a pass up the wing to Peters, who finds Ball inside. His pass straight up the middle is met by Lee, whose ankles are clipped by Brito. Lee taps the free-kick left to Peters, who rolls inside for Ball, who in turn chips up for Charlton, running down the centre. Charlton gets those ridiculous honey strands on to the ball, heading onwards to Lee, on the edge of the area, level with the left post. Lee attempts a low drive but it's blocked, and though Charlton nearly gets on to the loose ball, Félix is out to gather. England have a reputation as arch-pragmatists, yet few sides could put together a lovely end-to-end move like that.

23 min: Comic cuts from the Brazilians. First off, Everaldo fires a long-distance shot miles left of England's goal. Then Pelé cynically checks Ball as the England midfielder heads up the inside right. Moore taps the ball forward to place the free-kick. Tostão claims that's the setpiece taken and toe-pokes to Pelé, who embarks on a full-speed skitter upfield. Beautiful gamesmanship. England re-take the free-kick, Wright making ground down the right and sending in a cross, which Peters heads over from 12 yards. What a chance, England's best of the match so far.

26 min: It's a storm of unpredictable brilliance, this game. Pelé drags a shot wide left. Paulo César goes on a twinkle-toed run down the left to reach the touchline, but his pullback is intercepted by the wily Moore. Peters, away down the other end along the right, is flagged for offside. His cross is punched into the net by a frustrated Hurst, a good old-fashioned cockney downward right hook, the sort you'd land on top of a fellow drinker's flat cap dahn the fahkin rub a dub.

28 min: The pace is slowing a tad. Brazil are knocking it around a lot at the moment. Carlos Alberto skelps a long-range effort into Labone's back. Ooyah.

30 min: Rivelino could have forged a career in music hall as a tumbling act. Here he is with another theatrical showreel. First he flops over Ball's leg. The referee waves play on. Then he launches himself over Charlton's leg, causing the England star to mime a dive. Worth a try.

31 min: Pelé advances on the England area down the inside left. Moore goes to ground and crunches him with a no-nonsense tackle, sweeping the ball off his toe and sending the Brazilian No. 10 to the ground in one fell swoop. The two sit slumped on the floor, Pelé looking slightly disoriented for a split second, before he gets up, hauling Moore with him, and giving the defender a congratulatory/patronizing pat on the head.

32 min: Mullery once again sends Wright away down the right wing ahead of Everaldo. Wright loops a majestic cross into the centre of the box. The ball evades Piazza and Hurst by the near post, and drops to Lee, who sends a diving header straight at Félix. The keeper can't hold on, the ball spinning into the air. Lee sticks his left leg out in an attempt to hook home but only succeeds in planting his boot on the keeper's head. He immediately hugs the keeper to apologize and Brazil don't kick off too much, but Lee's booked for his trouble.

33 min: Félix is down getting a fair bit of treatment. Some quite stunning analysis from former England captain Billy Wright on ITV, who says: 'That's the difference between South America and English football. We go in on those balls, but in South America they leave those balls alone, and that's what's caused the trouble.' The keeper might suggest that a player going in, rather than all the players who left the ball alone, is what's caused the trouble here, but there's a sort of circular logic to Wright's argument.

34 min: Carlos Alberto hangs a leg out and absolutely clatters Lee as the England man races down the middle. Revenge is a dish best served at 98 degrees. At lunch. In fairness, Lee seems to understand what's gone on here and doesn't make a meal of it. England confuse themselves with a couple of overly clever dummies at the free-kick. They seem too embarrassed to compete for the ball after they finally get round to kicking it.

37 min: Ball comes straight through the back of Rivelino. A totally unnecessary challenge deep in Brazilian territory. This is getting a little bit testy.

38 min: Skirmishes in the England area. Rivelino crosses from the left. Moore clears into the stand. A gentleman in the crowd shapes to throw the ball back but practises his throw-in technique before returning it. A craftsman at work. Another ball in from the same wing, this time from Paulo César. A game of head tennis breaks out. Pelé tries to make space in the area down the right but Mullery is keeping a presence on his shoulder. As the two come together, Pelé executes a ludicrous belly flop. Come along, Pelé. The unknown Israeli referee, Abraham Klein, isn't fooled. No penalty. Mullery, no doubt in a state of high amusement, throws an arm round Pelé's shoulder as the pair get up.

41 min: Brazil are turning the screw a wee bit. Rivelino caresses a long diagonal ball towards Jairzinho on the right. Cooper clatters him. Jairzinho doesn't seem too happy about it. Free-kick in a dangerous area just outside the box. Rivelino curls a low shot around the wall on the left, looking for the bottom-left corner. It's threaded with great accuracy, but clever Moore has been lurking just behind the wall and pops out to intercept, trapping the ball between his shins before calmly sauntering upfield.

42 min: Lee is obstructed by Everaldo down the right wing and says his piece to the Brazilian, who has come off worse in the duel, by way of a little snarl. Tempers are fraying in the heat. The free-kick results in Charlton dragging a dropping ball wide right from a decent position on the edge of the area. Folk are getting tired, too.

HALF TIME: England 0–0 Brazil. A strong finish to the half by the Brazilians. Jairzinho skates past Cooper and then Peters down the right, gliding into the area. Pelé gets in his way, allowing Moore to swan over and mop up. Everaldo high-kicks Hurst in the back. Paulo César curls a cross into the six-yard box from the left, Banks nipping in ahead of Tostão to claim. The winger then shakes up Wright's blood a little by turning him this way and that, Labone heading the resulting cross clear. And that's that for a fantastic half. Who needs goals?

And we're off again! No changes. Brazil get the ball rolling.

49 min: Lee shoots straight at Félix from some distance. Tostão comes back at England down the inside right and heads for the area. Just before he gets there, Moore goes to ground and sticks out his left leg to whip the ball away. That's so clean and precise.

51 min: The excellent youngster Paulo César, only playing because Gerson is missing, cuts in from the left and launches a shot towards the bottom right. Banks is forced to palm out for a corner. From the setpiece, Jairzinho launches the ball into the crowd from a tight angle on the right.

53 min: Pelé makes with some determination down the inside-right channel. As he reaches the area Charlton steps in and sends a panicked interception deep into the crowd behind the goal on the left. The setpiece is worked all the way back to the halfway line and across the pitch, where Carlos Alberto launches a pass towards Pelé in the box. Pelé draws Mullery to the right and backheels the long ball into space, but Moore is the only player who's read his intention. World-class stars thinking alike.

55 min: Moore's one of football's gentlemen, no question, but here he is taking a handful of Jairzinho's shirt as the Brazilian chases a long Rivelino pass down the right. That wasn't on. Jairzinho is incandescent with rage as that attack looked promising and the referee hasn't clocked Moore's cheek.

56 min: Brazil certainly aren't afraid to launch it long on the counter. Pelé sprays a pass down the right for Jairzinho, who is just beaten to it on the edge of the area by Banks rushing out to sweep up and hammer the ball out of play. Banks is creating merry hell, like a child, claiming the striker had his foot up, but Jairzinho was entitled to go for that.

57 min: Clodoaldo comes in from the right and launches a shot that just about finds the top-left corner of the stand behind the goal.

58 min: This has suddenly opened up, with Lee nudging the ball inside from the right to Ball, who in turn shuttles it on for Charlton. Hoick! The ball sails over the bar but that only registers three out of ten on the Clodoaldometer.

59 min: Pelé skates past three white shirts down the right, then rides a thumping challenge by Moore as he enters the box. Mullery comes over to welt clear. That was a fantastic run. This is turning into a minor duel between Pelé and Moore. From the resulting throw-in, the ball's worked back to Rivelino, who lives up to his White Pelé billing by dropping a shoulder past Peters, then another to diddle Lee, before battering the ball towards the top right from 25 yards. Banks parries, the ball twanging off him miles upfield as though he'd erected a brick wall in double-quick time.

60 min: GOAL!!! England 0–1 Brazil (Jairzinho). England have done precious little wrong in conceding here: they've just been prised open by sheer brilliance. Tostão embarks on a baroque ramble down the inside left, elbowing Ball out of the way, then slipping the ball through Moore's legs and finally evading Wright's sliding tackle. Then, on the left-hand edge of the box, he turns back on himself before whipping a cross past Moore towards Pelé, just to the right of the penalty spot. The King's attracted three white shirts, none of whom have a mind for Jairzinho just to the right. Pelé traps the ball with one wave of his right boot, then glances it towards Jairzinho with another. Jairzinho takes one touch and lashes a shot across a despairing Banks and into the top left. Nobody's stopping that. The striker makes off towards the stand on an Olympic celebration, executing seven high-powered leap-and-punch combos before he's caught by his team-mates. On the England bench, Sir Alf Ramsey looks at his colleagues with an expression that couldn't be clearer in spelling out: 'Hot damn, but what could we have possibly done about that?'

61 min: There's nearly an instant response by England, with Peters bustling down the left. The ball breaks to Charlton on the edge of the D but his snapshot, intended for the top left, sails wide.

62 min: The crowd are giving it the full 'BRASIL BRASIL BRASIL' now. Paulo César goes on a long skedaddle from the left to the centre of the park, where Pelé takes up possession. Pelé slips another ball out right to Jairzinho, but the resulting shot is an over-excitable nonsense.

63 min: There is *one* thing Ramsey can do about goals like that: shake up his team. Charlton and Lee, the sun lashing down on their exposed pates, are replaced by Bell and Astle, both blessed with full heads of hair. Although you wonder whether Astle's favoured style, the Motorcycle Crash Helmet, is taking safety a bit too far. It'll offer good protection but that thing must weigh about five stone! And that's not accounting for the several litres of sweat it's surely going to soak up once he starts running around. He must have a neck like a reinforced concrete plinth.

65 min: Astle heads down a Mullery long pass for Ball, who rushes into the area and takes a fresh-air swipe. What a chance! Brazil hack clear. Moore launches it again. Astle goes up with Félix, who again prevails. Has Ramsey been reading the collected works of Commander Charles Reep, the statistician who argues that subtlety should be dispatched out of the window in favour of repeated long-ball blootering? This'll never catch on in England.

66 min: WHAT A TACKLE!!! Mullery swings another high ball into the area, this time from a free-kick down the right. Félix, for all his faults, is meeting these with some confident punches. Brazil stream upfield, Jairzinho rushing at full pelt down the inside right, pushing Moore back, and back, and back. He looks frankly unstoppable but just as he enters the area, Moore, holding his line on the inside, times an interception to the nanosecond, sticking out his right boot and taking the ball off the striker's foot. It would have been so easy to give away a penalty there. The temperature is nearing 100 degrees so how does Moore keep the ice in his veins from melting? That was beyond sensational.

67 min: WHAT A MISS!!! Upon divesting Jairzinho of the ball, Moore strokes a pass up the wing for Cooper, who exchanges a one-two with Bell before launching a long ball into the Brazilian area from the left touchline. Everaldo, just to the right of the penalty spot, meets the ball with a woeful volley. All he manages to do is clank it off his standing leg and cushion the ball to the left, where Astle is all alone on the penalty spot with only Félix to beat! But he flashes a left-footed shot inches wide right of the post! How on earth did he miss that? Dear Lord, that is an appalling effort, with the only excuse that it had to be executed at speed. Astle walks back upfield, his eyes boring thousand-yard-deep holes in the turf, his shoulders visibly slumping to the ground. What a chance to equalize and to embellish the instant legend of that Moore tackle on Jairzinho.

68 min: The game has yet to restart as Félix is down getting treatment. Is he paralysed with laughter? You could hardly blame him.

69 min: Moore goes on a Beckenbaueresque wander down the middle of the pitch. What a match he's having. You could make an argument that this performance will define him even more than the final of four years ago. Cooper eventually ends up with the ball down the left and flashes a shot from nearly 30 yards straight at Félix. That was a decent effort from the full-back.

70 min: Pelé kicks Mullery's arm while contesting a high ball and goes down clutching his knee, moaning. He does love a whine, you know. As he gets some wholly unnecessary treatment, Roberto comes on for Tostão.

72 min: Bell tries to break into the Brazilian area but Everaldo steps across him and sashays off with the ball. Bell makes a strangulated cry for a penalty, but gives up halfway through. Even he doesn't really believe it. He gets on with the game and is soon sending a cross in from the right, but Astle mistimes his run at the far post. His token after-the-Lord-Mayor's-show mini-leap represents nothing more than the twin concepts of disappointment and self-loathing expressed via the medium of interpretative dance.

73 min: Wright is down with cramp. Dr Pelé sportingly holds Wright's leg in the air. 'One hopes he's not trying to pull it off,' observes ITV commentator Hugh Johns, channelling the popular cosmopolitan thought processes of Sir Alf.

75 min: Jairzinho has a lot of space to run into down the right. Moore positions himself well so he can't head into the box. Jairzinho crosses for Pelé instead but Mullery rushes back to cushion a header to his keeper. That's marvellous defending by Moore and Mullery, who have both been excellent. The play goes down the other end, where Astle heads a long Peters pass down for Bell, who skies a shot from 20 yards.

78 min: BALL HITS THE BAR!!! Moore nicks the ball past Paulo César down the right and strokes a pinpoint diagonal ball on to the head of Astle at the left-hand post. Astle heads back down into space for Ball, who meets it just inside the box. The little fellow takes one touch to steady himself, then clips the top of the crossbar near the right corner. Félix was nowhere. So, so unfortunate!

80 min: Carlos Alberto jumps up and down near his own corner flag with the ball between his feet. Tigger's cameo ends with Cooper making off with the ball and crossing deep, where Everaldo calmly nuts behind for a corner. Bell's delivery is flat and easily cleared. Moore tries to come back at Brazil but Clodoaldo relieves the pressure with a typically idiosyncratic dribble. Near his own area, he beats Ball down the inside right, then turns back past him before U-turning again, abruptly past Cooper. Now facing the correct way, he makes Moore, sliding in, look like a Sunday-league hacker, before one-twoing with Jairzinho and then spraying a crossfield pass towards Paulo César. He cuts in from the left, advances on the area, and sends a daisy-cutter towards the bottom right that Banks smothers. That could have been such a picturebook goal. This has been such an open game.

83 min: Bell helps a bouncing ball into the area from the left. After punching so well for so long, Félix charges off his line and resorts to type, his awful fist landing at Ball's feet on the edge of the area. Ball hoicks over with the goal gaping. England have had their chances.

85 min: Moore comes wandering into the Brazilian half down the inside left, and is body-checked by the shoulder of Pelé. You couldn't get more blatant or cynical than that. Moore shakes his head less in anger or frustration, more in sadness that a great player has stooped so low. The resulting free-kick is easily cleared, Clodoaldo meandering up the left this time. He feeds Roberto, who bustles to the left-hand edge of the D before hitting low to the left corner. Banks turns the ball behind for a corner, from which nothing comes.

87 min: Moore is throwing caution to the wind now. He's playing as a left winger! Alf won't like that! He reaches the corner flag after a neat exchange of passes with Cooper. Carlos Alberto nips in to divert Moore's attempt at a cross out of play. The corner's punched clear by Coco, but the ball's soon sent back into the area by Cooper on the left. Astle relieves the pressure on Brazil by leaping above Everaldo and punching the ball down into Hurst's path. First Hurst's haymaker into the net, now this; turns out the world champions of association football are not that bad at volleyball either. Hope this willingness to handle the ball isn't running up any karmic debt that'll need settling in the future.

90 min: Piazza is caught snoozing on the ball near his own area by Astle. Cue hot-potato passing by two sides feeling nervous for very different reasons. Eventually Bell strides down the left channel and takes a shot but his weak pea-roller is easily gathered by Félix.

90+1 min: Jairzinho flies down the right, cutting inside. He lays off for Pelé, just to the right of the D. Pelé evades Wright's carthorse lunge and makes himself a bit of space in which to manufacture a glorious chip towards the top left. Just a little too much power and it flies over the bar. Banks makes out he had it covered and we probably owe him the benefit of the doubt given his heroics of the first half.

90+2 min: Pelé is gesturing to the referee, begging for the final whistle. He gets in the way of Peters, who is busying himself upfield in the hope of crafting one last chance of an equalizer. The referee blows his whistle. Brazil think it's all over but it isn't, it's a free-kick to England. The ball's sent out wide left to Cooper, who sends a Hail Mary into the area towards the unreliable Félix, whereupon . . .

THE WHISTLE GOES FOR FULL TIME!!! England 0–1 Brazil. That's that. So England didn't 'beat these'. Pelé shakes hands with Labone, then embraces Moore in the centre circle. It's a moment of genuine warmth, with Pelé holding Moore's face in his hands and the England captain throwing his arm around the Brazilian striker's shoulder. There's a *tableau vivant* for the ages: respect, friendship and sportsmanship distilled in a simple exchange of shirts. Of course, spool the film back a bit and you've got all those dives, body-checks and shirt tugs, and Pelé's just managed to totally blank poor Mullery, who was perhaps looking to swap shirts after marking him well through-out the game, but the overall point probably still stands. Despite Franny Lee's best efforts, that was a game played out in the grand spirit, both teams doing all they could to attack, both teams defending like lords. That's the first time Bobby Moore has lost a World Cup game, yet it's probably the best he's ever played in one. Figure that out. A draw would have probably been the fairest result, but then it was Brazil who managed to take the tin-opener to a steely defence, while England passed up their golden chance. Still, never mind. England will almost certainly progress to the second round and are still highly fancied to make the final. Which will probably be a rerun of this game, no?

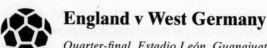

England v West Germany

Quarter-final, Estadio León, Guanajuato, Mexico,
Sunday, 14 June 1970

One thousand, four hundred and forty-five days. That's how long it's been since Geoff Hurst's hat-trick, the Russian linesman and all that. Now West Germany meet their bogey side England once more. England's hold on the Germans is pretty remarkable: nine wins in 11 with only one defeat – and that, two years ago, with a weakened side and a deflected winner from Franz Beckenbauer. 'The Germans,' as the superb young writer Hugh McIlvanney suggested in this morning's *Observer*, 'have to ignore more omens than Julius Caesar on assassination day.'

And yet, the Germans have been the more impressive side in this tournament. England were beaten by Brazil, even if they contributed fully to a charming match, and played dreadfully in Wednesday's unconvincing 1–0 win over Czechoslovakia that secured their quarter-final place. Then again, they started the 1966 World Cup pretty slowly too. And they do have Bobby Moore in simply majestic form despite the pre-tournament trouble in Bogotá.

Germany struggled a little in their first match, coming from behind to win 2–1 against Morocco, but then walloped Bulgaria 5–2 and Peru 3–1, with Bayern Munich goal addict Gerd Müller whacking hat-tricks in both games. Their wingful wonders have been a revelation, with Hannes Löhr and particularly Reinhard Libuda causing all sorts of problems. They seem content and relaxed: their coach Helmut Schön was ten minutes late for a press conference the other day because he had to change after being thrown in the pool by his players. You can't quite imagine Martin Peters and Francis Lee doing that to Sir Alf Ramsey, can you?

Leon is 6,200 feet above sea level. The sun is a fireball in the sky, so this will not be a day for haring around like madmen.

Team news: Gordon Banks has Montezuma's revenge and is unavailable, with Chelsea's Peter Bonetti standing in. That's one of five changes: Brian Labone, Francis Lee, Geoff Hurst and

Alan Ball come in for Jack Charlton, Colin Bell, Allan Clarke and Jeff Astle. West Germany are unchanged. There are five men on each side from the 1966 final: Moore, Ball, Bobby Charlton, Peters, Hurst; Höttges, Schnellinger, Overath, Beckenbauer and Seeler.

Charlton is winning his 106th cap, a new England record; he overtakes the great Billy Wright.

Referee: Norberto Coerezza (Argentina).

Kick-off: Midday for the players, 7 p.m. for the armchair viewers in England.

England: Peter Bonetti, Keith Newton, Terry Cooper, Alan Mullery, Brian Labone, Bobby Moore, Francis Lee, Alan Ball, Bobby Charlton, Geoff Hurst, Martin Peters.

West Germany: Sepp Maier, Berti Vogts, Horst-Dieter Höttges, Franz Beckenbauer, Klaus Fichtel, Karl-Heinz Schnellinger, Reinhard Lubuda, Uwe Seeler, Gerd Müller, Wolfgang Overath, Hannes Löhr.

1 min: West Germany kick off from left to right. They are in white, with England in red, just as in 1966. Could that be an omen? No, of course it bloody couldn't, you daft bugger. It's a different game in a different continent in a different year between two different sets of players! Anyway, it's a bit of a false start, because the referee has changed the ball after 35 seconds. Bobby Moore and Müller throw it up in the air, point at it like it's a piece of shit and hand the tatty orb to the referee. He squeezes it, decides it's not fit for purpose and boots it inelegantly off the field. You would think they'd have checked this beforehand.

2 min: While we wait for play to restart, the ITV commentator Hugh Johns – coming down the line from Mexico, although the distant crackle is such that he may as well be broadcasting from the moon – praises England's stand-in keeper Bonetti. 'It's not bad that England can have such a goalkeeper of such brilliance and skill to come in as reserve.' He's right. Of course, it's a blow to lose Gordon Banks but Bonetti must be among the best back-ups in the world.

6 min: Sepp Maier, the talented but erratic West Germany goalkeeper, comes flying out for a Newton cross with all the conviction of a wino chasing a pound note in the breeze. He actually runs ahead of the ball and has to leap back towards his own goal. He can't hold on to it but thankfully for Maier there are no England forwards around and he claims the rebound.

10 min: Charlton's deep cross from the right is headed back across by Geoff Hurst and Maier comes from his line to claim. As he does so Lee runs past him and Maier goes down dramatically, holding his face. Did Lee catch him with an arm? It's hard to tell. Lee is shoved by one of the German players and walks away with his arms outstretched, pleading his innocence. The referee stomps over to the linesman, putting his hand in his top pocket. He looks like he's about to book the linesman! Maier is holding his nose. On ITV, Hugh 'Buzz Aldrin' Johns calls it 'acting' by Maier. It seems impossible to tell from replays whether he touched him or not – but the referee has decided to give Lee a yellow card! If it was acting then method-man Maier did a comprehensive job of it: he was down for a minute and a half and needed treatment on the field.

16 min: Löhr is tackled well in the box by Moore. Löhr falls over, which seemed a natural consequence of the tackle, although Hugh Johns says, 'already these Germans looking like the tragedy actors from a touring Shakespeare show'. That seems more than a little harsh.

18 min: Müller has his name taken for a late, clumsy foul on Alan Ball, who goes down. The referee waves the card all around the ground, like a ring-card girl at a Vegas bout. A few moments later, Charlton runs at Beckenbauer and strikes a decent shot from 25 yards that is comfortably saved by Maier, plunging to his left. Charlton needs one goal to become the first Englishman to score 50 times for his country – what a double that would be on the day he becomes England's most capped player.

23 min: Hurst, under pressure from Fichtel, miscontrols Ball's sharp, driven pass into the area. Hugh Johns, sounding increasingly outraged, says, 'Hurst getting a kick from behind before he got the ball!' We haven't seen a replay so it's hard to tell, although there were no complaints.

29 min: Beckenbauer, 40 yards from goal, waves a pass over the top of the England defence with the outside of his right foot. Müller – who usually knows where the ball is going before the player in possession does – spins away from Labone and gets to it first but can't get any significant contact. Bonetti claims.

32 min: GOAL! England 1–0 West Germany (Mullery). Alan Mullery has scored his first goal for England! What a time to get it. It was a fine move from England, which started by their own corner flag when Cooper and Peters dispossessed Libuda. Mullery played a one-two with Lee and then, from just inside the Germany half, swept a long pass out to Newton on the right. He moved to the edge of the area, with Overath back-pedalling. 'Newton should take it past Overath now,' screams Johns. 'Run at him!' Instead of taking him on, he slipped a low cross towards the near post. Mullery – who had followed up his own pass – got there just before Vogts and crashed it first time past Maier from six yards.

37 min: Overath walks towards the referee, complaining about something just for the sake of it, so the referee shoves him away! Schnellinger jabs his finger towards the referee a few times and then wags his finger as if to say, 'Nah, you can't do that pal.' The referee quite clearly couldn't give a flying one what Schnellinger or anyone else thinks. He calls Overath towards him and administers what looks like a final warning.

43 min: Beckenbauer's 30-yard hit deflects wide off an England player. This is an odd game. It hasn't been awful technically. It's just that, with the exception of the goal, *nothing whatsoever has happened*.

44 min: Francis Lee goes on a bullocking 60-yard run from the right, infield past Höttges, before going over in the box under challenge from Schnellinger. 'That must be a penalty!' says Johns, before realizing that it wasn't a penalty and that not even Lee, the great pretender, had appealed. 'Good gracious me. That looked very much as though Schnellinger hit him with a sharp right cross.' Hm. There were no complaints from England. The 'Independent' Television commentator's ever-so-slightly partisan commentary has been the defining feature of this half.

HALF TIME: England 1–0 West Germany. Not much to write home about, but England will take it and so will the folks back home.

46 min: England begin the second half. West Germany have made a substitution at half time, with Willi Schulz replacing Höttges.

49 min: Lee is penalized near the halfway line, a little harshly, for leaning into Fichtel. The increasingly tiresome Johns is beside himself with apoplectic rage. 'And a foul is given!' chorus Johns and Johns. 'A foul against Lee which is almost unbelievable!'

50 min: GOAL! England 2–0 West Germany (Peters). England are surely heading for a semi-final against either Italy or Mexico! Martin Peters has put them 2–0 up! As with the first goal, this was a smooth length-of-the-field move. Moore blocked Seeler's shot and gave the ball to Ball. He played a crisp pass forward to Hurst, who was able to turn 40 yards from goal. He moseyed towards the right, waiting for a storming overlapping run from Newton, and then eased the ball down the wing. Newton chipped a fine first-time cross towards the far post, where Peters got to the ball just ahead of the sliding Vogts and forced it past Maier from ten yards. 'It's in the net! Geoff Hurst!' says Johns, but it was definitely Peters and he runs away in triumph. It was a slightly scruffy finish – one replay angle suggests Vogts may even have kicked the ball off Peters – but England will not care about that. It was West Ham who beat the Germans in 1966 and this time it's Spurs, in the shape of Mullery and Peters, who are doing the damage.

53 min: Müller goes in late on Newton, who instinctively turns round with a Why I Oughta look on his face. That was a pretty poor tackle, though not sufficient to warrant a red card for Müller, who had his name taken in the first half.

57 min: West Germany make their final substitution: Jürgen Grabowski, the speedy winger who has come off the bench in every game, replaces Libuda.

58 min: Grabowski's first touch is to take a short corner with Overath and then hit a fierce shot from a tight angle on the right that is blocked by Cooper. A few moments later, Löhr's high cross from the left is superbly claimed under pressure from Müller by the stretching Bonetti. That's pretty much the first thing the Chelsea keeper has had to do.

63 min: Overath runs forward, surveys the scene and then drills an entirely hopeless pass straight out of play with no German players within 20 yards of the ball. England look really comfortable defensively, with Moore and Labone in control.

66 min: A masterful interception on the edge of his own area from Moore starts another England attack. It goes through Charlton, Ball, Mullery, Moore, Cooper, Moore, Mullery, Cooper and then Peters, who clips over a cross from the left. Ball, near the penalty spot, escapes Vogts and takes it down on his chest, but with his second touch he treads on the ball and the half-chance has gone.

67 min: Beckenbauer's long-range shot – Germany's main threat thus far – deflects wide off Moore. England break sharply from the resulting corner when Ball nicks the ball off Beckenbauer on the edge of his own area. He gives it to Charlton, with four on three at one stage. Charlton runs 35 yards and moves smoothly past Overath to the edge of the D, but then mis-hits a fairly tame shot straight at Maier. He was under a bit of pressure from Schnellinger, although we have seen Charlton smash them into the top corner from that range so many times.

68 min: England keep the ball for over a minute, putting together 22 consecutive passes before Cooper's ambitious solo run proves unsuccessful.

69 min: GOAL! England 2–1 West Germany (Beckenbauer). West Germany are back in the game! This is a fine solo goal from Beckenbauer. He fronted Mullery up, 30 yards from goal, wiggled his hips for a couple of seconds and then moved sharply around his opponent to the right. Then, from just outside the area, he stabbed a low cross-shot that went under Bonetti and into the far corner. Bonetti should surely have done better. It wasn't a particularly well-struck shot and, although it dipped a little awkwardly, he basically dived right over the top of the ball. The camera lingers on Müller for a second. 'I don't quite know why we're showing a picture of Müller because it was Beckenbauer the scorer,' says Hugh Johns. Identities are easy to mistake, of course – as Johns shows a second later when he bemoans the fact that Beckenbauer scored while Moore was 'laid out' and out of the game. In fact, it was Lee who was down on all fours after being hit in the chest – or something swinging slightly lower – by a piledriver from Fichtel. Poor Johns.

He is an excellent commentator usually but he has had a nightmare today.

70 min: The kick-off is delayed while Lee receives some treatment. England have made a substitution, with Colin Bell replacing the slightly disappointing Charlton.

74 min: Grabowski leaves Cooper for dead, surges forward and plays a one-two with Seeler just outside the box. His first touch is poor, however, and forces him wide, from where he lofts a high cross that is well claimed by Bonetti. His pace and directness are causing a tiring defence some problems.

77 min: Moore flicks an elegant pass out to Bell, in loads of space just past the halfway line on the right. Bell runs to the edge of the area then comes across the line of the box, past Schnellinger's sliding tackle and also Vogts, before striking a left-footed shot that is smartly held by Maier, plunging to his left. That's the most significant save either keeper has made.

78 min: Hurst comes within an inch of putting England into the semi-finals! Peters and Ball combined to put Bell clear on the right, again in so much space. He chipped a careful cross towards the near post, where Hurst, Schulz and Maier all went for the ball on the six-yard line. Hurst got there, stooping forward to flick a delicate header that drifted tantalizingly past the far post.

79 min: Vogts hares into the box on the right and goes over after a tackle from behind by Cooper. It was a risky tackle, but it seems Cooper just got to the ball and Germany's penalty appeals are ignored.

79 min: WHAT A SAVE FROM BONETTI! Peter Bonetti may well have put England through to the semi-finals with a vital save from Müller. Löhr, in the centre circle, clipped an angled pass towards Müller, who was left one-against-one with Newton on the edge of the area. Müller, on the turn, stumbled straight through Newton and clear on goal. Germans would have been placing their house, car and favourite sausage on Müller to score. But no. He leathered a shot from ten yards that Bonetti not only stopped but held. It was pretty close to him; even so, that was a vital save, reminiscent of Manchester United's Alex Stepney against Eusebio of Benfica in the 1968 European Cup final.

81 min: England are going to make their second and final sub-stitution. Norman Hunter is coming on, although there is some confusion as to who is coming off. It was going to be Peters, but now Newton is limping. England have 12 players on the field at the moment while Newton is being treated. It seems he is going to continue so Peters is the one who is going off.

82 min: GOAL! England 2–2 West Germany (Seeler). It's all going horribly wrong for England: Seeler has equalized with a remarkable header! Löhr's cross hit Newton, prompting an appeal for handball. That was rejected but it didn't matter. The ball was only cleared as far as Schnellinger, 40 yards from goal to the left of centre. He drilled a long, high cross towards the far post, where Seeler pulled away from Mullery and sent a frankly ridiculous backheader over Bonetti and into the far corner. That's an astonishing goal. If he meant it, it's one of the greatest headers of all time. It's quite possible he was trying to flick it back towards Müller in the six-yard box and got lucky. Either way he needed neck muscles like the Incredible Hulk's. It was a high ball with no pace on it whatsoever. Seeler was facing towards the right wing, yet had enough strength to loop the ball back the other way and into the corner. He was off-balance as he did so and fell over, before lying on his back in celebration. We saw West Germany's capacity for a spec-tacular comeback in the 1954 final and now they have done it again, inspired by this remarkable little man. Where's there a will, there's Uwe.

84 min: BECKENBAUER ALMOST PUTS ENGLAND OUT OF THE WORLD CUP! England are all over the place here. How has this happened? They looked so comfortable for so long. Now they are hanging on to their World Cup title. Beckenbauer saunters forward from midfield and plays a sharp pass into Müller on the edge of the box. He has Moore, Labone and Hunter all surrounding him, but takes them – and also Mullery and Bell – out of the game with an ingenious first-time return pass, judged as if with a protractor. Beckenbauer roars on to it, slips past the weary Newton and drags his left-footed shot into the side-netting at the near post from ten yards. Bonetti would not have got there if it had been in the corner. What a chance!

86 min: Another chance for Germany! Löhr, running down the left wing, was fouled so obviously by the shattered Newton that even Hugh Johns called it a 'definite foul'. Overath curled it towards the six-yard line, where Löhr got ahead of Moore and headed over the bar. That's another very good opportunity, even if he had to jump slightly away from goal to meet the ball.

89 min: Hunter's long pass is headed needlessly behind for a corner by Overath. Is this England's moment? Alan Ball blasts the corner dangerously towards the near post, where Lee pulls away to try to meet the ball. He makes a bit of a hash of it, kicking it away from goal under pressure from Maier, although in his defence it was an awkward ball.

90+1 min: Overath plays a clever pass inside Newton, aiming for Löhr. It's heading for the referee, who lets it go with an elaborate stepover, and Newton beats Löhr to the ball to concede a corner. Is this Germany's moment? *Ach, nein*, Grabowski's corner is too deep.

FULL TIME: England 2–2 West Germany. 'You've won it once, go and win it again.' That's what Sir Alf Ramsey said to England before extra time in 1966 and he might well say it again here. England were cruising into the semi-finals before a dramatic comeback from West Germany. As the players prepare to kick off again, Hugh Johns reminds us that, if no side wins this game in 30 minutes of extra time, it will be decided by 'the rattle' – effectively a drawing of lots to decide who will play in the semi-final. We have seen this scenario before: Italy beat the USSR on the toss of a coin in the Euro 68 semi-final. And Italy will be the opponents for whoever gets through: they have beaten the hosts Mexico 4–1 in Toluca.

91 min: England begin extra time, kicking off from right to left, and Hurst has a chance within 12 seconds! Lee moved the ball down the wing to Bell, who bounced Beckenbauer aside and curved a dangerous cross towards the near post. Hurst got in front of Schulz and flicked his header wide of the far post from eight yards. That was a real opportunity.

96 min: Löhr's deep corner is headed away by Hunter. It comes to Beckenbauer 30 yards out. He controls the ball and then hits a vicious shot that is superbly tipped over the bar by Bonetti.

It might have been hitting the bar rather than going in, though Bonetti could not be sure: he leapt with both feet a long way off the ground to fingertip for a corner.

97 min: That Beckenbauer shot brought the second of five corners for Germany in a two-minute period. They come to nothing eventually but these are dangerous times for England.

98 min: Colin Bell has been England's most dangerous player since coming on and here he goes again on a 60-yard run. He sucks Beckenbauer in and leaves him for dead; then he zips around Schnellinger in the box, but his cut-back towards Lee is crucially intercepted by Fichtel.

102 min: A swerving run from Bell, away from Beckenbauer again, brings a corner for England on the right. And it leads to a great chance for Labone! Bell's corner was a poor one but it came back to him off Schnellinger. He took a touch and dragged a cross towards the penalty spot, where Labone got away from Fichtel only to spank it high and wide. He had to take it first time; we know he's a centre-half but, even so, that was a big opportunity. England have been the better team in this first period of extra time, recovering well from the shock of Seeler's equalizer.

105 min: Hugh Johns appeals for a penalty when Lee goes down in the box. It was a great run. He turned Fichtel smartly, beat Schnellinger on the edge of the box and came back inside the recovering Fichtel before falling over near the byline under challenge from Schnellinger. It looked like an easy fall, in truth. 'That must be a penalty!' said Johns, but there were no real appeals from England.

EXTRA TIME, HALF TIME: England 2–2 West Germany.

107 min: Hugh Johns tells us once again that, if the match is drawn, England will be the winner by virtue of being Englan— Sorry, lots will be drawn in the referee's room via 'the rattle'. You can be sure that the toys will come out of the losing pram and understandably so, for that's no way to decide a World Cup quarter-final between the 1966 champions and runners up. FIFA has proposed that the drawing of lots be discontinued and replaced with a competition of five penalty kicks per side, a suggestion that will be discussed at the International Football Association Board in a couple of weeks.

108 min: GOAL! England 2–3 West Germany (Müller). We may not need the rattle after all: West Germany are ahead! What an amazing comeback this has been. Moore played a ball forward to Hurst, who was slow to react and allowed Fichtel to get there first. He pushed it straight to Grabowski on the right wing. Grabowski turned the tired Cooper one way and then the other, bursting towards the byline before booming a cross beyond the far post. Löhr leapt above Newton to head it back whence it came, and Müller pulled away from Labone to volley it into the net from a couple of yards. It's his eighth goal of the World Cup. Even before the ball had reached Löhr, Müller was pulling away, his sixth sense telling him where the ball was going to go. Labone and Bonetti, by contrast, were drawn towards the near post, and that gave Müller the crucial couple of yards he needed. Müller and Löhr gallivant joyously across the pitch with their arms round each other. West Germany are on the brink of a sensational sort of hat-trick: an end to their England hoodoo in competitive play, their greatest World Cup comeback since the 1954 final – and, most importantly of all, a place in this year's semis.

109 min: HURST HAS A GOAL DISALLOWED FOR OFFSIDE! What has happened here? Lee hit a fierce cross from the right towards Ball. He was challenged by Vogts and the ball rebounded back to Lee by the right touchline in the box. He beat Schnellinger, moved around Maier and stabbed the ball towards Hurst. By then the flag had gone up, although Hurst put the ball in the net out of habit. It seems the linesman has given offside when the ball came back to Lee – but was the ball returned to him off Ball or Vogts? It's hard to tell as we have had no replays. Again, there are no complaints.

113 min: A couple of corners on the left for England, who understandably look desperate for the first time in the match. They come to nothing.

114 min: HOW IS THAT NOT A PENALTY TO ENGLAND? Hurst played a nothing cross into the box, where Bell met it under pressure from Vogts. His first touch was outstanding, spinning the ball around Vogts; with his second he got to the ball just before Beckenbauer, who sent him flying with a tired tackle. Again there are very few complaints but that looked a clear penalty. 'Colin Bell, a penalty!' said Johns. 'Surely!' He stopped just short of saying 'Please God!' But this time he was dead right: that was a clear penalty.

115 min: Maier collides with Labone as he claims a cross from the left. He staggers a couple of steps and then falls to the ground in slow motion. 'Oh what a dramatic moment!' growls Hugh Johns in disgust. 'Well, that was worth an Oscar!'

116 min: A few seconds later Mullery drills not far over the top from 25 yards. Maier is down again, lying in his six-yard box and pointing to his thigh. The referee ignores him and play goes on when Schulz takes the goal-kick.

116 min: England are really pressing now. Hunter, on the left, arrows a cross beyond the far post. Hurst rises majestically and heads back towards the penalty spot. Ball marauds on to the ball but, under pressure from Vogts, slashes it well wide with his left foot. That was a big chance.

119 min: Ball maims fresh air with his right fist after being penalized for what seemed a fair tackle on Beckenbauer. England know this is nearly over.

120 min: Newton's cross is touched off by Hurst to Ball in the D. He turns away from Vogts and squares it to Newton, who drags his weary legs on to the ball once more and hits a shot with the outside of the foot from 20 yards. It's a bit too straight and Maier jumps to touch it over the bar. England have a corner. This really is it now . . .

120+1 min: . . . the corner is cleared to Mullery, who hits a ridiculously ambitious half-volley over the bar from 35 yards.

Some people are on the pitch. Photographers, who are all crowding round Maier as he prepares to take his goal-kick. That's bizarre. Maier moves to the other side of the field to take the goal-kick – and when he does it's the last kick of the game! England's 1,445-day reign as world champions is over!

EXTRA TIME, FULL TIME: England 2–3 West Germany. The England players look like they are suffering from shock. It will take a long time for England not only to get over this defeat but also to understand it. At 2–0 they were so comfortable; then a mistake from Bonetti allowed West Germany back into the game and from that moment England had no control of events – even though they created plenty more chances themselves. West Germany move on to face Italy in the semi-finals; England go home, world champions no more.

Italy v West Germany

Semi-final, Estadio Azteca, Mexico City, Mexico,
Wednesday, 17 June 1970

Italy's post-war World Cup record is a disgrace. They were champions in 1934 and 1938 but could not get past the group stage in 1950, 1954, 1962 and 1966 – and they didn't even qualify in 1958. Their last campaign, in England four years ago, ended with humiliation by North Korea in Middlesbrough and a hail of overripe tomatoes when they got back home. Since then, things have improved spectacularly. They won the European Championship two years ago – albeit on home soil and after two draws in three games, including a win over the USSR in the semi-final decided by the toss of a coin – and now they are in the World Cup semi-final. They started the tournament slowly, sneaking through the group stages in binary mode (1–0, 0–0, 0–0), and then battered the hosts Mexico 4–1 on Sunday. They still have the problem of how to accommodate both Sandro Mazzola and Gianni Rivera; in the quarter-finals the coach Ferruccio Valcareggi simply gave them a half each.

If Italy are finally doing themselves justice at a modern World Cup, then West Germany want justice after losing so controversially in the 1966 final. They beat England in that dramatic quarter-final last weekend and have the swagger of a team who have beaten the holders. 'Once you have beaten England,' says Uwe Seeler, 'you know you can beat anybody.' But that win has taken plenty out of them and not just the extra half hour of energy sapping either: Horst-Dieter Höttges is out with a knee injury, while Beckenbauer, Seeler and Maier needed treatment.

Kick-off: 4 p.m. local time or 11 p.m. over here. Put the kettle on and snuggle in front of the Radio Rentals Hi-Vantage TV.

Referee: Arturo Yamasaki (Mexico).

Italy are unchanged, so Rivera stays on the bench: Enrico Albertosi, Tarcisio Burgnich, Pierluigi Cera, Roberto Rosato, Giacinto Facchetti, Mario Bertini, Sandro Mazzola, Giancarlo De Sisti, Angelo Domenghini, Roberto Boninsegna, Gigi Riva.

West Germany include Milan's Karl-Heinz Schnellinger – the only man on either side to play overseas – and Jürgen Grabowski, who tormented Terry Cooper from the bench on Sunday: Sepp Maier, Berti Vogts, Willi Schulz, Karl-Heinz Schnellinger, Bernd Patzke, Jürgen Grabowski, Franz Beckenbauer, Wolfgang Overath, Hannes Löhr, Uwe Seller, Gerd Müller.

The winners will meet Brazil or Uruguay, who are about to kick off in Guadalajara.

1 min: Italy kick off from left to right, with Boninsegna rolling the ball to Mazzola. They're in blue, West Germany in white, and there's an early free-kick for a foul by Domenghini on Overath.

4 min: Overath, just outside the area on the left, drives a surprise cross-shot that is not too far from Müller, lurking at the far post in pursuit of his *eighth* goal of the competition.

8 min: GOAL! Italy 1–0 West Germany (Boninsegna). Boninsegna scores his first goal for Italy! It was a beauty, too, rifled into the corner from 20 yards. But it came about indirectly from an appalling piece of defending from Schulz, who hoofed a miserable clearance straight into touch in the Italian half. Burgnich threw the ball to De Sisti, who pushed it forward to Boninsegna, 40 yards out and with his back to goal. He was allowed to turn by Schulz – who hasn't exactly covered himself in the glorious stuff in this goal – and ran infield before being challenged by a combination of Löhr and Overath. He tried to play a short-range one-two with Riva, whose mis-hit return pass deflected off the breast of Schnellinger and back to Boninsegna. He won the ball off the dithering Beckenbauer and then, as Schulz closed in, thrashed an instant left-footed shot that swerved away from the diving Maier and into the bottom-left corner. What a few weeks Boninsegna has had. Before the tournament he had made only one appearance for Italy and that in 1967; now he has scored his first ever international goal in a World Cup semi-final.

9 min: Almost an instant response from West Germany. Seeler is fouled by Domenghini in a central position 35 yards out. Beckenbauer waves a quick free-kick with the outside of the foot towards Müller, who loses his marker Rosato. The ball is just too far in front of him, however; Albertosi comes out and then, for some reason, decides to go with his feet rather than his hands, shanking it behind for a corner.

17 min: Beckenbauer oozes class in the centre of midfield. With nothing happening he goes on an urgent surge from the halfway line, beating Domenghini with his change of pace. Then he finds a brilliantly early touch just outside the area that takes Cera out of the game before he even knows he's in it. Beckenbauer gets into the box on the right before falling under a challenge from Facchetti. Should that have been a penalty? Certainly Facchetti did not get the ball. Beckenbauer fell a little easily but that does not mean it wasn't a foul. Beckenbauer and Müller are particularly radged off, waving their hands at the referee.

23 min: Riva thrashes well wide of the near post from a prohibitive angle on the left. He does what all brazen workmen do: he blames his tools, suggesting the ball pressure is not right. Maier agrees and so does the referee, who calls for a replacement. The same thing happened in the West Germany–England game. These Adidas Telstars look impossibly cool but it would be nice if, you know, they actually worked.

29 min: Löhr's cross from the left hits Müller, under pressure from Rosato, and is about to drop for Seeler ten yards out when Bertini stretches to flick it past his own goal for a corner. That was a crucial interception.

34 min: GRABOWSKI HITS THE BAR! Grabowski has done nothing all game but this was an explosive reminder of his threat. He received the ball from Schulz, ran directly infield at the defence, then smashed a rising left-footed shot from 30 yards. It grazed the head of Cera and rattled off the top of the bar! Albertosi may also have got a slight fingertip as he leapt backwards. It's hard to tell, although if he did it was a hell of a save.

36 min: Riva plays the ball wide left to Boninsegna, who dummies Schulz superbly and is butchered by him as a consequence. That was a dreadful tackle.

37 min: Beckenbauer crashes a 25-yarder wide of goal. It was only a couple of yards wide in fact, although Albertosi didn't dive; he just watched it whistle past the post with a kind of idle curiosity. From the goal-kick, Boninsegna gets his revenge on Schulz with a cracking elbow to the face as they jump for the high ball. He really caught him but Schulz didn't go down. He headed the ball clear and then felt his jaw tentatively, like someone checking their bank balance after a weekend on the sauce. The referee gave a free-kick, nothing more.

39 min: Seeler is fouled just outside the area and De Sisti is yellow-carded, probably for dissent. When the free-kick is taken by Löhr, the charging Riva is only a few yards away and blocks the ball. The referee orders a retake, whereupon Riva stomps away with a heroically misguided sense of injustice. Take two: Löhr drills it over the bar.

42 min: That was almost a second for Italy. Albertosi's long goal-kick was headed on by Domenghini towards Boninsegna. He miscontrolled it and it would have run through to Maier had Schnellinger, uncertain as to what was behind him, not stuck a foot out on the edge of the area. He diverted it into the area to Riva, who had ran off Vogts and lifted his left foot gymnastically to head height to try to meet the ball. He missed but Vogts headed it back towards his own goal. It bounced up awkwardly in front of Maier, who nonetheless made a bit of a meal of what should have been a routine save, chesting the ball behind for a corner. Before which, there's a **PITCH INVASION!** What's going on now? Domenghini was preparing to take the corner on the left when a supporter in a turquoise blue suit jacket ran towards him. The supporter doesn't seem to want any trouble – in fact, it looks like he just wants a hug. Or maybe to touch the World Cup ball. Domenghini shrugs him off, grabs him by the shoulder and drags him back towards the stands, whereupon the man skips jauntily back into anonymity. That was bizarre.

43 min: A long free-kick from Bertini is headed back out towards the edge of the area by Vogts. Riva runs back after it, lets it bounce a couple of times and then drags a slow shot across goal and not far wide. Maier again didn't look entirely convincing there.

44 min: Italy are finishing the half very strongly. Boninsegna takes a long pass from Bertini on the right wing and comes inside Schulz, cradling the ball on his left foot. He spots Mazzola making a great run off the back of Beckenbauer in an inside-left position and plays a gorgeous angled pass between Vogts and

. . . .MAGIC MINUTES . . . . .MAGIC MINUTES . . . . .

Brazil 3–1 Uruguay (1970, semi-final)

At Mexico 1970, Pelé had already nearly scored from the halfway line against Czechoslovakia – unheard of in those days, when David Beckham was minus five years old – when he produced an even more sensational attempt in the semi-final against Uruguay.

90 min: PELE REDEFINES FOOTBALL! Pelé comes within a whisker of scoring a goal like no other. He was put through by a lovely pass from Tostão, played towards the D. As Pelé hurtled towards the ball, Ladislao Mazurkiewicz ran outside his area in an attempt to intercept. Pelé ran straight past the ball and round Mazurkiewicz, who was so befuddled that he tried to paw at Pelé's legs, missed and ended up on his knees in total confusion. Pelé was moving so fast that he had to put the brakes on like a cartoon cat and run back away from goal to meet the ball before shooting on the turn. He wrongfooted Atilio Ancheta, the defender on the line, who was so thrown that he ended falling over and doing a forward roll, but the ball drifted fractionally wide of the far post. Perhaps that's the true level of Pelé's genius: that he's becoming better known for the goals he doesn't score rather than those he does. He is stretching football's parameters in the most astonishing ways. This is the cinematography in *Citizen Kane*, the Beatles's melodies, a moment of pure inventive genius that will live in the mind for ever. Actually, sod that: this is football's equivalent of putting a man on the moon.

Schnellinger. Mazzola takes it on the edge of the box, moves in to the area and then, as Schnellinger comes across, stabs wide of the near post from 12 yards with his right foot. The referee played a good advantage and has now given a free-kick on the edge of the area for shirt-tugging by Beckenbauer on Mazzola.

Mazzola nods his head approvingly at the referee and claps his hands approvingly at Boninsegna.

45 min: Riva's free-kick hits the wall and Bertini's long-range follow up is saved by Maier. Hang on, now Maier has been penalized for taking more than four steps! He had about 12 – and the referee has given Italy an indirect free-kick 12 yards from goal. The German wall is six yards away at best. Mazzola touches it off to Riva, whose shot is blocked.

HALF TIME: Italy 1–0 West Germany. Italy have been much the better side. West Germany look a little like a team who played their World Cup final the other day.

46 min: This new half-time substitution malarkey from Italy, with Gianna Rivera replacing Mazzola.

48 min: GREAT CHANCE FOR WEST GERMANY! Seeler should probably have equalized then. Beckenbauer, halfway inside the Italy half, lofted a nothing ball forward towards the edge of the area. Bertini slipped and ended up lunging at the ball like a dog. He missed and it came to Seeler, just inside the area. He controlled the ball as he back-pedalled, ran round it and then scuffed a tame shot straight at Albertosi.

50 min: Domenghini steals the ball in midfield and carpe diems down the right wing. He drills a flat cross beyond the far post, where Riva pulls off Vogts and forces a vital save from Maier! Actually, Riva should have done better: his diving header was too close to Maier, who plunged to his right to save. On ITV, Hugh Johns suggests the flag has gone up for offside against Riva, although the referee did not stop play so presumably it would have counted had he scored.

52 min: West Germany swap one winger for another, with Stan Libuda replacing Hannes Löhr.

55 min: Beckenbauer's long-range shot hits one of his own players, Grabowski, and rebounds to Overath. He gets it out of his feet on the edge of the D and whistles a left-footer wide. It looked pretty close, although it's not easy to tell from the TV angle, and Albertosi didn't bother diving.

62 min: GREAT CHANCE FOR GRABOWSKI! West Germany should probably be level. Müller was fouled from behind by Rosato, which meant a free-kick 25 yards from goal.

Italy were still preparing their wall when Beckenbauer stabbed a quick free-kick to Müller on the edge of the box. He flicked it cleverly around Burgnich to find Grabowski in space eight yards from goal to the left of centre, and he dragged a poor left-footed shot across goal and wide. It was a tight angle but he should at least have worked Albertosi.

64 min: OVERATH HITS THE BAR! What a chance that was for Overath! Libuda's mis-hit cross from the right was patted over the bar by Albertosi; corner to West Germany. It was half cleared to Bertini on the right, who then played a woeful back-pass towards Albertosi. Müller got there first near the touchline and, with Albertosi at his back, played it to Grabowski on the left. He skinned Bertini, swerved away from Facchetti and, with everyone running towards the goal, cleverly played it the other way, rolling it back for Overath near the penalty spot. He charged on to the ball and spanked it off the top of the crossbar! That's a poor miss. He had a number of bodies to get through; even so, he had to score there.

65 min: Suddenly West Germany are all over Italy like malevolent shingles. Beckenbauer takes a square pass from Patzke 35 yards out and explodes on another of his exhilarating runs. He ignores Rivera's tackle from the side and then zags past Cera right on the edge of the box before being cynically body-checked. Was that inside the area? The referee has given a free-kick, and it did look *this* far outside the box, but you can understand why West Germany are so aggrieved because he would have been through on goal. Patzke points to the spot – and to where Beckenbauer landed, which was well inside the area – and now Müller is going ballistic. He points the referee towards the linesman, who has wandered over to say something or other. The referee isn't going to change his mind. When Müller realizes this he puts his hands on his head and then clasps them together in horror at the injustice of it all. His noggin has gone! He moves away for a few seconds and then decides, nah, I'm not done here. Müller walks over and tries to move the ball – which is currently about 20 yards from goal – right to the edge of the area or maybe even to put it on the penalty spot. As he does so the referee boots it out of his hands! Müller's head snaps round towards the referee, a look of almost violent contempt on his face; then, just in time, he finally accepts the way things are and moves back into the area for the free-kick.

67 min: Almost two minutes after the foul on Beckenbauer, Overath finally gets to take the free-kick. He stabs it to Held, whose shot dribbles comfortably wide.

68 min: Italy can't breathe. It's all West Germany. Seeler's looping header towards Müller is punched away nervously by Albertosi. The last five minutes have been like a highlights reel.

69 min: Another chance for West Germany! Overath's long, deep cross from the left was flapped away by Albertosi, who did well under considerable pressure. It came to Libuda on the right and he volleyed it quickly back into the area. Müller controlled the ball on the penalty spot but couldn't quite wriggle away from Rosato, whose tackle inadvertently gave the ball to Seeler. His rising snapshot on the turn from 12 yards was straight at Albertosi. Either side and that would probably have been in.

70 min: YET ANOTHER CHANCE! West Germany have turned it up quite devastatingly in the last ten minutes, in which time they could have scored five. Overath moves easily away from Rivera, beats Burgnich with sleight of shoulder and then plays a lovely pass to the left of the box for Grabowski, in a weird amount of space 12 yards out. He controls it calmly, slams a left-footed shot past Albertosi – and Rosato appears out of nowhere to clear spectacularly off the line! He leapt and shinned the ball away, falling into the goal in the process. Seeler gets to the rebound first, goes over after a tackle from Bertini, then Müller, back-pedalling away from goal to meet the ball, slices wide from ten yards! That was mayhem. It should probably have been a penalty, and Bertini knew it because he fell over holding his face in an attempt to distract the referee. Müller, although there were bodies everywhere, will feel he should have scored. Bertini is still on his back. Half the West Germany team are asking the referee why it wasn't a penalty, with Seeler particularly insistent. Replays suggest it was a clear penalty. Bertini wrapped his legs round Seeler's like it was a game of Twister!

74 min: The ball goes into the West Germany half for about two seconds.

76 min: ANOTHER CHANCE GOES BEGGING FOR WEST GERMANY! And this time it's the usually lethal Müller. Beckenbauer swept an insouciant long pass out to Grabowski on the left. He moved it infield to Held, who made a beeline for the Italian defence, neatly evaded a challenge from Cera 25 yards out and then pushed an angled ball into the area for Müller. He shifted the ball on to his left foot and, with Rosato leaping into a tackle, slashed it wide from 15 yards. West Germany are slaughtering Italy 0–1.

80 min: Italy have finally restored some order after that traumatic 15-minute spell, although their policy of sitting on this one-goal lead has been seriously tested.

82 min: Seeler lobs the ball over Bertini and is dragged down approximately 0.0001 yards outside the box. Seeler punches the air with rage. One of these free-kicks surely has to go in. Not this time: Overath drills it straight into the wall and Beckenbauer's long-range follow-up dribbles through to Albertosi. Following which . . .

83 min: AN ASTONISHING INCIDENT! This is ridiculous. After collecting Beckenbauer's shot, Albertosi rolled the ball across his area to waste a few seconds. Then he tried to launch it downfield – except his kick hit the back of Grabowski just a couple of yards away. It deflected towards goal and started spinning across the line. Müller was in a race for it with Albertosi, who got there a fraction before him. Actually, it wouldn't have counted – the referee has given a foul against Grabowski for blocking the goal-kick – although Albertosi didn't know that and made a last-ditch sliding tackle of which Bobby Moore would be proud.

88 min: West Germany are running out of time. Müller, who has been frustrated all day, has a full and frank exchange of views with Domenghini, who then goes down holding his face! It was off camera so we don't know what happened, although a number of Italian defenders are pointing the finger. Domenghini motions to the referee that he was punched in the face but then undermines his argument by pointing to the wrong man, Overath. Play eventually resumes with an Italian goal-kick nearly two minutes after the ball went out of play.

90 min: Riva could have sealed it then! Rivera's long cross from the left towards Riva was brilliantly defended by Vogts, who headed it out under extreme pressure. Domenghini sauntered over to collect it by the right corner flag, turned and drove a cross back into the area. It cleared the leaping Schnellinger but Riva, six yards out, planted a tame header into the ground and straight at Maier. He had no pace to work with, although it was still a great chance. Germany go straight down the other end. Grabowski skips down the right and past De Sisti, who rugby tackles him quite ludicrously. 'He almost had his trousers off!' says Hugh Johns on ITV. A cushion is thrown on to the field and just misses Grabowski. It's still sitting there, in space on the right wing, when West Germany take a short free-kick. Overath moves down the right and wins a corner in the pursuit of a goal that would keep the Germans in this, the first World Cup with bespoke soft furnishings.

90+1 min: One corner leads to another, this time on the left. The corner is taken short by Held to Libuda, who lofts it towards the far post. Seeler gets up above Facchetti to loop a header towards the top corner and Albertosi leaps dramatically to volleyball-smash it behind for a corner!

90+2 min: Italy have been given a free-kick for a foul by Müller on Rosato. That surely is that.

90+2 min: GOAL! Italy 1–1 West Germany (Schnellinger). Unbelievable! West Germany have equalized through the most unlikely source: Milan defender Karl-Heinz Schnellinger! What a perverse twist! Held took a short throw on the left. He burst down the wing, resisting a challenge from Boninsegna and a token, weary effort from Domenghini, and curled a hopeful cross into the middle. It dipped over Müller and Rosato at the near post to find Schnellinger, in a staggering amount of space six yards from goal, and he leapt towards the ball with what was basically a star jump before sidefooting a volley wide of the motionless Albertosi. That is astonishing! He fell over in the act of scoring, landing on his back, whereupon Müller writhed joyously on top of them. As Schnellinger jogs past to the halfway line, Beckenbauer puts his arm round him and bursts out laughing at the sheer absurdity of it all.

FULL TIME: Italy 1–1 West Germany. That's the fourth time in this tournament that West Germany have come from behind. Amazing.

91 min: Italy begin extra time. Beckenbauer has his right arm strapped to his chest and has apparently done his shoulder, perhaps when he was sent flying by Cera on the edge of the area in the second half. West Germany have used both substitutes so he can't be replaced. Italy have made their second substitution, with Fabrizio Poletti replacing Rosato.

92 min: FINE SAVE FROM ALBERTOSI! West Germany almost took the lead right at the start of extra time. The substitute Libuda went on an exhilarating run down the right, beating Facchetti on the outside and then coming back the other way to crunch a left-footed cross towards the near post. Müller, eight yards from goal, hung in the air like Denis Law, getting above Poletti and Cera to head towards the bottom-left corner. Albertosi got down very smartly to his right to help the ball behind for a corner.

94 min: GOAL! Italy 1–2 West Germany (Müller). It had to happen. Gerd Müller has been almost entirely useless in this match and now he may have put West Germany into the World Cup final! They have started extra time superbly and now they lead for the first time. It was ostensibly one of the worst goals you will ever see, almost comically scruffy, but with this amazing goalscorer there are no bad goals, no accidents. Libuda drilled a deep corner from the right and Seeler, on the edge of the box, looped a header into the danger area. Poletti, caught in umpteen minds, chested it back towards his own goal in the vague direction of Albertosi. At the precise moment the ball touched his chest, he realized somebody else was lurking and ran after the ball. Too late. Müller ran across the area, used his enormous arse to block Poletti barely three yards from goal and, while in the process of falling over, dribbled a shot past Albertosi that trickled goadingly over the line. That was the slowest shot you will ever see: it took almost three seconds to travel the three yards it needed to go to be over the line! To compound the misery of both Albertosi and Poletti, they turned in time to see the ball moving apologetically towards the line – but not quite quickly enough that they could do anything about it. That was astonishing from Müller. He knew what Poletti was going to do even before Poletti and started running towards that side of the area just in case. He scored in every game in qualifying, and he has scored in every game so far at the World Cup.

97 min: De Sisti's long shot deflects wide for a corner, after which he has a hand-waving row with Rivera, who wanted a pass. The corner is taken short and sprayed pathetically out of play at the near post. Italy are all over the place.

99 min: GOAL! Italy 2–2 West Germany (Burgnich). But now they are level! It was dreadful defending by West Germany. Vogts mistook Riva for a stepladder 40 yards from goal, which meant a free-kick to Italy. Rivera's clipped ball into the area dropped over the head of Burgnich and hit Held on the chest before dropping perfectly for Burgnich. He kissed the gift horse in the mouth, ramming the ball past Maier from ten yards with his left foot. What was Held doing?! He could have let the ball go out for a goal-kick or let it bounce and hoofed it clear. He could have done anything. But he lost concentration for a split-second and that was enough.

103 min: Held struggles past Poletti before Cera halts his progress with an emphatic foul on the edge of the area. Held stumbles into the box, trying to stay on his feet, before giving up and falling over. De Sisti is yellow-carded for not retreating ten yards at the resulting free-kick, and then Grabowski's effort is blocked.

104 min: GOAL! Italy 3–2 West Germany (Riva). Italy are back in front through Riva! He actually started things off deep in his own half. Libuda fell over under challenge from Riva, the referee gave nothing and Riva waved at him to get up before pottering off downfield. The ball went to Rivera, who made 30 yards and pushed it down the left wing to Domenghini. He clipped an early pass to Riva, in a little bit of space 20 yards from goal. Riva cushioned the ball into the area expertly, shifted it away from the covering Schnellinger – who was haring from right to left as Riva moved the other way, the two like ships passing in the night – and then drove a low shot across Maier and into the corner! What a beautifully placed finish! Riva runs 20 yards in celebration and then falls over joyously after being embraced by Rivera. West Germany will feel aggrieved, however, after that tackle on Libuda. As play restarts Riva is gulping almost dementedly for air after that 80-yard charge. And he's one of the substitutes.

EXTRA TIME, HALF TIME: Italy 3–2 West Germany. These players are utterly exhausted. Many of the players are flat on their back in this short break.

106 min: West Germany begin the second period of extra time.

109 min: WHAT AN ALMIGHTY BOLLOCKS FROM ALBERTOSI! The Italian keeper almost gives the Germans an equalizer. After a storming run, Held played an attempted through ball to Müller that was intercepted by Burgnich. He tapped it back to Albertosi, who picked it up and then tried to roll it out to Poletti. Except Poletti wasn't looking and the ball hit him on the backside before rebounding to Müller, just outside the area on the left. Albertosi followed Müller, all the way out of his box, and brought him down with a desperate tackle from behind to give West Germany a free-kick. That was indicative of the tired bodies and particularly minds that have made extra time so error-strewn – and so exciting.

110 min: ALBERTOSI ATONES FOR HIS MISTAKE! Overath clipped the resulting free-kick to the far post, where little Seeler somehow got above Riva eight yards out. He headed the ball down into the ground, from where it bounced up sharply and was punched over the bar spectacularly by Albertosi – a showy save, in truth, but still a vital one.

110 min: GOAL! Italy 3–3 West Germany (Müller). Gerd Müller has saved West Germany with his tenth goal of the World Cup! It came from the corner after Albertosi's save. Grabowski took it short to Libuda on the right and he curled it high towards the far post. Seeler managed yet another immense leap, this time above Poletti, to head it into the six-yard area. It was dipping over the head of Müller, who improvised and jumped backwards at a 45-degree angle before twisting his body in mid-air to head it past Rivera on the line and just inside the post. That's another deceptively superb finish. Rivera shapes to kick the post in frustration and instead wraps his arms and legs around it like a fireman about to go down a pole.

111 min: GOAL! Italy 4–3 West Germany (Rivera). Italy are in front again! They've scored within 22 seconds of the kick-off! Facchetti clipped a pass down the left to Boninsegna, who ignored a tired tackle from Schulz and made a beeline for the box. Once inside he cut the ball back to Rivera, in all sorts of space on the penalty spot, who passed it into the net with his right foot with Maier's weight going the wrong way! We've had six goals in 22 minutes. In a World Cup semi-final. It's legitimate to point out that most of those goals have been through poor defending from shattered players, but even so.

112 min: Held wins a corner with a scorching run down the left past Cera and Poletti, who came back to block the cross. The corner comes to nothing.

116 min: Grabowski's direct 40-yard run is ended calmly by Cera. Italy look relatively comfortable, certainly compared to what has gone before. In fact, we haven't had a goal for five minutes. What kind of basketball match is this?

118 min: Bertini jumps for a high ball with Seeler and takes the opportunity to lie back and think of the World Cup final. He's wasted a good minute there and it looks all over for West Germany. Just as it did before Schnellinger's equalizer.

EXTRA TIME, FULL TIME: Italy 4–3 West Germany. Italy are into the World Cup final after a deranged and often brilliant match that exploded in extra time. Italy are almost – almost – too tired to celebrate. Boninsegna lies on his front and slaps the ground in triumph with both hands. Then he embraces with Facchetti on the halfway line. They will play Brazil, who in the other semi have beaten Uruguay in the World Cup for the first time ever. England's conquerors, meanwhile, are out, but with a home tournament to come in four years, all hope is not lost.

Brazil v Italy

Final, Estadio Azteca, Mexico City, Mexico, Sunday, 21 June 1970

It's beginning to look like Brazil will realize their dream of becoming the first country to win the World Cup three times and take home the famous Jules Rimet Trophy for keeps. They're hot favourites to win this afternoon and little wonder: en route to the final they've scored 15 goals in five matches, beaten the reigning champions England and seen off the ghosts of 1950 by finally defeating Uruguay at a World Cup. They've raised the bar to such an extent that their two most memorable moments are misses, for goodness sake, Pelé nearly scoring from the halfway line against Czechoslovakia, and freezing the Uruguayan keeper in amber during the semi with an outrageous dummy, rounding him on one side while the ball went t'other, before finally yanking a shot inches wide. Can anyone stop this famous forward five of Pelé, Rivelino, Tostão, Gerson and Jairzinho?

If anyone can, Italy are your men, for the 1934 and 1938 champs are looking to bag Jules Rimet for good as well. The current European champions eased their way through qualification, with Luigi Riva, a newly crowned Serie A champion with Sardinian minnows Cagliari, scoring seven times. After a quiet start in the group stage, they've reached the final after pelting four goals past hosts Mexico and the highly fancied West Germans. The only problem has been keeping midfield maestro Gianni Rivera happy. Coach Ferruccio Valcareggi doesn't much like the cut of the Milan star's jib, it would seem, preferring Sandro Mazzola of Internazionale, who it was thought had been brought to Mexico merely as cover for Rivera. When he replaced Rivera at the start of the tournament, so abrasive was the Golden Boy's response to being dropped that he was nearly sent home. But as things have panned out, Mazzola's been playing the first half of the knockout games, with Rivera coming on for the second. What a carry-on. And to think Valcareggi is paid to make decisions! It's a decision of sorts, I suppose, and eight goals in two games suggests it's working, but you have to wonder how this might pan out now we're down to the nitty-gritty.

Whoever plays, this final is being viewed as a battle for the philosophical heart of soccer, the flair and panache of the South Americans versus the wily *catenaccio* **(the 'door-bolt' defensive system) of the Azzurri.** Broad brushstrokes, of course, but it's not totally unfair. Either way, it's expected to be a close one, with Brazil fancied to edge it, much as they did against England. In fairness, the contest would be a damn sight harder to call if it wasn't being played in this heat and altitude. Gerson, the brains of Brazil, is on 40 gaspers a day and a faster game at sea level would surely be beyond him.

Kick-off: The highest of high noons: 12 midday.

Referee: Rudi Glöckner (East Germany).

Valcareggi has made another decision! And it's to keep that preposterous Mazzola–Rivera *staffetta* **(relay) policy going:** Enrico Albertosi, Tarcisio Burgnich, Giacinto Facchetti, Mario Bertini, Roberto Rosato, Pierluigi Cera, Angelo Domenghini, Sandro Mazzola, Roberto Boninsegna, Giancarlo De Sisti, Luigi Riva.

Brazil, a teamsheet that conjures up so many vivid images it reads like a modernist poem: Félix, Carlos Alberto, Everaldo, Clodoaldo, Brito, Piazza, Jairzinho, Gerson, Tostão, Pelé, Rivelino. So much depends on Brazil, glazed with rain water. It's a humid, oppressive afternoon.

A heady atmosphere in the Azteca, then, which is filled to the brim, 112,000 people. Sailing off into the ether are four humongous beachball-balloons, one bedecked in the blue-and-green of Brazil, another in the Italian *tricolore* and therefore totally out of sync with the national team strip, and a couple with huge Mexico 70 logos stamped on them. That brazen branding's going to give someone at FIFA ideas. They can't rely on coin generated by pitchside ads for Mothercare for ever.

The players line up to get their photos taken, Brazil looking grim-faced, the weight of expectation pressing heavily. The scene quickly descends into mayhem. Bedlam bedlam bedlam. The pitch fills with some official-looking folk and very many unofficial-looking folk. An awful lot of photographers and assorted hangers-on. The World Cup final's going to kick off in less than 60 seconds, for goodness sake, will you all please bugger off?!

Amid the madness, Pelé swooshes around, warming up, completing several little circles to make one big, baroque, semi-circular swoop of the field, a one-man whirling waltzer. Attempt to avoid clichés all you like but just try watching him move without picking up a samba earworm. Speaking of stereotypes, up the other end of the field the Italians are huddled around several severe gentlemen in trenchcoats, looking for all the world like they're striking an import–export agreement that won't necessarily involve passing through any of the major designated ports.

Handshakes between captains Giacinto Facchetti and Carlos Alberto, the latter winning the toss and insisting the teams switch direction. And with the field quickly swept of clingers-on, we're off! Boninsegna gets the ball rolling. It's not long before Italy lose the ball and Jairzinho is skittering down the right. Pelé goes down looking for a free-kick but he's full of sauce.

2 min: Pelé's full of energy, too, and speedily exchanges passes with Tostão down the inside-left channel. For a second it looks like he'll break clear, but Bertini is covering and passes back to the keeper. Italy waste no time in tearing down the right themselves, the ball eventually being shuttled inside to Riva, who unleashes a rising heatseeker towards goal. What a shot! Félix tips over magnificently. The corner is an easy one for the keeper. What a start, though.

4 min: Bertini hacks down Pelé as the latter chases after a sliderule Carlos Alberto pass down the right. What glorious hoodlummery. Free-kick. Gerson looks to bend it, but slips as he takes, and his low left-to-right curler is easily gathered by Albertosi.

5 min: This is a high-octane start. Brazil are coming down the middle at pace after Jairzinho picks up a loose Domenghini pass from the right wing. He's clattered to the floor on the edge of the D by Facchetti. Another free-kick.

6 min: Pelé dummies. Rivelino blooters the setpiece on to the roof. Haw.

7 min: Mazzola exchanges passes with Riva to advance down the inside left, but his eventual shot is weak and wafts into the arms of Félix.

8 min: Carlos Alberto floats a cross into the Italian area from the right. At the far post, Albertosi should let it fly out for a goal-kick but panics and punches behind. He's not the only one not quite on his game; Rivelino, after that free-kick, now hits a corner miles into the sky and straight out of play on the other side.

9 min: Rivelino slips on the turf and skitters across it on his arse. An undignified climax to an undistinguished start.

15 min: Italy have settled into this a little bit now. Domenghini tries to score from the best part of 40 yards while out on the touchline, some respect please, for the love of God. The shot pings off poor Wilson Piazza's coupon and out for a corner on the left.

16 min: De Sisti is clattered by Pelé. Free-kick, 35 yards out, just to the left of goal. Brazil line up a wall but there's a laughably large gap in their defence to its right. Mazzola floats the ball over the head of the lurking Boninsegna and right on to the forehead of the onrushing Riva, who really should score from a slight angle, 12 yards out. Instead his effort loops over the bar. That's an appalling miss, really, and nearly as bad as Brazil's defending.

18 min: GOAL!!! Brazil 1–0 Italy (Pelé). Tostão drops a shoulder down the left and whips a cross towards Pelé, but it's headed out for a throw by the stooping Facchetti. The Italians do not heed the warning. Receiving Tostão's throw, Rivelino leans back and loops a high cross into the box, Pelé getting the jump on Burgnich and clattering a majestic header into the bottom right, Albertosi late to react. That's Brazil's 100th goal in World Cups. Not bad timing, eh? Pelé is lifted into the air by Jairzinho's bearhug and punches the sky three times. You'll see that celebration again.

19 min: Hilariously, and preposterously, Brazil make no effort whatsoever to regroup for the kick-off, and are all buggering around deep in their own half when Italy get the ball moving again. The ball's flicked out to Domenghini, who powers down the wing, cuts inside and hammers a low shot towards the bottom right, Félix doing well to claim. That was staggeringly inept.

20 min: Gerson sends a crossfield ball to the right for Carlos Alberto who, ten yards from the touchline and with the angle preposterous, decides to go for the spectacular. He achieves it: a spectacularly awful slice off the side of his boot straight behind and into the crowd. He has the chutzpah to look down and blame his footwear. At least there's plenty of time left in which to showcase better technique, Carlos.

23 min: After a period of sterile Brazilian possession, a cock-up. Everaldo passes back down the left wing to Piazza, who side-foots inside to Brito. Brito attempts to flick a casual one back to the left for Clodoaldo, but Riva nips in to block the lazy pass and hare after it down the middle. Félix comes out of his box, wallops clear and waves angrily at his defence. Don't. Do. That. Again. Or else!

25 min: Free-kick to Brazil, 20 yards out on the left, level with the left-hand side of the area, after Bertini scythes through the back of Rivelino. The Italians line up a five-man wall. Rivelino shapes to have a shot but sprints straight past the ball. Pelé rushes in and chips a perfectly weighted ball after Rivelino. The five Italians spin and turn, then crash to the floor like pissed-up circus performers. Rivelino, on the run, shapes to whip a cross into the middle, where Gerson, Jairzinho and Tostão are lining up to belt home from six yards. But he hesitates for a fatal microsecond, allowing the ball to skid off the turf and out for a goal-kick, despite a desperate late lunge. Such a clever pass from Pelé, though, threaded along a route to the left of the wall and the right of Rivelino, inviting the cross.

26 min: Italy so nearly cleave Brazil in two. From the centre circle, Domenghini slides the ball forward to Riva, who with his back to goal 30 yards out plays a first-time flick onward to Mazzola and gets clattered by Piazza for his trouble. The referee waves play on, as Mazzola is clear of the backtracking Tostão and advancing towards the area, but on the edge of the D, Brito slides in majestically. He's not letting that ball get past.

27 min: Pelé goes on a meander down the inside-right channel and is upended by Burgnich. He rolls over on his side once, then executes two head-first roly-polies, all in one smooth Olympic-gymnast-standard movement, a technique that comes with a difficulty tariff of 6.0. Applause. The Italian is shown the yellow card and doesn't seem to care very much. Brazil's trainer trots on with bucket and sponge to attend to Pelé, but is angrily told to chip off by the referee, who furiously flaps his hands in dismissive style. Pelé is still on the floor moaning, but there's naff-all wrong with him, the big gurner.

28 min: Rivelino's resulting free-kick finds the top-left corner. Of the stand behind the goal. That's the worst free-kick ever taken in a World Cup final, surely. Rivelino looks down at his wet boot and the soft turf, but is fooling nobody.

32 min: Félix reverts to type, throwing an awkward ball out wide to Carlos Alberto, who sees it balloon over his head for a throw to Italy. As the sun comes out, Mazzola takes up possession from the throw and slides the ball left to De Sisti, who draws three men before twinkle-toeing the ball back inside to Mazzola. From a standing start, Mazzola turns on the burners, dances past three challenges, flicks a quick one-two off De Sisti to his left, then powers into the box and takes a shot from a tight angle. But Brito and Gerson have crowded round him, and the ball's blocked out for a corner. From the setpiece, Félix, mopping up his own mess, sends a punch almost to the halfway line.

34 min: A mad scramble on the edge of the Italian area. Jairzinho bombs down the middle and attempts a one-two with Tostão. On receiving the return, he's stopped mid-flight by Burgnich's sliding tackle, but still manages to nick the ball down the inside left for Pelé, who immediately flicks one back into the middle for Tostão. The forward breaks into the box before hitting a weak cross-cum-shot in the general direction of the left-hand corner and the onrushing Jairzinho. Italy hack clear.

35 min: Rivelino drops a shoulder to glide past Bertini down the inside right. As he cuts inside, Bertini is so wrong-footed he inadvertently performs the splits across the skiddy turf. That might make a couple of bobbles on the pitch. Rivelino pokes an awful effort miles left of the target and as high as a house to boot. He gets pelters from the bench. A full and frank exchange of views ensues. His shooting has been hilariously poor so far.

37 min: FARCICAL GOAL!!! Brazil 1–1 Italy (Boninsegna).
Pelé looks to turn Burgnich in the Italian area but the defender's

having none of it, banging an interception upfield with no little authority. Everaldo chases back down the Italian right flank to collect, turning the ball inside to Piazza, who floats a needlessly dangerous chip across his back line. It drops towards Brito, who has Riva nearby but still enough time to deal with the problem. He doesn't, though. He heads inside to Clodoaldo who, unaware Boninsegna is lurking, attempts an adventurous blind backflick out towards Piazza, still on the Brazil left. Boninsegna intercepts and, though never quite in control, barrels clear down the inside right. Brito is coming over to meet him from the middle, while Félix races rashly out of his box. Cue komik kutz on the edge of the D and proof that Brazil really did learn nothing from all that fannying around at 23 minutes. Brito's sliding challenge, coming in towards Boninsegna from the left, is weak and mistimed, the ball clattering off his heel and into the middle. His useless contribution has also had the effect of taking Félix out of the game, the keeper having turned up to the melee a millisecond too late. Félix puts the brakes on and attempts to change direction, but he knows the game is up. Boninsegna scampers after the ball and, although Riva gets in the way with a view to nabbing the goal himself, wraps his left leg around his cheeky team-mate to hook the ball into the bottom right of the empty net. He races off with arms out wide before being smothered by Domenghini and Mazzola. Riva doesn't join in, the mardy get.

41 min: The sun is shimmering now. Mazzola instigates a gorgeous sweeping Italian move from deep, jigging his way out of trouble near his own area down the left before clipping a ball out to Facchetti, who shuttles the ball up the flank to Boninsegna. Facing back down the pitch, he draws two Brazilian players and, with the full knowledge he's going to be cleaned out by Carlos Alberto, plays a reverse ball down the wing to Riva, who makes good for the box and wins a corner off Brito, the defender doing well to stop the striker taking a shot. Back upfield, Carlos Alberto and Boninsegna are both receiving treatment, the former having been clocked in the coupon upon clattering the latter. The pair respectfully apologize to each other like adults, proving that this game really can be beautiful even when the participants are wantonly fouling each other.

43 min: Domenghini launches a low, rising shot straight at Félix, who nearly dives all around it but eventually gathers midway through the pudding course.

44 min: Rivelino is booked for a petulant backflick on Bertini, who has come from behind to whip the ball off his toe. Bertini holds his thigh. For a second, it looks like the referee is going to show the Brazilian a red – the card's in his hand, visible to all – but he ostentatiously flashes yellow to all four stands. But then he lets Rivelino see the red card, pointing to the bench as if to say: 'One more like that, son, and you'll see this one too.'

HALF TIME: Brazil 1–1 Italy, though it probably should be Brazil 2–1 Italy! So how's this for a farcical end to the half? Despite Rivelino's booking for retaliation, the referee has awarded a free-kick to Brazil for the original Bertini challenge. Very strange. From the left touchline, Gerson loops a high ball into the area. It drops over the head of an out-of-position Burgnich, who falls backwards as the ball lands at Pelé's feet, ten yards out, level with the far post and with only the keeper to beat. But instead of playing on, Pelé throws his hands up in disgust. Why's he pausing?! It's half time, that's why! The referee's blown his whistle early – 45 minutes aren't quite up – and Pelé is understandably beside himself with the rage! He still manages to convert, despite the red mist, flicking the ball into the bottom-left corner and clattering Cera, coming across to cover, on the shoe while he's at it. Cera gets right up in Pelé's grille to remonstrate, pointing at his instep, and Pelé's suddenly surrounded by a raging sea of blue shirts. Nobody's got a clue what's going on, until the referee, ball wedged under his armpit, strides through the melee and wanders off the pitch for a fag and a cup of tea.

And we're off again! No changes, which is something of a surprise as Valcareggi was expected to continue with this *staffetta* malarkey and replace Mazzola with Rivera at the break. Brazil set us in motion again.

47 min: Carlos Alberto is sent striding clear on the overlap. He fires a ball straight through the six-yard box. Pelé slides in at the far post, but misses the ball and clatters his wrist on the post.

50 min: Gerson clips a high ball down the middle, into the

Italian area. Pelé stumbles as he tussles with Facchetti, then races off after the referee, miming a tug on his sleeve. The big man's bopping around with the heat on. It really wasn't much of a challenge.

52 min: Burgnich upends Pelé in roughhouse fashion, 30 yards out on the right. Rivelino takes what Hugh Johns on ITV calls a 'fast-bowler's run-up' and batters a rising, swerving shot towards the right of goal. Albertosi parries it with strong arms and Italy hack clear. Brazil come straight back at them. Gerson goes on a Power Jog down the inside right. His one-two with Tostão on the edge of the box doesn't quite come off but the ball loops towards Pelé, who is obstructed by Burgnich as the Italian attempts an overhead clearance. Indirect free-kick! Or, as the caption has it: *tiro indirecto!*

53 min: On ITV, Bobby Moore thinks it should be a penalty for dangerous play. But *tiro indirecto* it is. Pelé feathers the ball to the right for Gerson, who blooters hopelessly into the Italian wall. Insult is nearly added to injury as Facchetti breaks upfield along the left. The ball's funnelled inside and across the pitch to Domenghini, bombing in acres down the right. He hammers a shot towards the bottom-left corner. Everaldo comes across, sticks a boot out and nearly deflects the thing into the bottom right. That was inches away. Domenghini waves both of his fists, then pumps them, in frustration.

55 min: Gerson is looking increasingly dangerous, a testament to his daily multipack cheroot regime. Again he bursts down the inside right, again a one-two with Tostão doesn't quite come off. He was very nearly through on goal there.

56 min: Rivelino twists on the ball through 360 degrees, takes a couple of steps down the inside-right channel, drifts inside then hoicks an effort over the bar. Italy go up the other end through the increasingly attack-minded Mazzola, who has a sortie down the inside-right flank himself and shovels a poor shot miles over from distance. This is good to-and-fro stuff and not wholly predictable, even if Brazil are gaining a little momentum.

58 min: Rivelino begins a determined sashay towards the Italian box, drifting in from the left. He's scythed down by Bertini, who cuts his feet off with one cynical swish from behind. Pelé's free-kick from a central position 25 yards out is a new Worst Of All Time, some going given Rivelino's attempt half an hour earlier, shooting off at a 45-degree angle towards the top-right corner of the stand behind the goal. A place-kicker in rugby would struggle to set a ball off along that flight. Ee, he's a poor lad.

59 min: RIVELINO HITS THE BAR! Another free-kick for Brazil, just outside the area, after Facchetti linked arms to do-se-do Jairzinho out of a one-two with Tostão. *Tiro indirecto!* From the edge of the D, Gerson knocks the ball to the right for Rivelino, who twangs the crossbar with a rising thunderer. Goal-kick. Bobby Moore reckons it's the first time Rivelino has used his right foot all tournament. 'It's a wonder he doesn't use it more often!' Especially the way he'd been shooting up to this point.

61 min: Brazil are becoming the dominant force now. Pelé looks to dance round Burgnich down the right and into the area, but he's barged off the ball and appeals to the referee by waving his hands in the air as he falls backwards. *Tiro directo!* Rivelino batters it over the bar and is battered himself by Riva as he's taking it. Another free-kick! Riva looks astonished and dis-gusted at the same time, an Italian speciality. Rivelino skelps the second effort into the wall, a trick Gerson repeats with the loose ball.

63 min: An increasingly rare sojourn upfield for Italy as Boninsegna finds space down the left and loops a cross to the far post for Riva, who bangs a header into Everaldo's back from a tight angle, a couple of yards out. The corner's met by Mazzola, whose header sails along a gentle parabola towards Félix. The keeper skips into the air in the style of a morris dancer after one mead too many and punches a feeble effort a couple of yards to his right. Fortunately Carlos Alberto is on hand to sweep up. 'What an incredible man to have behind you if you're a defender in this brilliant Brazilian side,' notes a tinder-dry Hugh Johns.

65 min: Gerson has the run of the middle of the park. He's been running the show since half time, only moving upfield since the restart, after which the Italians have had no time to formulate one of their trademark defensive lockdowns. Clever Gerson. Clever Brazil. He sets a move in motion down the right,

Clodoaldo feeding Carlos Alberto, who whips a cross towards Tostão at the far post. The forward can't control his header, which screws well wide left.

66 min: THIS HAS BEEN COMING!!! Brazil 2–1 Italy (Gerson). Gerson has the run of the park all right. His beautiful reverse ball sets Everaldo on a probe down the inside left. Jairzinho takes up possession and makes for the edge of the D. He's tracked by Facchetti, who sticks a toe in. The ball breaks to Gerson, who has been loitering in the middle. He takes two little taps to the left, before twisting and walloping a mid-height cross-shot into the right-hand side of the goal. Boninsegna slid in with a tackle, while Albertosi flung himself across goal, but neither made it in time. Gerson races off with arms aloft, a cheesy grin across his boat. Reserve keeper Ado leads a delegation off the bench to celebrate the achievement. Brazil are 24 minutes away from becoming world football's first three-time champions!

67 min: Straight from kick-off, Domenghini is brought down by Everaldo along the right touchline, 12 yards from the byline. The Italian gets up and attempts to beat Félix at his near post with an outrageous effort but it goes straight out of play, ten yards to the right of goal. He walks back upfield with his head hung low, abjectly defeated and humiliated. Pelé's reign as taker of Worst Free-kick Of All Time has lasted all of nine minutes.

68 min: The stunning Gerson eats up most of the pitch as he scampers down the inside right. He rolls a pass inside to Tostão, who attempts to turn Facchetti but fails and executes a rather embarrassing dive instead. Italy move upfield through Domenghini, who is checked by Pelé. He responds by shoving the Brazilian in the chest. Pelé falls backwards like he's catching a cannonball, then rather absurdly grabs his left shin as he hits the ground. The ref clearly considers this a whole load of nonsense and ostentatiously refuses to allow Pelé to receive any treatment, ordering the bald guy with the bucket and sponge back off the field for the second time. And just like before, Pelé's soon back on his feet again. Good old ref.

69 min: Gerson has been brilliant since the restart, having kept his cards close to his chest for so long, though whether he's within his rights to attempt to score from 40 yards now is a moot point.

70 min: Domenghini leaves a leg in as Pelé glides past. Pelé flips himself miles into the air, a triple salchow with pike and a difficulty tariff of 34. This is gloriously petulant behaviour all round. The referee can't be bothered with any of it, and simply gestures that they're to get up and stop behaving like a couple of spoilt brats.

71 min: SURELY THE CLINCHER!!! Brazil 3–1 Italy (Jairzinho). From the resulting free-kick, just to the left of the centre circle, Gerson left-foot-wands a raking crossfield ball into the area towards Pelé, level with the right-hand post. Burgnich is completely lost. And beaten. He turns around to see Pelé rise above him. Pelé plants a header down and across the face of the six-yard box. Jairzinho races in and thighs the ball into the bottom-left corner, evading the desperate lunges of Cera and Albertosi. He tries to finish with a flourish, but his wild hoof becomes a fresh-air swipe and the ball makes its own way in, almost apologetically. That's a goal in every game of the finals for the Botafogo striker, who races off in the arms-aloft Gersonian style, before sinking to his knees in prayer.

72 min: To illustrate the ragged mental state of the normally impervious Italians, as they kick off six of them are loitering around the centre spot, like folk waiting for the bus home. They look broken. This has been a Gerson masterclass. He attempts to replicate his goal by launching another left-footed stinger from the edge of the area but it's straight at Albertosi.

74 min: Gerson walks through the centre circle with the ball at his feet. We've got to the stage where nobody even bothers to challenge him.

75 min: Rivelino is checked by De Sisti on the left-hand edge of the area. Free-kick. Before it can be taken, a limping Bertini falls in the centre circle and is replaced by Juliano, the first substitution in any World Cup final. Gerson taps the free-kick to the right for Pelé to embarrass himself with a witless blooter that's high and miles wide right.

79 min: Mazzola cuts in from the right and feeds Boninsegna, who turns and looks for the bottom left from the edge of the D. It's accurate but without power. Félix saves comfortably, which is a phrase for the ages. Brazil break upfield. Tostão pokes Pelé clear into the area. Pelé should score but his sidefoot towards the right-hand side of the net is smothered brilliantly by the desperate Albertosi. The flag's up, so none of this counts, a real shame for the keeper, who'd just won a personal showdown with the best player in the world.

80 min: The last chance for Italy to get back into this match, perhaps, is squandered. Juliano, from a position down the inside right, scoops a clever pass forward towards Mazzola, who is screaming for the ball in space, 25 yards from goal in the centre. He turns and has time to shoot, but takes a second too long and is forced to drift to the right and clip a cross into the mix instead. There's a brief stramash involving Riva and Boninsegna, the latter eventually thrashing a wild effort miles over from the left-hand side of the box, but by then the Brazilians were swarming around and the door of opportunity that had opened momentarily for Mazzola had long been slammed shut.

84 min: As Albertosi receives a wet sponge to the head, Boninsegna is replaced by Rivera. So much for the half-time *staffetta*.

86 min: THE ICING ON THE CAKE, THE BOW ON THE BOX, THE CROWNING ACHIEVEMENT! Brazil 4–1 Italy (Carlos Alberto). What a thing of beauty this is, nothing short of a masterclass, football's pinnacle finally reached, Brazil planting the flag. The Italian substitute Juliano hares down the right, but Tostão takes the ball off him like candy from a baby suffering from heat exhaustion and altitude sickness despite only being in the pram for 11 minutes. Tostão dispatches the ball back to Brito, who rolls it forward to Clodoaldo. The ball's clipped in a short-range triangle, first Pelé, then Gerson, then back to Clodoaldo, who drops and raises his shoulders like a laughing policeman, tying Rivera, Domenghini, De Sisti and Juliano up in knots. He strokes the ball wide left to Rivelino who, inside his own half, curls a pinpoint pass down the line to Jairzinho. Just ahead of the box, the striker cuts inside past Italian captain Facchetti, then clips the ball across Cera to Pelé, facing goal in front of the D. Burgnich closes him down but Tostão – who's made it all the way upfield after starting the move and is now behind Burgnich, also facing Pelé – gives the King the eyebrows to the

Brazilian right. Pelé takes the hint and rolls a perfect ball out wide; it sits up, allowing Carlos Alberto to evade the despairing lunge of Rosato, who has attempted to come across and block, and skelp it into the bottom corner past Albertosi. Only two out-field Brazilians were not involved in that move – Everaldo and Piazza. With a beautiful symmetry, only two Italians, Mazzola and Riva, were completely out of the picture and can therefore wash their hands of it. God almighty, what a move, what a strike, what a final statement to make in a World Cup!

87 min: As the Brazilians cavort behind Italy's goal, the Mexican television caption – **ANOTADOR! SCORER! *4 CARLOS ALBERTO** – washes out the entire picture. It's almost as though we've reached the end of the reel, this is the end, we can go no further, Brazil have finished off football as well as Italy. Where else can the story be taken from here?

88 min: Carlos Alberto is surrounded by photographers – on the pitch! Finally they bugger off and we restart. Rivera has a resigned shot, which Félix swallows up without fuss. Pelé sends another ball goalwards from the halfway line but this time it's a gentle backpass. Rivelino goes on a determined run down the inside-left channel and is upended by Juliano when he makes the box. If this was 0–0, that'd be a penalty but the referee decides to show Italy some mercy. Brazil deserve to win and have been so good during the second half that the three-goal margin doesn't particularly flatter them. And yet this excellent Italian side doesn't deserve to be spanked in the biggest match of all by a margin of four.

90 min: There's been plenty of bloody awful shooting in this match and perhaps the most egregious hack has been saved for last, a Domenghini shank that nestles in row Z, but only after rebounding from the seats behind. The crowd refuse to give the souvenir back. Time's up, but the referee refuses to blow until a ball's on the pitch. This is farcical. Eventually a new orb is presented to him. He hands it to Rivelino to give to Félix.

90+2 min: This is bedlam. Now the original ball has been dispatched back on to the field of play! One fan pops out of the stand and goes on a speedy skitter down the Brazilian right, which is better than some of the Italians have managed. Félix restarts the game and Rivera nearly takes his ankles out with a petulant lunge. The ball's hoicked upfield, in the general environs of another encroaching punter who's sporting a sombrero and poncho. ¡Arriba! At which point referee Rudi Glöckner raises both arms . . .

IT'S OVER!!! BRAZIL ARE CHAMPIONS OF THE WORLD FOR THE THIRD TIME AND WILL GET TO KEEP THE JULES RIMET TROPHY!!! Brazil 4–1 Italy. Within seconds of the final whistle, Pelé is mobbed. Hundreds of fans are on the field. Firecrackers crack their fire. Pelé is lifted shoulder high. He's already been divested of his shirt. But someone does give him one of those sombreros to wedge on to his noggin, so it's swings and roundabouts when it comes to wardrobe inventory. This has quickly descended into a rare old brouhaha. But there's Carlos Alberto lifting the glistening Jules Rimet trophy to the sky. You look after that thing, now!

The 1974 Finals

Holland 0–0 Sweden (1974, group stage)

Holland's Total Footballers only reached the 1974 World Cup because of a shocking offside decision in the last minute of their final qualifier, but once they got to West Germany they wowed the world before losing in the final. The most YouTube-able moment did not produce a goal and came in a game they didn't win.

23 min: Johan Cruyff hoodwinks Jan Olsson with a piece of genius. He receives a long pass just outside the box on the left wing and gets it under control as he faces away from goal. Then, as Olsson closes in, Cruyff shapes to kick the ball one away only to sidefoot it behind his standing leg and into space down the left wing. By this point Olsson is running in completely the wrong direction: not so much a fire engine going to the wrong fire – as *The Times* described Billy Wright when he was tricked by Ferenc Puskás at Wembley in 1953 – as a fire engine going to the scene of an armed robbery. He doesn't have a solitary clue what's going on, although he's far from alone in that. Cruyff's deep cross eventually comes to Van Hanegem, who bounces off Bo Larsson and falls over. That's not a penalty. What a flat ending to a memorable attack. He's probably done it a million times for Ajax, but it's the first time we've seen it. Somebody should give it a name. The Cruyff Spin maybe?

West Germany 0–1 East Germany (1974, group stage)

West Germany, beaten by East Germany, at 'their' World Cup? In one sense it was unthinkable; in another, preferable. Both sides had already qualified and the loser would have a much easier second-round group. So it proved: East Germany won the battle, West Germany won the World Cup.

GOAL! West Germany 0–1 East Germany (Sparwasser 77). Jürgen Croy claims Bernd Cullmann's looping header and throws the ball out to Gerd Kische, who makes ground without challenge on the right and then wafts a long ball towards the D. The ball bounces up towards Jürgen Sparwasser, who was in his own box a moment earlier before pelting it downfield. He chests it neatly past Horst-Dieter Höttges on the edge of the area, waits for Sepp Maier to sit down and roofs the ball emphatically from six yards. He celebrates with a roly-poly that, given the significance of the goal, measures about 8.2 on the Richter scale. Take that, capitalism!

Brazil 3–0 Zaire (1974, group stage)

The footage of Zaire defender Mwepu Ilunga taking a Brazil free-kick himself is a staple of any World Cup banter show on BBC3, but the story had a sinister background: the team had been threatened by presidential guards, working for the despot Joseph Mobutu, before the game who told them that, if they lost by four goals, they would not be allowed to return home.

85 min: ILUNGA IS BOOKED IN BIZARRE CIRCUM-STANCES. Mirandinha is taken out by Kilasu Mussamba, just outside the D. Nelinho tries to demonstrate that the wall is not ten yards, whereupon he is shoved away brusquely. Carpegiani, Rivelino and Marinho Chagas are all standing over the ball. Who will take it? None of them will because a Zaire defender has just bolted from the wall and hoofed the ball down the other end of the field! That's extraordinary. The right-back Mwepu Ilunga had decided, 'Nah, not on my watch.' He is booked, not so much for kicking the ball away as blootering the ball away. He pleads his innocence and sort of bows towards the referee. Eventually Carpegiani's free-kick hits the wall.

West Germany v Holland

*Final, Olympiastadion, Munich, West Germany,
Sunday, 7 July 1974*

The Dutch have been the stars of the show at *Fußball-
Weltmeisterschaft 1974,* **charming and beguiling with their
swashbuckling, thoroughly modern ways.** They've seen off
Uruguay, Bulgaria, Argentina, East Germany and reigning champions Brazil. Even when they were held to a 0–0 draw by Sweden,
Johan Cruyff unveiled what will surely become his signature turn
to an audience of millions, a twist of rococo delicacy worth much
more than anything so crass and base as a goal. They've been
operating on a different planet to the rest of the world. Totally.

But there's always an exception that proves the rule. The hosts
West Germany aren't quite the slick proposition of two years
ago, when they humiliated England at Wembley on their way
to glorious triumph at Euro 72. They've stuttered badly during
their World Cup, the low point an abject defeat to neighbours
and ideological rivals East Germany, which sent manager
Helmut Schön into such a depressive funk that someone had to
chop up his dinner and spoon-feed him like a baby. But despite
the absence of Gunter Netzer, the star of 1972, they've managed
to swash a bit of buckle themselves. Their winning goal against
Chile was scored by Paul Breitner, who if you blinked, appeared
to be patrolling both flanks at once. The left-back thrashed one
in from 30-odd yards down the inside-right channel with his
right peg. Total Football? Not totally. But nearly total.

**So the best two teams in the competition have reached the
final for the first time in a World Cup since 1950.** Holland are
favourites, with the will of the world behind them. They should
just about have enough to prevail, though few pundits think it'll
be anything other than close. And there's one thing worrying
the Dutch. The Germans have already competed in a World Cup
final as rank outsiders against a supposedly superior team who
captivated the world's heart: the Hungarians of Puskás, Boszik
and Hidegkuti back in 1954. And look what happened there!
This could be a thriller.

Kick-off: 4 p.m.

Referee: Bobby Davidson of Scotland was told he had the gig by FIFA officials' official Ken Aston, he of Battle of Santiago infamy, only for the committee to perform a U-turn 24 hours later and award it to Jack Taylor of England instead. 'He is not a man,' said Davidson of Aston as he fumed in the airport, waiting for his plane home. 'He is a mouse.'

West Germany: Sepp Maier, Berti Vogts, Paul Breitner, Rainer Bonhof, Hans-Georg Schwarzenbeck, Franz Beckenbauer, Jürgen Grabowski, Uli Hoeness, Gerd Müller, Wolfgang Overath, Bernd Hölzenbein.

Holland: Jan Jongbloed, Wim Suurbier, Ruud Krol, Wim Jansen, Wim Rijsbergen, Arie Haan, Johnny Rep, Johan Neeskens, Willem van Hanegem, Johan Cruyff, Rob Rensenbrink.

The teams are out, and we're good to go! Or are we? Where are the centre flags? Not there, that's where! Have they forgotten to replace them after the intriguingly scheduled pre-match closing ceremony? Or has Bobby Davidson stuffed them in his luggage and nicked off with them out of spite?

Holland kick off! AND WIN A PENALTY WITHIN 54 SECONDS!!! The Dutch knock it around the back awhile, hither and yon. After 16 passes, Cruyff takes up possession on the edge of the centre circle. He drives forward, drifting towards the inside-left channel, ignoring the yapping challenge of Vogts. As he enters the area, Hoeness slides across and sticks out a telescopic leg. Oops!

1 min: 32 seconds: GOAL!!! West Germany 0–1 Holland (Neeskens pen). Beckenbauer comes across to argue but he's waved away by the referee. Neeskens hammers the penalty down the middle, Maier diving to the left. What a start! The Germans haven't even touched the ball yet and they're a goal down!

2 min: Almost an immediate response by the hosts. Breitner cuts in from the left, 35 yards from goal, and sliderules a pass down the channel for Müller, who with his back to goal on the edge of the six-yard box tries to spin past Rijsbergen. But the blond defender isn't having any of it and shuts the door. The ball eventually finds its way back to Breitner, who shoots but doesn't even find the corner flag on the right.

4 min: Vogts is booked for persistent fouling, some achievement given we've only completed three full minutes of play. It's a hilarious sequence. Cruyff slightly miscontrols a ball down the left and pauses, giving the defender the opportunity to slide in, hack the ball away and take his ankles with it. Cruyff stays on his feet and trots back up the wing to take up possession again, and is immediately clattered on the right ankle by Vogts, who has followed him in the rabid style. The free-kick's tapped to Cruyff. In comes Vogts again, an over-excitable puppy with a string of sausages on his mind. It's a facsimile clatter to the ones that have gone before and the referee shows him the yellow card with a great sigh. Vogts makes a show of disbelief, hands on hips, but you can tell he knows it's a fair cop. The camera cuts to the bench and the grim face of Helmut Schön, Jackie Stewart sideburns jutting out of an outsized green tartan bonnet. And yet Vogts is still the one who looks most ridiculous during this particular sequence.

5 min: From the free-kick, Krol is found in a bit of space down the inside left. He reaches the box but leaves himself a tight angle, blootering into the side-netting.

8 min: This is being played at 100 miles an hour. Müller twists and nearly turns Rijsbergen inside-out down the left, but the defender stays staunch.

9 min: Breitner takes two touches inside from the left wing and launches one towards the top right. A decent effort but the ball's deflected out for a corner. Jongbloed claims it easily.

12 min: The German fans are whistling loudly as Holland stroke it around the back. Schwarzenbeck tries to get things going with a big-boned sashay down the right past three men. After a fashion, the passage of play ends with a throw-in down the left, from which Hölzenbein drags a low shot wide of the goal.

14 min: Haan spots a huge gap in the German midfield down the inside left and goes for it. He one-twos with Cruyff on the edge of the box and races for the return with Schwarzenbeck coming in from the left. Schwarzenbeck puts in a robust challenge, a comprehensive double shoulder barge that sends Haan scrambling momentarily on all fours, Bambi on ice, to stay upright. It could so easily have been a penalty, if the Dutchman had opted to land on his face instead of staying honest. As it is, Schwarzenbeck overpowers the unsettled player and stomps off with the ball.

17 min: Holland are enjoying the lion's share, though there's little end product to show for it. Meier hasn't had a save to make yet and, no, we're not counting the penalty. The Oranje spend 51 seconds stroking 11 lazy passes upfield from Jongbloed to Haan, who flings a cross into the box from the right. It's immediately headed clear by Breitner, allowing Germany to break upfield through Müller. Germany are more direct and pile forward to assist: Breitner chases after a Schwarzenbeck pass down the inside right, the ball breaking to Müller, who is only just stopped from racing clear by a determined Rijsbergen. Breitner is magnificent, he's here, there and everywhere, as Total as a Football player can get. The Dutch wouldn't say no, put it that way.

20 min: Schwarzenbeck spins on the spot through 360 degrees to nip past Cruyff and Rensenbrink. Vogts bursts down the inside right and slides the ball forward to Müller, who is flipped into the air by Rijsbergen. After one false start, Germany take their free-kick, 25 yards out. Bonhof blooters it idiotically into the wall. It should be gathered by Jongbloed, but he makes an awful hash of collecting and concedes a corner, the ball squirting under his arms. He does better with the setpiece, punching a Bonhof header clear.

22 min: From the centre circle, Beckenbauer waves his arms around, ordering Hoeness down the right. He sprays a delicious ball in the player's direction. Hoeness cuts back and moves infield, executing a one-two with Müller of tissue-paper delicacy, then feeding Overath in the centre. Overath fires a low pass down the inside left for Hölzenbein, who immediately flicks inside to Müller. The striker, his back to goal on the edge of the box, goes down in a heap with Rijsbergen, having backed into him. He springs up to claim a penalty and is quickly sprung down again as an incensed van Hanegem shoves him in the back as punishment for harping on at the ref. As Müller skates across the turf on his teeth, having acrobatically propelled himself to make sure the referee saw the disservice brought upon his person, the referee takes van Hanegem's name. Plenty of boos ringing around the ground.

23 min: Cruyff is needlessly hacked down from behind by the incessant Vogts, who really wants to watch himself. To be fair to the Dutch star, he picks himself up and gets on with business.

24 min: AND NOW IT'S A PENALTY FOR THE GERMANS!!! What a minute for Jansen. He sends Neeskens off down the right with a prompting pass from the middle of the park. Neeskens reaches the byline and pulls the ball back into the centre. Jansen, having meandered up the channel, nearly gets on the end of it, but Beckenbauer steps in calmly with a one-touch interception-cum-pass that sets Overath heading up the other end. Jansen puts the brakes on, Roadrunner style, then turns to track back. He's trotting as Overath sprays a pass wide left to Hölzenbein, but breaks into a panicked sprint as the winger cuts in from the flank and makes good for the box. Jansen thinks about a challenge on the edge of the area, checks, then as Hölzenbein keeps heading goalwards, decides to go in properly this time. He slides in rashly, sticking out a leg that the winger is all too happy to flop over. Penalty! There wasn't much contact, in fact there's a hint of the dive, but Jansen stupidly gave Hölzenbein the option to go down and the referee was always going to fall for it.

25 min: GOAL!!! West Germany 1–1 Holland (Breitner pen). Breitner places the ball on the spot – only just, mind, the thing's nearly in front of it – and confidently slots it into the bottom left. Jongbloed just stood there. For goodness sake, man, it's the World Cup final, put some effort in, will you?! Breitner certainly gives his celebration a good old go, thrusting his arms into the air with such passion it seems for a millisecond that they might extend telescopically and touch the heavens. Breitner, in thrall to communist doctrine, would probably prefer a more secular altitude-related metaphor, but he's wrapped up in the moment and will presumably let that slide.

26 min: A crunching tackle by Vogts, this time totally legit! It's on Haan down the Dutch left. As Vogts gets up to scamper off with the ball, the crowd roar their approval. There's a real sense now that the hosts are going to give the favourites a run for their money.

27 min: Van Hanegem tries to set Cruyff away with a long ball down the middle. Charles Reep in the house! Total Football, huh? Meanwhile, Beckenbauer sashays forward and tries to cleave the Dutch back line in two with an ostentatious pass forward for Müller, a gentle scoop off the turf, but the saucy looper is intercepted as it sails along its aesthetically pleasing parabola, cleared by the head of Rijsbergen. There's a discernible change of attitude in the two teams.

28 min: Oh, there's a change of attitude all right. The Dutch are trying to beat West Germany in their own manor, and now the Germans are trying to beat Holland in their own manner. If you want Total Football (or, in the German parlance, *Ramba Zamba*) explained in a nutshell, you can't do much better than Vogts going on a charge down the inside left, exchanging passes with Hoeness, skating past Neeskens and whipping a right-foot shot towards the top left. Jongbloed palms the ball out for a corner. Vogts, past the last man, probably should have scored, but nevertheless what a run from a player not usually noted as a barnstorming goal threat. The corner comes to naught.

29 min: Germany aren't giving the Dutch any time on the ball now. Cruyff tries to get something going by coming in from the right on a powerful run but he's upended by Vogts. Down on his knees, he hollers for a free-kick and should get his wish, but play moves on upfield. Frustration already appears to be setting in.

30 min: Grabowski goes on a Garrincha-esque twist and turn down the right. Having reached the byline, he makes it into the area and stands one up for Hölzenbein at the far post, but Rep gets in with a crucial header and Jongbloed sweeps up.

32 min: Hoeness charges down the left. He's checked. The ball's worked around awhile until Overath takes a turn down the same flank. He swings a cross high into the area. Jongbloed comes to collect and nearly makes a proper pig's lug of it, palming down into no-man's-land on the edge of his area and only just getting to the ball ahead of Grabowski, blootering clear upfield.

33 min: Cruyff sends Suurbier away down the right, but his cross into the area is unimaginative and easily mopped up by Meier. Hoeness goes on another sortie down the left, breaking past

Rep and into the area. He doesn't quite have the power to finish the job off and opts to cross into the centre for Müller, but his ball is cut out by Rijsbergen. This is an increasingly impressive performance by the Germans.

34 min: Grabowski skedaddles down the right from the halfway line and comes inside. Just before he reaches the D, van Hanegem makes an agricultural intervention. Free-kick. Beckenbauer stabs an exquisite chip over the wall with the outside of the foot, the sort of effort that should be set to porn-film wah-wah guitar. It's dropping under the bar but Jongbloed does well to tip over. Nothing comes of the corner. This is pretty much all Germany now, what a sea-change.

35 min: Springing out on the break, Cruyff and Rep find themselves two on one with Beckenbauer, bombing through the German half! Breitner and Schwarzenbeck, the dozy eejits, were stood appealing for offside even though Cruyff received the ball in his own half. It's like *One Man and His Dog*, as the German shepherd holds his position so Cruyff, taking the central line, can't get a comfortable shot away. He's forced to feed Rep on the left, who enters the area with the whites of Maier's eyes in his sight. Thanks to Beckenbauer's brilliantly awkward positional work, he's shooting from an angle that allows Maier to come off his line and parry brilliantly.

38 min: This is end-to-end brilliance. Grabowski twists and shakes down the left, pulling the ball back for Hölzenbein on the edge of the area. His snapshot is deflected out wide right for a corner.

39 min: Hoeness, with Jansen stood still and appealing for offside down the right, plays to the whistle and piles into the Dutch area. His low drive goes straight down Jongbloed's throat. He should have done so much better.

40 min: Neeskens, the salt in Holland's stew, is booked for an outrageous clip on both of Hölzenbein's ankles as the winger hares down the left. The keeper punches the resulting free-kick clear of danger.

42 min: A couple of minutes dominated by Holland, but there's no pace in their play and Germany seem comfortable letting their opponents enjoy possession. Van Hanegem curls in a cross from the left, but a Neeskens header from 12 yards is weak and well wide left.

43 min: GOAL!!! West Germany 2–1 Holland (Müller). Suurbier strides into the German half from his nominal right-back position. He drifts inside and nearly pings Cruyff clear down the inside left with a crossfield pass, but Bonhof has tracked back well and directs a spectacular diving header into the arms of Maier. The keeper feeds Hoeness down the right. He reaches the centre circle and leaves the ball for Grabowski, who holds it up on the right before sliding Bonhof into acres down the wing. Bonhof storms towards the box, drops a shoulder to beat Haan on the outside, then pulls a short pass back into the middle for Müller, catching up and level with the right-hand post. The striker takes a touch to kill the ball, leaving it sitting eight yards from goal. Krol follows the striker's run and not the ball, so when Müller takes an immediate step backwards to meet up again with the ball he's just stopped, the defender is out of the game and all is lost. Müller twists and in one deadly movement drags the ball into the bottom left. It's an astonishingly clever finish. He raises his arms, then jogs back to the halfway line with a look of inscrutable insouciance, just another day at the office. It's his 68th goal in 62 international matches, an obscene record. He's also now the top goalscorer in World Cup finals with 14, one ahead of Just Fontaine. And a second World Cup for West Germany is now a very real prospect.

44 min: Beckenbauer dribbles around in his own area awhile, just because he can.

HALF TIME: West Germany 2–1 Holland. And that's that for the half. Van Hanegem responds to the half-time whistle by aiming the ball straight at the referee's head. He's lost the plot completely! The referee goes up and has a quiet word. Cruyff races over and has a loud word. The official threatens to book the Dutch captain if he doesn't quell his yakking neck. Cruyff thinks about it awhile and decides he's not the sort of guy to be told what to do. There's only one outcome here and that's a booking for Cruyff, who departs the scene sporting an affronted coupon. He'll need to calm down because this isn't going to script for the Dutch.

And we're off again! The Dutch have made one change: René van de Kerkhof coming on in place of Rensenbrink, who never quite got into the match and was carrying an injury anyway. Someone in the crowd is waving a placard that says (in German, naturally): 'We know Bonhof, but who is Cruyff?' Bonhof has been one of the stars so far, while Cruyff has by his own high standards been a disappointment. The Dutch captain has got 45 minutes to reveal himself. Germany get the ball rolling again.

47 min: All Germany in the opening 60 seconds or so. Grabowski nutmegs Krol down the right, but quickly loses possession. Krol, powered by the steam coming out of his lugs, goes on a sortie upfield, a lung-bursting 50-yard romp, but his pass forward in the general direction of van de Kerkhof is way too strong.

48 min: Suurbier clatters into Overath down the left. From the free-kick, Hölzenbein twice causes bother down the inside-left channel. The second baroque ramble ends in a corner. Hoeness takes, finding the head of Bonhof, on the right-hand edge of the six-yard box. He's all alone, but sends a dreadful header wide left of the goal with only Jongbloed to beat. The German fans may know very well who Bonhof is, but they don't particularly like him very much at the moment.

49 min: And who is Cruyff? He's the bloke palming off Vogts in the centre circle, having had more than enough of the professional irritant's attention. He sets Holland going down the inside right. Neeskens chases a ball into the area and falls over, claiming Müller, tracking back, had bundled him to the ground, but the referee is quite rightly having none of it.

51 min: Holland press Germany back awhile. Van de Kerkhof sends a ball into the area from the left. Neeskens, level with the far post ten yards out, heads back to Rep who stretches to fire a low shot towards Maier. The keeper claims and is clattered by Cryuff as he snaffles the ball. Cruyff had every right to attempt to divert the ball into the goal before it reached the keeper, though a cheeky Beckenbauer is quickly on the scene, hands on hips in pantomime disgust, to cause bother. The referee has a quick chat with Cruyff but he's done little wrong and is in no danger of being sent off.

52 min: This is end to end. Maier bangs a goal-kick downfield. Hölzenbein chases after a Müller flick-on but can't reach the ball before Jongbloed comes out to claim. Holland race upfield through Rep and Haan, winning a corner down the right. Rep floats it to the near post. Maier comes off his line to punch clear but only manages to send it squirting backwards towards his own net. Luckily for the keeper, who was about to become synonymous with haplessness, Breitner is on the line to head clear. Hardly a surprise. Breitner is everywhere. He's omnipotent.

53 min: Schwarzenbeck hacked the loose ball out for a corner on the left. From which there's another scramble, the Germans suddenly unconvincing in defence. The ball drops to Neeskens in space, eight yards out, but his snap shot is blocked and balloons away. Panic over for the Germans. For now.

54 min: All-new panic for the Germans! Overath takes Cruyff down along the right wing. Cruyff takes the setpiece himself, sending a bouncing bomb through the German six-yard box. At the far post, van Hanegem comes in to meet with his head, guiding the ball down and bounding back up towards the top right. But there's no power in the effort, and even though Maier seems to have gone the wrong way, and too early to boot, he's still got enough time to make adjustments in mid-air and clasp the ball. It's not clear what Beckenbauer was up to there, other than fannying about. He should never have allowed van Hanegem to get across him with the goal at his mercy.

57 min: Overath creams a pass down the right for Bonhof to chase. Bonhof reaches the byline and hooks a cross into the area. Müller is lurking on the edge of the six-yard box but Suurbier extends a leg to divert the ball out for a corner. Müller claims for handball, ludicrously. The corner sees Grabowski duff a chip on to the top of the goalnet, a dismal nonsense.

59 min: GERMANY SCORE!!! BUT IT'S RULED OUT!!!
Hölzenbein goes on a high-speed wheech down the inside left. Just as he looks to turn the burners on with a view to reaching the penalty area, he's brought crashing to the floor by Rep, who isn't in the mood. Overath hoicks the free-kick wide right to Grabowski, who is one-on-one with Krol, Holland having fallen asleep in the trademark Amsterdam-afternoon-on-the-

Oranjeboom-and-bong style. The German feints to break down the wing but instead takes two nudges to the left and cuts inside. On the edge of the area, he clips a clever little diagonal pass into Müller, who was standing on the penalty spot but is now breaking for the right-hand edge of the six-yard box. Müller chest-controls as he runs across, then spins and sends a shot through Jongbloed's hands and into the left-hand side of the goal! It's a superbly worked goal, but the flag's up for offside. That's an atrocious decision: when Grabowski played the ball in, Rijsbergen was standing a good three or four feet in front of the striker, whose movement has made everyone look very daft. Lucky, lucky Holland.

60 min: Cruyff is complaining to the referee over an insignificant decision in the midfield. Is this news?

61 min: Van de Kerkhof cuts inside a heavy-footed Schwarzenbeck down the right and, flicking the ball with the outside of his right boot like a dandy flourishing a lace kerchief, finds Cruyff at the far post. Cruyff heads down for the incoming Rep, who is beaten to the ball at the near post by Breitner, lunging in to concede a corner. Cruyff's near-post setpiece is easily dealt with by the white-and-black wall.

64 min: This is attack versus defence, though at the moment Holland are doing little more than launching balls into the box from either wing. It's not so sophisticated. In times of desperation, even football's artists resort to the base ways of Charles Reep.

66 min: Cruyff executes one of his trademark turns on the edge of the German area but even that fails to prise open much space. He's got that face on again, though the aggressive irritation of earlier has now been downgraded to impotent frustration and is threatening to dissolve into resigned defeatism.

68 min: Cruyff lets the ball roll clumsily under his foot. Coming so soon after his blunt-can-opener turn, this really isn't a good sign for the Dutch.

69 min: Theo de Jong comes on for Rijsbergen.

70 min: Hölzenbein betrays German nerves with an awful back-pass down the German right. Neeskens latches on to it and races for the area, down the Dutch inside left. Luckily for the home side, Beckenbauer is on hand to gently nudge Neeskens out wide and then heads his cross behind. The corner is a waste of time and Holland don't have a whole load of that left.

71 min: More questionable newsworthiness involving a whining Cruyff.

72 min: Corner to Holland. Germany deal with the setpiece easily enough. Krol is brushed off the ball on the edge of the D and plonked on his arse, and as the Germans rush off upfield with their prize, tittering, the Dutchman could only look more queasy and confused if he was patting the top of his head with an open palm.

73 min: GREAT SAVE FROM MAIER! Germany switch off, assuming Cruyff's clipped pass down the left is going out. Van de Kerkhof chases after it, stops it dead by the corner flag, turns and loops a cross to the far post. Neeskens powers in to volley goalward but his hammer is met at the near post by Maier, a spectacular and brave stop. Nothing comes of the corner.

75 min: Hölzenbein's overhead clearance down the right is hoofed straight into poor Neeskens's grid at point-blank range. Playing through the pain, Neeskens romps into the space left down the wing and spoons a cross to the left-hand post, where the ball's headed back into the path of van de Kerkhof. The sub miskicks an effort from 12 yards so comprehensively that it corkscrews out of play down the right. He holds his knees, then his hips, in shame and sorrow.

77 min: AN ASTONISHING MISS! Suurbier is sent twinkling into the German area down the right and whips a low ball through the six-yard box. Rep, extending his leg, should connect and equalize, but doesn't. The ball sails harmlessly out of play on the other side. Maier is on his knees in embarrassed relief, while Bonhof loiters with the discombobulated air of a man who has been divested of his wallet, keys and watch by a street magician, then been given them back in a big envelope, and is trying to work out how it all happened. Germany are living dangerously and yet it's beginning to feel like it won't be Holland's day, or indeed year.

78 min: An astonishing and possibly illegal example of Vogts's tenacity as he beats Cruyff to a loose ball on the halfway line by pelting down the inside-right channel and launching a head-high studs-up challenge. He gets away with it, too, his bustle earning a throw for Germany deep in Dutch territory, some much needed relief, and comic relief at that. But for how long? Not long, is the answer. Grabowski dawdles in the centre of the field and is crunched by Cruyff, who strides upfield and flies a pass wide right to Rep. Rep, conscious that opportunities will be running out soon, makes a basic beeline for the penalty box, steaming past Schwarzenbeck. A fine opportunity to shoot but his effort is dragged across the face of goal, another painful near miss.

80 min: Holland are gifted a rather dubious corner down the left. Cruyff puts it in the mixer but Maier for once claims with confidence. The Dutch are soon coming back at Germany through van de Kerkhof, who drops a shoulder and fizzes a low shot to the near post. Maier snaffles but once again a questionable corner is awarded. And once more, Maier claims! He launches the ball upfield, where Jongbloed is forced to come out of his area to head clear under pressure from Müller.

82 min: Maier comes out to claim a high ball. Upon catching it, he's scratched by Neeskens's outstretched leg and makes his displeasure known through the medium of petulance. You can't blame the Dutch midfielder for going for that. Maier hoofs upfield. Müller nearly sends Hoeness clear down the left but Jongbloed is out quickly again to hack clear.

84 min: Comic cuts in the German box as Beckenbauer, under a high ball down the inside right, lobs his own keeper! Bonhof is forced to rush back and hack clear off the line. But it's all something and nothing, as Rep, making his presence felt in the melee, is penalized for a foul.

85 min: PENALTY TO WEST GERMANY??? NO!!! BUT IT SHOULD HAVE BEEN! Beckenbauer wallops a clearance down the left wing, an artful blooter. Hölzenbein makes good for the box and, as he enters the area, has the beating of Jansen on his right. Noddy Holder sticks his left leg out and stops the winger in full flow. Gudbuy T. Hölzenbein! The German again makes the most of it but that was unquestionably a foul and a penalty, more so than the one that was awarded in the first half! How costly could that decision be to West Germany?

86 min: Nearly very costly indeed because Holland go straight up the other end and almost score. Schwarzenbeck's headed clearance from the edge of his own box is poor. Neeskens intercepts, cuts in from the left and sends a low right-to-left curler a couple of inches wide of the left-hand post.

88 min: Hoeness sends Grabowski away down the right. He's into the area and wins a corner off Jansen. Suffice to say there were few passing options for the winger in the centre. Germany aren't taking any risks. The corner comes to naught.

89 min: Rep hammers the ball into the ground after needlessly fouling Breitner down the left and conceding a foul. He knows the jig is up.

FULL TIME: WEST GERMANY ARE THE NEW WORLD CHAMPIONS!!! AND POOR OLD HOLLAND ARE THE NEW HUNGARY. West Germany 2–1 Holland. The last kick of the final is Müller's as he chases the ball out of play down the right. The whistle goes and the striker, whose stunning piece of opportunism in the first half has won a second title for the Germans, holds his hands up in triumph before sinking to his knees and putting his face in his hands. The Olympic Stadium is awash with red, black and gold tricolours, what's there of the spider's web roof nearly shearing off, such is the noise. Beckenbauer strongarms his way through a riot of photographers to hug Müller, before the striker is lifted shoulder high. As Germany cavort, the Dutch stand on the sidelines, ashen-faced, keeping their counsel. Cruyff is also in the middle of a melee, but if the drained, numb look on his face is anything to go by, he could not be more alone.

Argentina v France

Group 1, Estadio Monumental, Buenos Aires,
Argentina, Tuesday, 6 June 1978

Group One is living up to its expectation as both the best and the toughest in the tournament. Italy, France and Argentina all played some outstanding football in their opening games, and Italy were at it again this afternoon with a 3–1 win over Hungary, which almost certainly puts them into the last eight. Argentina know that victory tonight will do the same.

The last eight is not enough, however. Argentina don't just want to win the World Cup. They *need* to win it. The worldwide deploring of the military junta, who are accused of torturing and 'disappearing' – i.e. killing – thousands of people since taking charge two years ago, has taken a lot of goodwill away from an Argentina team who can be spectacularly good to watch. They didn't need any help to come from behind to beat Hungary 2–1 on Friday – but they got it from the spineless referee, who allowed Argentina to kick the Hungary players around like pieces of ticker tape and whipped out two red cards when the Hungarians responded in kind.

It's hard to know what France expects. This is probably their best team since the one that reached the semi-finals in 1958 and they played some fine football in Friday's 2–1 defeat by Italy, but their campaign has been completely overshadowed by off-field nonsense. The coach Michel Hidalgo has threatened to quit over the ongoing Adidas row, with the players demanding more money from the team kit-supplier, some painting over their Adidas stripes before the first match. There have also been some arguments over whether wives should be allowed to visit, with Mrs Platini and Mrs Bathenay joining the team. If they lose tonight they are out. But if they win, they will be in a great position to reach the last eight, potentially at the expense of the hosts.

Team news: Argentina had a number of niggles after that fibrous encounter with Hungary, but all are fit, which means no place for the local darling, Norberto Alonso of River Plate. The wonderfully named defender Daniel Killer does not make the bench. For France, Dominique Bathenay, whose absence from the opening match caused Michel Platini such ire, is deemed fit enough to return. A numerical quirk: tonight's goalkeepers are wearing the numbers 5 and 21. To explain: Argentina have numbered their squad in alphabetical order, so their No. 1 is the midfielder Alonso, while the keeper holding France's No. 1 shirt, Dominique Baratelli, is on the bench.

Kick-off: 7.15 p.m., 11.15 p.m. in Blighty.

Referee: Jean Dubach (Switzerland).

Argentina: Ubaldo Fillol, Jorge Olguín, Luis Galván, Daniel Passarella, Alberto Tarantini, René Houseman, Osvaldo Ardiles, Américo Gallego, José Daniel Valencia, Leopoldo Luque, Mario Kempes.

France: Jean-Paul Bertrand-Demanes, Patrick Battiston, Marius Trésor, Christian Lopez, Max Bossis, Dominique Bathenay, Michel Platini, Henri Michel, Didier Six, Dominique Rocheteau, Bernard Lacombe.

1 min: Argentina kick off from left to right. They are in light blue and white; France are in dark blue.

2 min: Some nice early movement from both sides, with Valencia nutmegging Michel to spark an attack that ends when Luque is crowded out.

7 min: The camera cuts to the Argentina manager César Luis Menotti, who has a fag on.

9 min: The first big chance goes to France. Platini, Bathenay and Michel combined smoothly before Michel curled a nice cross behind the defence from an inside-right position. Lacombe got between Galván and Olguín but his diving header from ten yards was too close to Fillol, who saved at the second attempt. Lacombe might have done better.

11 min: Nice Work If You Can Get It dept: after 11 minutes, the BBC co-commentator Bobby Charlton speaks for the first time. He is full of praise for France's start. They have been extremely confident and don't seem intimidated by this raucous crowd. Nor does the referee, who has started with splendid authority – just what we needed after the weak performance of the Portuguese referee Garrido in Argentina's first game.

16 min: Another chance for France! They are playing beautifully here. Six, the mischievous left-winger, teased the right-back Galván before screwing a low cross towards the near post. Rocheteau – who had started the move on the other side of the pitch – got there a fraction before Fillol and flicked it just wide with the outside of the right foot. It was a clever effort, with Rocheteau stabbing at the ball in an attempt to spin it around Fillol, but he didn't quite soften his foot sufficiently.

18 min: Now it's Argentina's turn. Ardiles plays a one-two with Kempes, struggles past a couple of France players in the box and then moves neatly around Trésor before cutting the ball back from the byline. Kempes and Valencia get in each other's way but it comes to Luque, whose slightly mis-hit shot is cleared off the line by Lopez! It might have been drifting wide but Lopez played safe.

19 min: Argentina have a goal disallowed for offside! Gallego's quick free-kick put Houseman through on goal and he squeezed the ball past the goalkeeper Bertrand-Demanes; but the flag had gone up. We haven't seen a replay from a decent angle, although there were no complaints from Argentina. He was probably level and therefore offside.

21 min: Argentina have woken up big time and so have this uniquely intense crowd. Valencia makes space neatly on the left and chips a cross into the small space between Bathenay, Lopez and Trésor at the near post. He was probably looking for Kempes but Luque got there first and welted a spectacular volley from a narrow angle that hit Bertrand-Demanes and flew to safety. A vital if essentially unwitting save.

23 min: The camera closes in on Tarantini's shorts, which are leg-crossingly tight. They look like they've been painted on. Whatever they're made of – cotton, polyester, matt emulsion – that really can't be healthy.

27 min: A slippery run from the impressive Six, past Ardiles, Olguín and Galván, ends when he falls over in the box and is penalized for handball. An exasperated Six directs a double limp-wristed wave towards the referee.

30 min: The camera cuts to Menotti, who has his trouser leg rolled up and is meticulously pulling his socks up almost to the knee. Perhaps he's getting fidgety, on account of not having a fag on.

32 min: Argentina are the masters of slow-slow-bloody-quick attacks, usually through direct running. When they speed things up they do so devastatingly, as if you've accidentally fast-forwarded the tape on the old Radio Rentals Betamax. There were two examples there. First Luque charged infield from the left, beating Lopez, Michel and Bathenay before playing it to Kempes, whose return ball on the edge of the area was intercepted by Trésor. Then Ardiles nicked the ball off Bathenay, played it right to Houseman and ran into the area before volleying the return ball into orbit. It was a difficult chance, with the ball almost behind him as he took the shot from 15 yards. The consequence was that air-traffic controllers in Argentina have an unexplained dot on their screen.

35 min: Luque's pace is blistering. He rolls Lopez and skedaddles down the left, past Michel and into the area before going over after contact from Trésor. The crowd beseech the referee to give a penalty but in fact he's given an indirect free-kick for obstruction. That was a tough call: the ref could easily have given nothing – or even a penalty. It's on the left side of the box. Argentina take it quickly and Houseman whips his shot over the bar from the edge of the box.

41 min: KEMPES HITS THE POST! Actually he doesn't just hit the post, he assaults it with a stunning effort. The move started when Passarella stepped decisively from defence to win the ball off the hitherto disappointing Platini. He pushed it forward to Kempes, who ballerina'd away from Trésor and pushed it wide to Luque on the left with all the France defence running desperately towards their own goal. Luque moved into the area and then came back the other way before flicking a short pass off to Kempes, just inside the area to the left of centre. He wrapped his foot around the ball and belted a stunning effort that boinged off the near post before Bertrand-Demanes had twitched a freshly plucked eyebrow.

45 min: IS THIS A PENALTY FOR ARGENTINA? We have controversy on the stroke of half time! Kempes slipped Bathenay with a lovely drag-back on the halfway line to start yet another

Argentina attack. Michel made a half-challenge 30 yards out, and then Kempes lobbed the ball over the top of the defence for Luque. Trésor tracked him all the way into the area, forcing him slightly wide. Eventually Luque struck a shot that hit the hand of the falling Trésor and went behind for a corner. Argentina appealed for a penalty but Trésor was in the process of falling backwards and had little idea what day it was, never mind where his hand was in relation to the ball. Argentina – the country, not the team – demanded a penalty and the referee has come over to talk to his linesman on the near side.

45+1 min: HE'S GIVEN THE PENALTY! The referee jogs back towards the area, with two Argentina players pointing towards the spot like owners telling a dog where to go, and then stands on the spot to signal he has given the penalty. Argentina celebrate as if they have already scored. That's extremely harsh. All the good work in an outstanding refereeing performance has been undone in one moment of weakness, although it may have been the linesman's decision.

45+2 min: GOAL! Argentina 1–0 France (Passarella pen). The captain puts Argentina ahead with a decisive penalty, rammed into the bottom-right corner as Bertrand-Demanes goes the other way.

HALF TIME: Argentina 1–0 France. How about that for an end to the half? Menotti saunters down the tunnel, presumably taking the opportunity to slope off for a fag.

46 min: France start the second half with a bit of a cavalry charge that produces a half-chance after 30 seconds when Michel's half-volley from the right of the box is well blocked by the stretching Tarantini.

47 min: A couple of comically inept clearances from Argentina in the space of five seconds. First Galván shins Michel's free-kick right across the face of his own goal; then Kempes, trying to clear the ball from near the touchline, blitzes spectacularly over his own bar for a corner on the other side of the field. That is quite possibly the worst attempted clearance in the history of all football.

51 min: Another storming run from Luque. He bursts past Lopez before flicking the bouncing ball one side of Trésor and running round the other. He gets into the area and tries to slither and stumble through the entire France defence, with only the last man, the recovering Lopez, eventually stopping him.

53 min: Six is lucky not to have his name taken for an inept and laughably late lunge at Ardiles.

56 min: France have had more of the ball since the goal – as they have all game really – but Argentina carry such menace when they attack. And there's an example: Valencia plays a one-two with Kempes, addresses the bouncing ball 35 yards from goal and hits a booming, dipping shot that is beautifully fingertipped over the bar by the back-pedalling Bertrand-Demanes. The keeper may have hurt himself badly here; as he fell backwards after making the save his spine slammed into the post. Kempes and Lopez rush to see how he is; he's hardly moving. France are already at this World Cup without their first-choice goalkeeper, André Rey – who broke his wrist saving a shot from his own man, Battiston – and now it seems Bertrand-Demanes may have to go off. There's a stretcher on the field and substitute goalkeeper, Baratelli, is stripped and ready. At least he's wearing No. 1, that's got to count for something?

58 min: Bertrand-Demanes is still being treated. The camera cuts to Menotti, who had a fag on. The BBC's Barry Davies describes him as a man with 'a face like a well-kept grave'.

59 min: After three minutes, the keeper is replaced by Baratelli, which means we've lost the most phonetically appealing name in the tournament: Bertrand-Demanes. Short of having a player called Cellar Door, it can't be improved.

61 min: GOAL! Argentina 1–1 France (Platini). France score within 90 seconds of the restart! They deserve this for their intrepid performance throughout. Battiston ran 40 yards down the right unchallenged and then dinked a lovely chip over three defenders to find Lacombe in space in the area. As Fillol charged out Lacombe lobbed the ball gently over him. It bounced off the crossbar – two Argentina defenders and Rocheteau leapt for it as it dropped on to the bar, with their momentum taking them into the net – but Lacombe had followed up his own shot and the rebound came to him six yards out. He either passed it or mis-controlled it square to Platini, depending how generous you are feeling. No matter because Platini rammed it through Olguín – who was behind the line anyway – and into the net. Platini has been fitful so far in this tournament, despite all the hype, but what a vital goal this is. France are back in the World Cup – and if they get another they will be favourites to qualify from this group!

62 min: WHAT A CHANCE FOR LUQUE! Kempes, found by Ardiles, pirouetted delightfully away from Trésor and Platini on the edge of the D before flicking an angled through-pass to the right with the outside of his left foot. Luque took it in his stride and then hit a right-foot shot from ten yards that was deflected wide by the sliding Lopez, who has injured his shoulder in the process. He should be fine. What a vital tackle that was.

64 min: Battiston plays an awkward ball down the right to Rocheteau, who improvises with a game of keepy-uppy: chest, a flick of the right foot and then an up-and-under towards the far post. Six wins the header above Olguín but can't get any power on it and Fillol makes what should have been a routine save at the second attempt, scrambling after the ball like a drunk pensioner trying to find his dentures.

65 min: We now have two No. 1s on the pitch. The public darling No. 1 round these parts, River Plate's captain Alonso, has replaced Valencia. Many feel he should be a regular in Menotti's team. He greases his thighs like a homoerotic wrestler and charges on to the field.

68 min: This is pulsating stuff. There is a slight nervousness in the crowd, who are maybe just starting to think the unthinkable: if Argentina are beaten here, they will almost certainly have to beat the impressive Italians in four days' time to avoid an ignominious early exit.

69 min: Alonso has only been on the field a few minutes and he's already struggling with injury. That's some dumb luck indeed. It looks like it might be a hamstring problem. He obviously didn't grease his thighs enough.

71 min: SIX MISSES A GOLDEN CHANCE! Argentina should be on the brink of defeat. Platini picked up the ball halfway inside his own half, wandered 50 yards unchallenged and then suddenly quickened up the pace. He ran past Gallego, drew Passarella towards him and then teased a through-pass to Six on the edge of the D. Six's first touch was beautifully smooth, easing the ball past the sliding last man, Tarantini, and with his second he slipped the ball past the outrushing keeper Fillol. It drifted excruciatingly wide of the right-hand post. You could call that a bad miss but he seemed to have done everything right.

73 min: Ortiz replaces poor Alonso, who is unable to continue. What a miserable World Cup this is turning into for him.

74 min: GOAL! Argentina 2–1 France (Luque). This epic match has yet another twist! Argentina, under so much pressure for the last ten minutes, are ahead through a wonderful goal from Luque. The move started when Kempes dropped deep to pick up possession inside his own half. He gave it to Ardiles, who moved it on to Luque, in far too much space 25 yards out. The ball bobbled awkwardly when it reached Luque, whose first touch sent it spinning up in the air to head height. It bounced once and then twice, with Luque waiting impatiently for it to sit right, like a tired parent waiting for their kid to stop pissing about and brush their teeth before bed. As it dropped the second time he turned 90 degrees and thrashed a marvellous right-footed half-volley that swerved away from Baratelli and into the corner. 'The crowd have gone mad!' says Barry Davies. And they have every right to go mad. That is an outstanding goal, which may well put Argentina into the last eight. But France will be so disappointed with their defending: only Trésor went to close Luque down and by the time he did it was too late. It may be too late for France: they have 15 minutes to get an equalizer or they will be out of the tournament.

75 min: The camera cuts to Menotti, who has a fag on. Then Six draws a vital save from Fillol! Bathenay's ball forward towards Trésor was half cleared by the head of Passarella. Six controlled it and then, as defenders converged, walloped an impatient – almost angry – half-volley from 25 yards. It was rising towards the top corner and Fillol leapt to his left to palm it behind for a corner.

78 min: The camera cuts to Menotti. Yes, he's still sucking them down. He might be halfway through a new one, mind.

79 min: A sniff of a chance for Six, who takes a through-pass from Platini and falls over after a challenge from behind. Six appeals alone for a penalty, to no avail. It was a clumsy tackle at best and France might have a case there.

80 min: The atmosphere is unreal. Kempes dances across the face of the area, past Lopez, before striking a fierce shot that is superbly blocked by Trésor.

82 min: Kempes is fouled just outside the area on the right, almost by the touchline. It's a crazy angle but he has a go anyway, chipping languidly into the side-netting as the poorly positioned Baratelli dives desperately across his goal. Moments later, Luque falls awkwardly after a challenge from Lopez. He has done something to his right elbow and looks in serious pain. He's has gone off the field and is receiving treatment.

85 min: Luque is still off the field and in obvious agony too – it looks like his elbow is dislocated. So Argentina are down to ten men as they have already used both substitutes. France, with the extra man, are moving the ball around nicely without ever really penetrating.

88 min: Six, fouled by Passarella, gives the referee another double limp-wristed wave – his second of the evening. In accordance with the laws, he is booked for repeat double limp-wristed waving.

90 min: Argentina's ten men are camped in defence. Lacombe hooks a volleyed pass down the left wing for Rocheteau, who wriggles past Galván into the area but then hits his cross over the head of Bathenay on the six-yard line!

90+1 min: This is a storming finish, with France pushing everyone forward. Luque comes back on, holding his right arm very carefully down by his side, bringing to mind Franz Beckenbauer's heroism in the 1970 semi-final.

FULL TIME: Argentina 2–1 France. That's it! After only two minutes of injury time, the referee ends a classic match. Argentina go through to the second group stage, and France go into the history books as one of the better sides to be eliminated in the first round of the World Cup. Next time, perhaps?

Holland v Scotland

Group 4, Estadio Libertador San Martín, Mendoza,
Argentina, Sunday, 11 June 1978

When Scotland arrived a fortnight ago at Alta Gracia, their training retreat in the hills just outside Córdoba, hopes were high. Comic crooner Andy Cameron might have been the only man to vocalize great expectations of really shaking them up and winning the World Cup, but manager Ally MacLeod had delivered a downgraded promise of 'a medal of some sort'. And was he so wrong? Was a place in the last four such a (bag)pipe dream for a squad containing the European champions Kenny Dalglish and Graeme Souness, newly crowned English champ Archie Gemmill, and big-club talent such as Joe Jordan, Martin Buchan and Asa Hartford? The bookies certainly didn't see it as out of the question. Scotland were priced at 9/1 for a successful shoogle. They might not have been the greatest football team, as Cameron claimed, but fifth greatest isn't so bad, behind Brazil, Argentina, West Germany and Holland. Ally's Army on the march!

But just before Scotland reached Alta Gracia, the clutch on the team bus burned out. In farcical scenes, the clapped-out vehicle had to be nudged down the street to its final destination by the coach travelling behind. If there's ever been a more obvious harbinger of doom, we'd love to hear about it.

Cue the wholly inevitable. First up – and these were MacLeod's words – came the 'old men' of Peru. Then the 'minnows' of Iran. Oh Ally! And let's not even go into the destabilizing Willie Johnston pep-pills scandal; Don Masson's false drug confession made in misguided support of the banished Johnston; the rows in the camp over bonus money; and the post-Iran press conference which saw MacLeod bend down to pat a stray dog, reflecting that 'this wee fellow is my only friend at the moment'. The dog, needless to say, sank its teeth into him. Scotland have, not to put too fine a point on it, made a royal arse, balls and sack of this. And the fans aren't best pleased, if the chant spat at MacLeod after the Iran draw was anything to go by: 'We want our money back!'

All this leaves Scotland needing to win their final group game *by three goals* **if they're to advance to the second round.** No problem, eh? Who's up next? Ah.

It's Holland. The good news: they're not a patch on the 1974 vintage. No Johan Cruyff, for a start. They've also looked fairly unconvincing against Iran (though they did at least manage to beat them) and Peru, against whom they barely crafted a single chance. Not an impossible dream, then. Though on the other hand, this Dutch team still contains Ruud Krol, Johnny Rep, Johan Neeskens and Rob Rensenbrink. And while Scotland's abundance of talent surely has to click sometime, Holland's abundance of talent surely has to click sometime.

Kick-off: 4.45 p.m. local, 8.45 p.m. back home.

Referee: Erich Linemayr (Austria).

Not picking Souness, who along with Dalglish won the European Cup for Liverpool last month, hasn't helped Scotland, but MacLeod's finally seen some effing sense: Alan Rough, Stuart Kennedy, Willie Donachie, Bruce Rioch, Tom Forsyth, Martin Buchan, Archie Gemmill, Asa Hartford, Joe Jordan, Graeme Souness, Kenny Dalglish.

Holland: Jan Jongbloed, Wim Suurbier, Wim Rijsbergen, Ruud Krol, Jan Poortvliet, Johan Neeskens, Wim Jansen, Johnny Rep, René van de Kerkhof, Willy van de Kerkhof, Rob Rensenbrink.

Meanwhile back hame . . . A brick has been hurled through the window of the Scottish FA offices in Glasgow. Seems the punters are placing the blame for this debacle on the amount of promotional activity before the tournament, the most embarrassing of which has been the telly ad for Chrysler Avenger cars. 'They both run rings round the competition' ran the slogan, which has already been consigned to history, the chastened manufacturer pulling the ad before any more damage to its brand can be done. 'It was time to call a halt as the team just did not live up to the copywriters' claims,' jabbered a spokesman for the company, who at least can count their lucky stars they didn't manufacture the team bus. Chrysler's lack of ad spend isn't stopping ITV as well as BBC showing the match, though. Presumably the newly vacant slots will sell for a pretty penny in England, where tonight's entertainment could prove strangely popular.

The Austrian referee, sporting a very brash none-more-red kit, gets proceedings under way. Scotland, in their famous dark-blue shirts and white breeks, kick off. Souness gets his first touch of this World Cup after two seconds. The ball's launched up the right wing and picked off by Krol. Holland, in their second-choice white shirts and orange shorts, to avoid a colour clash for those watching in black and white, move upfield, but René van de Kerkhof gifts the ball to Hartford, who sends Kennedy away down the right. Krol deals with the cross and, despite Souness battling to get on the end of the clearance, the ball's eventually shuttled back to Jongbloed. A positive start by Scotland, though it's not as if they're left with the whole gamut of approaches to pick from.

2 min: There are around 35,000 spectators here in a stadium that holds 40,000. A few empty yellow seats dotted around. And a strange, strangulated noise coming from the crowd: a wispy yet defiant chant of 'Scotland! Scotland!' from a gang of fellows who are holding on to hope despite the vast scale of the task facing their countrymen.

4 min: Neeskens attempts a smartarse backheel down the Scottish right but succeeds only in finding Jordan, who lays off to Hartford. The Manchester City midfielder advances down the channel and whistles a low shot wide right of goal. Not fantastic but not the worst either, which just about sums up Scotland's start; they've enjoyed more of the ball and appear to be on the front foot at least.

5 min: SCOTLAND RATTLE THE WOODWORK! Oh they're on the front foot! Souness glides into space down the right, stops for a wee moment of contemplation, then wedges a cross into the six-yard area. Rioch rises and plants a header on to the crossbar. You'd say the Scottish captain was unlucky, especially as his effort twangs away from danger, but he was unmarked in the middle and really should have scored.

7 min: SCOTLAND FIND THE NET! BUT IT WON'T COUNT! Souness finds Donachie in a ridiculous amount of space down the left. The cross is abysmal. Gemmill then has a go down the same wing and is fouled. He hits the free-kick into the first man and wins a corner. Dalglish takes, setting up

Donachie to send an outswinger into the area. The Dutch step up for offside as Forsyth traps on the penalty spot and plants the ball on to the bottom of the left-hand post and into the net! But the flag's up. That's a really close call. Forsyth looked onside, although there's maybe a suspicion that Kennedy, lurking away to the right and well out of the road of the action, might have been half a yard off. That probably should have been the opener but at least it might give the Scots some much-needed succour.

9 min: Rijsbergen is clambering all over Dalglish, just to the left of the D. Free-kick. Rioch blooters an idiotic effort straight at the wall. Souness picks up the loose ball and tiptoes gracefully past a couple of Dutch lunges, but as he pokes the ball through to his front men, the flag goes up for offside again.

10 min: During that skirmish, Neeskens went in hard on Gemmill and has managed to injure himself. He was carrying a knee injury anyway. He's whisked away on a stretcher and replaced by Jan Boskamp.

13 min: Scotland pass it around sweetly in the middle of the park awhile. Souness then pings a ball down the inside left but Holland push up once again, leaving three Scots stranded.

14 min: SCOTLAND HAVE THE BALL IN THE NET *AGAIN*!!! BUT, ONCE MORE, TO NO AVAIL! Rough, his preposterous white peaked cap defying the laws of physics by staying on his head despite being tasked to contain that springy perm, squints and launches long into the evening sun. Krol, more by accident than design, heads the dropping ball back towards his own area. Dalglish chases after it, a step behind Rijsbergen. As the pair reach the edge of the box, Dalglish sticks his right peg out and pokes the ball past the advancing Jongbloed, sending it bouncing into the corner of the net. But he's adjudged to have clipped the heels of the defender as he made his move, a decision that looks harsh as the defender appeared to have gone over by his own design. Dalglish stares at the referee with an intensity that can best be described as Glaswegian.

15 min: Scotland are winning most of the ball in the middle of the park. Holland can't get going. Gemmill slides a pass down the inside-right channel. Rioch, his back to goal, lays off inside to Dalglish, a gorgeous first touch. Dalglish, 20 yards out, meets the dropping ball with his right foot and sends a low shot screeching past the left-hand post. Scotland should be ahead by now. It's quite possible, on another day, they'd be four(!) goals to the good already, but such are the slim margins at World Cup level.

16 min: And yet Holland could have had a couple themselves by now, with Rensenbrink taking a pass from the left wing, stepping inside, and thrashing a shot across goal and wide of Rough's right-hand post. Scotland stepped off a wee bit there, perhaps intoxicated by their relative successes up the other end.

18 min: Jordan is given a stern talking-to by the referee after clattering Jansen, seconds after he himself was battered by Suurbier, who had gone unpunished. A case of mistaken identity when the red mist came down, one would suggest. Will that literal boot give Holland a metaphorical kick up the jacksie? They've been strangely quiet so far, few passes sticking. At one point, Boskamp was standing around in the centre circle with his back to play, having a wee chat to a pal, it would seem, allowing Rioch to snatch the candy. They need to up their game.

19 min: THE SCOTS ARE DENIED A PENALTY! Rioch drops a shoulder to dance past Krol down the left and fires a low cross into the centre. Jordan, from the right, makes a run inside to meet it, with a view to sidefooting home from 12 yards. But he's clumsily hacked from behind by Poortvliet, who having got Jordan out of the way guides the ball back to his keeper. That surely should have been a spotkick. A clumsy challenge by a player winning only his third cap.

24 min: Rioch goes on a powerful skitter down the right. He's being held back. That's a free-kick, just outside the area, near the byline. Souness clips it to the near post but can't find Dalglish.

27 min: René van de Kerkhof has perhaps been Holland's most consistent performer so far. His twin brother Willy decides to take up some of the slack, cutting in from the left and powerfully curling a shot just to the left of the target. Rough probably had it covered, although he's struggling with the sun and shadows under the peak of that hat, which makes him look like an extra from *Smokey and the Bandit*.

28 min: Jensen skins Gemmill down the right and loops a cross to the far post. It's a bit overcooked but Rensenbrink manages to extend a giraffe's neck to send it arcing towards the right side of goal. Rough has to stretch high to collect, and as he does so he's unceremoniously dumped to ground by Rep. Rough's got shot of the Confederate Cap since the last attack and could have done with the extra protection, as he rattles into the post and sits dazed awhile, propped up in the style of the alfresco drinker.

30 min: Holland are turning the screw a bit. Donachie, inside the Dutch half out on the left, rolls a ball inside for Gemmill but the wee man is away with the fairies, perhaps trying to recalculate his wage packet minus the Chrysler money. Krol steps in to intercept and takes a few strides towards the centre circle before rolling a pass down the left channel for Rensenbrink. The striker's clear but he's not getting to the ball ahead of Rough, who races from his area and slides along the ground to smother with his hands! Either he's still suffering from that bang to the noggin or more likely that was as cynical as it comes. He trots back to his goal-line with the ball tucked under his arm, not a trace of guilt or regret on his face. All Holland get is a free-kick just to the left of the D. Boskamp hits an idiotic shot straight into the wall and Jensen skies the rebound miles over the bar. One of the great professional fouls, not bad going for a player who is only part-time with Partick Thistle.

34 min: PENALTY TO HOLLAND! Rough throws the ball out to Kennedy on the right. The full-back rolls a ball forward to Souness, who gives it him back. Rensenbrink rushes in to press Kennedy, who experiences a hot flush and, such are the paradoxes of football, freezes. He turns, contemplating a backpass, but his dithering allows Rensenbrink to prod the ball away from him, down the Dutch left. Rep swarms in to pick up the loose ball and race into the area. He looks to go outside the advancing Rough but he's bundled over by Kennedy, desperate to catch up and atone. A no-brainer for the referee. So typical of this Scotland vintage, after playing so well. Gemmill is booked for giving the referee lip.

35 min: GOAL!!! Holland 1–0 Scotland (Rensenbrink pen). Rensenbrink whips a low penalty, his third of the group stage, into the bottom-left corner. Rough went the right way and wasn't far off the ball either, but it was such a well-placed kick the poor keeper had no chance. That's the 1,000th goal in World Cup finals. The way the last week's gone for Scotland, they'll feel like they've conceded the whole lot. They now need four to progress. Four. Against the 1974 finalists. Good luck, boys!

36 min: An immediate response by the Scots, who have clearly decided they may as well be hung for a sheep as a lamb and are piling forward in the gung-ho fashion. Donachie is sent scampering into space down the left. His cross shaves the top of Jordan's head, six yards out. The ball flies to Rioch, racing in from the right. His low drive towards the bottom right is met well by Jongbloed and Boskamp mops up the rebound.

40 min: For the 948th time this afternoon, Scotland have several men caught offside. They're not thinking on their feet at all.

43 min: René van de Kerkhof turns on the burners to embarrass Kennedy down the left. The full-back does enough to ensure he doesn't make the area but Holland win a corner. The ball's worked out to the right, allowing René's twin Willy to send a weak shot down Rough's throat. Scotland are beginning to be pulled this way and that. After that superlative start, they've lost a lot of momentum since the goal.

45 min: GOAL!!! Holland 1–1 Scotland (Dalglish). But suddenly the picture changes! Souness, loitering on the left, just outside the area, caresses a cross towards Jordan, ten yards out, level with the right-hand post. The big striker rises above Rensenbrink, heads back across goal and down towards Dalglish, who sets himself, lets the ball bounce and welts a rising shot into the top right past Jongbloed's despairing wave. What a stunning finish that is, from a player who has rarely replicated his Celtic and Liverpool form on the international stage!

45+1 min: Rijsbergen can't continue, and is replaced by Piet Wildschut. Kennedy reaches the byline down the right and whistles a cross towards Rioch, level with the far post on the edge of the area. He heads across for Souness, who swishes his boot through thin air. Holland sweep up the left wing through René van de Kerkhof. His cross finds Rensenbrink free in acres on the edge of the box, but the striker can't control.

45+3 min: Boskamp attempts to beat Rough from 40 yards. Even allowing for the keeper's somewhat idiosyncratic style, that's taking things a wee bit too far, isn't it? 'We'll support you ever more!' holler the Scotland fans, which is quite a step up from intemperate demands for a refund. The volte-face has been earned.

HALF TIME: Holland 1–1 Scotland. And that's that for the half. A draw's no more than Scotland deserve at this stage. You could make a case that they should be comfortably in the lead, but then Holland came back at them strongly and could have had two or three themselves. A fine performance so far but let's not get too carried away with the plaudits; they still need three goals and now they've only got 45 minutes left to get them.

And we're off again! Hats off to the BBC, who miss the start of the second half, Jimmy Hill forced to cut off pundit Jock Stein in mid-flow as the pictures from Argentina demand attention. Souness is immediately sent clear down the left and his cross is only half dealt with by Holland. Kennedy takes up the attack down the right, where he wins a corner off Rensenbrink. From which . . .

47 min: PENALTY TO SCOTLAND!!! Dalglish crosses to Jordan, ten yards out and level with the left-hand post. He nods down for Souness, who can't quite get the ball under control but nevertheless takes it towards goal. He's bundled over, six yards out, by Willy van de Kerkhof! Souness springs to his feet and slowly raises his right arm into the air, a look of quiet, calm determination on his face, a deliberate show of gentle power. This could be a perfect start to the half for MacLeod's side!

47 min: GOAL!!! Holland 1–2 Scotland (Gemmill pen). Gemmill threads the spotkick into the bottom-right corner with a flip of his left foot. This couldn't be on, could it? Surely not. Still, all of a sudden, thanks to a couple of goals bookending the interval, the picture certainly looks very different!

49 min: It's all fairly subdued in the wake of that goal, almost as though both sides are carefully recalibrating their positions.

50 min: Rep has a slash from 25 yards, an awkward low ball bouncing along the scarred turf towards the bottom left. Rough is down to parry to the right, then springs up to claim.

52 min: This game remains a couple of decent final balls away from turning into a scoring spectacular. First Kennedy is released in acres down the right, zipping past a mistimed Suurbier lunge, but his cross is awful. Then René van de Kerkhof takes up the ball to the left of the Scottish half, plays a loose pass into the middle behind Rep, chases after it himself, skins Buchan on the outside down the right, then upon reaching the byline hoicks the cross out of play. Try predicting this! Okay, it's Scotland at a World Cup. But *how* are they going to go out? Because it's far from clear how this will finish.

55 min: Holland seriously click for the first time in the match. Rep takes a quick free-kick down the right, tapping to Jansen who slips the ball wide to Boskamp. The blond substitute curls a cross into the centre, where Rep connects with a spectacular bicycle kick from just inside the box. The ball flies well over the bar. It's starting to look like Johnny boy's left his shooting boots at home today.

56 min: 'You'll never walk alone,' trill the Scottish fans, which is either staunch support for their beleaguered but brave team or arch comment on the state of the team bus, and the fact Chrysler have taken back the keys to all the Avengers.

58 min: Dalglish snaps around Boskamp's ankles and wins possession marvellously. Souness finds Forsyth, who rakes a long pass down the inside-right channel for Dalglish, who for a second looks like breaking clear. But he doesn't quite have the pace to reach the pass, Poortvliet coming across to cover and welt the ball out of play on the right. From the throw, Souness whips in a cross and Dalglish flashes a header wide right. If that was on the postage stamp, it's not clear Jongbloed would have had it covered. 'He's grown up today,' sniffs the BBC's David Coleman, of a player who has won four Scottish titles, scored 19 international goals and notched a winner in a European Cup final.

61 min: The Dutch look a bit rattled here. Three rash fouls transport Scotland from box to box. First Rensenbrink pulls Gemmill back by the neck, then Boskamp slides through Jordan like spatula under fried egg, and finally Poortvliet clatters Dalglish just outside the Dutch box on the left. Souness floats the free-kick to Jordan, level with the right-hand post. He's the boss of the Dutch defence and wins yet another knock-down, but Forsyth, six yards out in the middle, isn't paying attention properly and is on the back foot when the ball flashes across goal and out of play on the left. He was flagged offside anyway – another questionable decision by the linesman – but he should have skelped that into the net, if only to put the willies up Holland.

62 min: Jansen sends René van de Kerkhof away down the right. Closing towards the byline, he breaks left, poking the ball past Rioch and into the area. Rough races towards him and decides to stay upright and tackle with his feet. Van de Kerkhof doesn't fancy a dust-up and shirks the challenge, ceding possession to the keeper. Scotland were living dangerously there.

63 min: René van de Kerkhof curls a high cross into the box from the right. Rensenbrink is clear on the penalty spot but his attempted volley is sliced into the air. Rough comes out to collect under pressure from Rep but can't get a proper hold of the ball. Luckily for Scotland – a tattered mess at the back, having presumably decided it's Buenos Aires or bust – Forsyth is on hand to mop up and clear the lines.

65 min: Jordan isn't too far from latching on to Hartford's speculative pass down the middle. Holland aren't looking particularly comfortable at the back.

69 min: BRACE YOURSELVES . . . IT'S HARD TO BELIEVE, BUT . . . *THIS IS ON!!!* Holland 1–3 Scotland (Gemmill). Kennedy scoops the ball down the right to Dalglish, who picks up possession ahead of Poortvliet on the right-hand edge of the area. He steps out towards the wing and makes space to turn, then looks to burst into a gap between Poortvliet on his right and Jansen on his left. He manages that but Krol slides in to tackle. The ball breaks back up the wing to Gemmill, who takes six of the best touches you'll ever see in a World Cup! One: he nips the loose ball inside and away from Jansen. Two: he turns and faces goal. Three: he nudges the ball past Krol, desperately sliding out but destined to skitter hysterically upfield and out of the picture. Four: he prods the ball into the area past another hapless slide from Poortvliet. Five: he takes a touch to allow himself to open his body up to goal. Six: he caresses an exquisite chip into the middle of the goal, over the hopeless spread of Jongbloed. Gemmill is entitled to race 16 times round the stadium after that, but he satisfies himself with a few fist clenches and a jog back to the halfway line. That's a thing of artistic beauty, made better by poor Jongbloed's position during the money shot: splayed chest down on the turf, but looking up and backwards in impotent distress as the ball sails into the net.

70 min: AFTER THE GREATEST GOAL, NEARLY THE MOST LAUGHABLE OWN-GOAL! Scotland are within one goal of qualifying and knocking Holland out! This can't be possible, can it? Jansen goes on a lumber down the right and wins a free-kick, shoulder-charged with unnecessary force by Buchan. Boskamp takes the setpiece, whipping the ball through the six-yard area. Rough flaps. Kennedy connects at the far post, knocking a downward header behind for a corner – but only missing the left-hand post by an inch or so! It's a small wonder that didn't find the net for the craziest own goal you'd ever have seen; he was under no pressure whatsoever! Nothing comes from the resulting corner but dearie me.

72 min: INSTANT DEFLATION FOR SCOTLAND!!! Holland 2–3 Scotland (Rep). Hartford slides a pass forward to Dalglish on the edge of the D. The striker looks to turn to his right but is crowded out. So close to breaking through for that killer blow. But then comes the killer blow Scotland didn't want. Krol jogs towards the halfway line and finds Rep on the right, just inside his own half. Rep flicks back to Krol, who has advanced down the channel. Krol then returns the favour, with Rep underlapping him on the inside, picking up speed. Scotland don't close him down and from 30 yards he unleashes a rising shot towards the top-left corner. Rough does his best to get a hand to it – the ball might even have brushed the tips of his gloved fingers – but that just can't be stopped! Rep turns, a toothy grin spreading over his face more in relief than celebration. In the background, Gemmill looks totally distraught, his once-in-a-lifetime achievement, his career pinnacle, his work of art, rendered worthless junk after 202 seconds.

73 min: Gemmill takes his frustration out on the ball, blootering it down the left to set Donachie into space. His cross to the far post is contested by Jordan but overly so. Peep!

74 min: Hartford, to the right of the centre circle, rakes a superlative diagonal pass towards Dalglish, sending him clear down the inside left. But not for the first time Dalglish's lack of pace lets him down and he hasn't got the power to break into the box. He hesitates, allowing Krol to cover. Dalglish clips the ball inside for Souness, who has time to shoot on the edge of the area but opts to knock a pass back to Rioch. Hartford tries to Gemmill his way through the Dutch back line with a little chip, but the ball's blocked and Dalglish is stranded offside.

75 min: The Scottish fans are still giving it plenty but there's a sense that the jig is up. Souness walked away from that last burst of action with his head hung low. Or as low as the Sounessian pride will allow.

79 min: The Dutch have been well below par tonight but Rep's movement is wonderful. From the corner, he's found to the right of the Scottish D, his back to goal. He plays the ball downfield to Willy van de Kerkhof, who chips forward down the middle, Rep having swung round in a gentle arc to beat the offside trap and break into the box. Such a smooth move and a shame that he ends it by rather absent-mindedly sending a soft header forward into Rough's arms.

80 min: Kennedy is robbed down the left by Willy van de Kerkhof but with his brother René begging for a pass down the middle, he wangs a ludicrously heavy pass straight towards Rough.

85 min: Gemmill slides Forsyth away down the right. Forsyth is upended. Gemmill swings his free-kick on to the penalty spot, where Krol heads confidently clear. Suurbier hits long down the left. The chasing Rep jinks past Kennedy and makes good for the box, but his low pullback for René van de Kerkhof is cut out brilliantly by Donachie. Scotland, despite all reason, haven't given this up by any stretch.

86 min: Jansen boofs a long ball up the left. René van de Kerkhof steals a march on Buchan and enters the area. From a tight angle on the left, he fires straight through the six-yard box, the ball missing the right-hand post by a couple of feet. Rough had shown him far too much of the near post there, so much so that he was diving *back towards goal* in his attempt to stop the shot! What comically dreadful positioning.

89 min: 'It really is sad, when you look at the ability these Scottish

Argentina 3–1 Holland (1978, final)

With eight minutes of the match remaining and the Dutch trailing the hosts by Mario Kempes's first-half goal, Dick Nanninga headed an equalizer. Extra time loomed. Could either team snatch it?

90 min+15 seconds: Ruud Krol, in the centre circle, belts a high free-kick down the inside-left channel. A one-bounce precision pass, it drops to the feet of Rob Rensenbrink, who has stolen a march on the snoozing Jorge Olguín and is romping towards the left-hand corner of the six-yard box. Ubaldo Fillol is off his line to close the angle but can't get there in time, and Rensenbrink sticks out a long left leg. He prods past the keeper but the ball bounces up, off the middle of the left-hand post and out, in super-slow motion. René Houseman hacks the loose ball clear. And 51 seconds later, that's it! Extra time. So unlucky for Holland, who have come as close as you can to winning the World Cup without actually doing so. Argentina have been gifted the mother of all reprieves; you'd fancy them to seal the deal in extra time now.

players have got, that they find themselves in this position at all,' sighs Coleman on the BBC. Well, quite. MacLeod has a lot to answer for, not least the non-selection of Souness in the first two games.

90 min: Donachie finds Hartford down the left. Hartford whips the ball to the far post, where Forsyth, unchallenged and six yards out, heads over when it was far, far easier to score. He picks himself up from the turf, his body heavy with depression. That should have been four. But it wouldn't have mattered because before Jongbloed can take the goal-kick . . .

SCOTLAND ARE OUT OF THE WORLD CUP!!! Holland 2–3 Scotland. Well, that's that. 'Scotland can at least go home and look people in the face,' suggests Coleman. Indeed. Some dignity has indeed been reclaimed: Scotland were brilliant tonight, and yet had no luck whatsoever. But this Scottish campaign will go down in history as one of the most needlessly farcical failures in all World Cup history. Sent homeward, tae think again. *Again*.

Brazil v Italy

Second round, Group C, Estadi de Sarrià, Barcelona, Spain, Monday, 5 July 1982

If today's match were on a movie poster, the tagline might be: *Brazil v Italy. Attack v defence. Joga bonito v catenaccio. Good v evil.* Brazil are, depending on your preferred metaphor, playing football from the future or playing a different sport altogether. Of the 12 goals they have scored in four consecutive wins, nine have been genuine belters. They have soundtracked España 82 with the unfettered joy of samba beats. (Literally, as their fans give it *plenty*.) The world has fallen hopelessly in love, our hearts beating to every jazzy syncopation.

Italy have engaged a different sense: they have stunk the place out with a clunking, ersatz form of *catenaccio*. They were lucky to get through the group stage without winning a single game. And although they were better in beating Argentina 2–1 six days ago, only their third win in the last 15 games, that victory was down to well-rationed counter-attacks and Claudio Gentile's man-marking job on Diego Maradona – not so much a case of persistent fouling as occasional non-fouling. There has been no great attacking fluency. And yet, for all that, in two hours' time, Italy could be in the semi-finals ahead of Brazil.

The scenario is simple: Italy need a win, Brazil need a draw. It is a nicely contrary state of affairs – the attacking side need the draw, the defensive side the win – but we would still expect both sides to assume their usual archetypes. Most people feel that Italy have two chances today – and slim is unavailable through suspension. If they do pull it off, childhood discoveries about Santa and the Tooth Fairy will have nothing on the distress that will envelop the watching world of football.

Team news: If it's perfect, don't fix it: Brazil are unchanged from the team that ransacked Argentina 3–1 on this ground three days ago. This is the fourth consecutive match in which they have named the same XI. Their team includes Roma's Falcão, the only man on either side who plays his football overseas. Falcão wasn't guaranteed a place a month ago but he has probably been the player of the tournament. There was talk that the veteran Franco Causio might replace Paolo Rossi, whose last goal for Italy came over three years ago, but they are also unchanged.

Kick-off: 5.15 p.m. local time, 4.15 p.m. for those in England who want to escape work early.

Referee: Abraham Klein (Israel).

Italy: Dino Zoff; Gabriele Oriali, Fulvio Collovati, Gaetano Scirea, Claudio Gentile, Antonio Cabrini; Bruno Conti, Marco Tardelli, Giancarlo Antognoni; Paolo Rossi, Francesco Graziani.

Brazil: Waldir Peres; Leandro, Oscar, Luizinho, Junior; Falcão, Cerezo, Socrates, Eder; Zico; Serginho.

• • • •MAGIC MINUTES • • • • • • • •MAGIC MINUTES • • • • •

BRAZIL 4 – 1 SCOTLAND
(1982, group stage)

The hot favourites for the 1982 tournament annihilated Jock Stein's side in sweltering Seville, but not before they were made to momentarily think again. Dundee United right-back David Narey opened the scoring with one of the goals of the tournament. The BBC's Jimmy Hill would later dismiss the strike as a 'toe poke'; Scotland fans would respond by dismissing Hill in song as 'a poof'.

18 min: GOAL!!! Brazil 0–1 Scotland (Narey 18). Graeme Souness, standing just ahead of the centre circle, sweeps a diagonal pass to John Wark, on the right-hand edge of the area. Wark heads back into the centre, in the path of Narey, bustling in from the right. His first touch, with his left, is a wee bit heavy and draws three yellow shirts towards him on the edge of the D. But before any Brazilian can reach the ball, Narey sticks out a long leg and sends it whistling into the top-right corner, Waldir Peres left with no chance of reaching it. Narey, arms aloft, bounces up and down gently, Tigger hooked on downers, with a look of sheer disbelief plastered across his coupon. Souness bombs in to give him a suffocating bear hug and take the celebrations up a notch.

1 min: Brazil kick off from left to right to the distinctive peep of caxirolas that have been such a part of this tournament. The pitch markings look like they have been done by Jackson Pollock's marginally more methodical brother. There are straight lines along one part, angled lines across another and little white circles dotted all around the pitch. It's a seriously hot afternoon in Barcelona, the kind we are contractually obliged to describe as either sultry or steamy.

2 min: The good news for Zico is that he was passed fit to play today. The bad news for Zico is that he's going to be marked by Gentile. For an attacker that invariably means pain in the post, and usually by special delivery.

3 min: It's a very open start, at both ends. Whisper it but Italy may have come to play.

4 min: What a chance for Paolo Rossi! A patient move from Italy ended with Cabrini lofting a fine pass down the left for Tardelli, who fizzed a superb cut-back to Rossi, in space 12 yards out. He made a dreadful mess of it. He completely missed his kick, beaten by the pace of the cut-back. Then at the second attempt he fell on his backside after running into Cerezo. That's Rossi's tournament in miniature. We know he is a class act but he is having a miserable time. His last goal for Italy was 1,118 days ago, and he looks terribly rusty after his two-year ban for his involvement in the Totonero betting scandal.

5 min: GOAL! Italy 1–0 Brazil (Rossi). Can we edit that previous entry, please?! Precisely 60 seconds after that miss, Rossi has given Italy the lead! It was a beautifully worked goal. Conti circled lazily away from Cerezo near the halfway line, made 15 yards, swerved away from Eder's token challenge and then swept a regal outside-of-the-foot crossfield pass to the onrushing Cabrini on the left. He coaxed an excellent cross to the far post where Rossi, given far too much space between Luizinho and Junior, planted a decisive header back across Waldir Peres from six yards. Could we have a major shock on here? As things stand, Italy will be playing Poland in the semi-final!

6 min: The good news for Italy is that they are a goal up. The bad news for Italy is that they are a goal up. The last team to stir the beast by taking the lead against Brazil, dear old Scotland, were dismantled 4–1. The kick-off has been delayed because an Italian fan has lobbed a firecracker into the Brazilian penalty area in celebration. The delay is over a minute until, with the camera lingering on the firecracker, a shoe appears from out of shot to hoof it straight back towards the Italian fans. You can have that back!

8 min: Zico is fouled by Gentile, not for the last time we'll be bound, 30 yards from goal and a little to the left. This is the first chance for Eder, whose storming free-kick against Argentina hit the bar and led to Zico's opening goal. This time his run-up starts somewhere near La Rambla and he hammers it straight into the wall.

9 min: The left-back Junior is contemptuously dispossessed by Conti, who launches a counter-attack with a long pass to Rossi. Leandro gets there first but then haplessly miscontrols it straight into the path of the striker. Rossi backheels to Graziani, who thrashes his 20-yard shot over the bar. That was pathetic defending from Brazil. The camera cuts to the Italy coach Enzo Bearzot. With his rimless sunglasses, stern visage and bright lilac shirt, he looks like the greatest nemesis Theo Kojak never had.

11 min: WHAT A MISS! The knives have been out for Serginho for most of this tournament and a few more rusty, serrated ones will be unsheathed after this appalling miss. Socrates started the move with a crisp ball into Serginho, 35 yards out. He was dispossessed by a combination of Cabrini and Collovati, but then, in a whirl of collisions and cartoon clouds, Scirea's attempted clearance hit Serginho and went to Zico. He played a simple pass to put Serginho through on goal. He was 14 yards out, with just Zoff to beat – and he lummoxed a hopeless shot well wide of the far post. That was desperate. He attacked the ball with all the calmness of control of a teenage boy attacking his first bra, and his hamfooted shot bobbled past the post. 'The sort of miss that a Sunday morning player shouldn't have been guilty of,' says the BBC commentator John Motson.

12 min: GOAL! Italy 1–1 Brazil (Socrates). This is a masterpiece of elegant simplicity. It involved just two players, Socrates and Zico. Socrates, just past the halfway line, slipped a straight pass into Zico and kept running. Zico, 25 yards out, ignored

Gentile's burgeoning plan to defile him with a majestic Cruyff turn and then stabbed a sudden, disguised pass for Socrates down the side of the sweeper Scirea. Socrates ran off Tardelli, past the slightly flat-footed Scirea, lit up a Ducados and then, from a tight angle, simply passed the ball in at the near post. Zoff will probably feel he should have done better but Socrates may have given him the eyes.

13 min: That's a fitting addition to Brazil's absurd portfolio of goals in this tournament. If scoring a goal is comparable with sex, as so many players say, then Brazil's work at this World Cup is the greatest porn you will ever see. Who needs *Debbie Does Dallas* when you have *Socrates Does the Sarrià Stadium*?

14 min: Gentile is out of the semi-final! He's been booked for taking a shortcut through the back of Zico. Yellow cards are usually a bit of an event but you can't really call this a surprise, can you? Gentile got away with maimage against Maradona the other day but Abraham Klein has shown him a yellow card for his first bad tackle. The happiest man in the world might be Poland's Zbigniew Boniek: if Italy get through to the semi-final, Gentile will not be there to mark him.

16 min: There's a cracking pace to this game. 'I've never known anything like it,' says BBC summarizer Bobby Charlton. 'The most fantastic start to any World Cup match I've ever seen.'

17 min: Falcão, inside his own half, plays the ball into Zico and keeps running. Zico holds off Gentile, turns to face him and plays a wonderful angled pass back towards Falcão. With a better first touch he would have been through on Zoff, but the ball bobbled awkwardly and he was pushed wide. Brazil have been so good at these long-range one-twos in the tournament, usually through Zico: Junior's goal against Argentina, Socrates's today and now Falcão's chance. Forty seconds later, Cerezo's teasing cross is headed further across the area by Falcão. Serginho is just shaping to blooter a volley into orbit when Collovati stretches to head clear eight yards from his own goal.

19 min: Brazil are playing beautifully now, with the wonderful midfield pair of Cerezo and Falcão galloping forward at every opportunity. This looks a bit ominous for Italy, who are on the back foot for the first time.

24 min: A bit of respite for Italy, with Tardelli fouled 25 yards from goal. Antognoni's deflected free-kick loops gently into the arms of Waldir Peres.

25 min: GOAL! Italy 2–1 Brazil (Rossi). What an appalling mistake from Cerezo! Italy are back in front! It all came from that Antognoni free-kick. Waldir Peres faffed around a bit and then threw the ball out to the right-back Leandro. He laid it square to Cerezo, 30 yards from the Brazil goal, and he knocked another lazy square pass towards a pocket of Brazilian players. The problem was that they were loitering with all the urgency of civil servants at a watercooler and had no idea the ball was coming. It also bisected them perfectly. Luizinho was trotting upfield, Falcão wasn't expecting the pass and it was too late by the time Junior realized what day it was. He dived in; Rossi beat him to the ball, ran to the edge of the area and thrashed a shot straight through Waldir Peres. I know this Brazil team want to be the spiritual heirs to 1970, but there's no reason to play homage to Clodoaldo's cock-up against Italy. That didn't cost Brazil; this one might.

27 min: The fact and manner of the goal don't seem to have affected Brazil one iota. They have picked up exactly where they left off, playing the same beach football we have seen in the last two weeks. Italy look dangerous, though, in a way they previously haven't in this tournament.

32 min: Collovati goes down in the area. There's no suggestions of maimage most foul – I don't think there was anyone near him – but he's struggling and the referee has called for a stretcher.

33 min: Eder spanks the free-kick straight into the wall. A few seconds later, with Italy temporarily down to ten, Socrates almost grabs his second goal! Cerezo curled over a good cross from a deep, narrow position on the right, which cleared a big posse of bodies around the penalty spot. Socrates, arriving late in space at the far post, headed spectacularly but straight at Zoff from 12 yards.

34 min: Collovati is replaced by Giuseppe Bergomi, who is making his second appearance for Italy. He's only 18, but has one of the thickest moustaches you'll ever see.

36 min: Rossi is flattened as he goes for a high ball with Luizinho.

The referee Klein, like a father telling his weeping son it's only a scratch, wanders over, pats him on the side and then lifts a wincing Rossi to his feet.

40 min: A languid relay run down the centre of the field, involving Leandro, Cerezo, Junior (whose nominal position of left-back really is little more than a basis for negotiation) and Serginho, ends with Falcão's first-time shot from the edge of the area being deflected wide. The resulting corner from Eder flashes right across the face of goal with Zoff flapping.

42 min: Zico becomes the first player to be undressed in a World Cup match. You don't need me to tell you that Gentile is the one doing the disrobing. He's ripped Zico's shirt in half! Socrates's through ball somehow found its way through to Zico, who managed to escape Gentile's wandering hands just long enough to strike an off-balance shot that was beaten away by Zoff. By then he had been flagged offside, so the goal wouldn't have counted. Zico shows his shirt, which has a huge hole around the right side of the stomach, to referee Klein, but it's irrelevant as he had been flagged offside. And Klein doesn't have his sewing kit with him today, so he can't help.

43 min: There have been some mighty performances in this half: Rossi, Zico, Falcão, Scirea, Antognoni, Cerezo (that shocking mistake aside) and Klein have been particularly good.

44 min: Oriali introduces Socrates to an advertising hoarding – Caloi bicycles, since you ask – with a gentle shove. Socrates signals an elbow at Klein with mild irritation. The referee gives him oogatz.

45 min: Graziani combines with Antognoni on the left, gets past a woolly challenge from Cerezo and is denied a simple chance by a vital challenge by Oscar. For all the brilliance of Brazil's attacking play, Italy have arguably had the greater chances.

45+2 min: A Junior corner from the left causes havoc and almost leads to an equalizer. The ball deflects to Zico on the byline, in front of the near post. He improvises and lobs over Zoff towards the far post, where it hits the under-pressure Serginho on the back before being hoofed to safety by Oriali. That's an unbecomingly agricultural end to a stunning half of football.

Spain 0–1 Northern Ireland (1982, group stage)

The Irish needed a win or high-scoring draw to make the second round. As they had only scored twice in their last six games, and were facing the hosts, the odds were against them. But Spain were under pressure themselves: they weren't playing well and a two-goal defeat would see them knocked out. The second half started with a bang.

And we're off again! The Irish have come out in determined mood, and spend 60 seconds or so in the Spanish half, getting nowhere in particular. The hosts attempt to break forward themselves, López Ufarte feeding the ball down the inside left for Rafael Gordillo, who tries to flick the ball out left for Enrique Saura. But the Watford striker Gerry Armstrong intercepts and . . .

GOAL!!! Spain 0–1 Northern Ireland (Armstrong 47) . . . barrels off down the Irish inside right. Drifting inside, past challenges from Enrique Saura (who tries to clip his heels) and Miguel Angel Alonso, coming in from the left, he slides the ball out to Billy Hamilton on the right. Hamilton drops a shoulder to get past Miguel Tendillo and fires in a low cross. Luis Arconada slides out to gather but only succeeds in pushing the ball out with a flap of his right arm to Gerry Armstrong, who has been keeping up and skelps a low shot home. He turns immediately with arms raised in triumph.

HALF TIME: Brazil 1–2 Italy. Nobody predicted this scoreline. But then nobody thought Italy were going to come out and play gorgeous football.

46 min: Italy kick off from left to right. It remains unthinkable but Brazil are only 45 minutes away from going out of the World Cup.

47 min: Gorgeous football again from Brazil. Falcão, just inside the Italy half to the right of centre, feeds an angled pass to Junior and sets off. Serginho and Zico drag the defenders the other way, allowing Junior to play a return pass into the area for Falcão, who bursts past Tardelli and then sidefoots just wide of the far post from a tightish angle. Zoff may have had it covered but most credit goes to Scirea, the only man who didn't buy Serginho's and Zico's off-the-ball runs and got across just in time to ensure Falcão had to take the shot under considerable pressure. That was outstanding defending from a brilliant sweeper.

48 min: We talk a lot about what Brazil do with the ball, not unreasonably, but their movement off the ball in this game has been outrageously good, particularly the late runs from midfield of Socrates and Falcão.

50 min: Brazil have eight men forward in attack – eight! – but Junior wafts a poor pass out of play.

51 min: Oriali wins the ball decisively from Eder, who has hardly had a kick apart from the free ones, and launches another Italian counter-attack. Conti plays the ball to Antognoni, runs on to a beautifully chipped return pass, comes inside Oscar on the left corner of the box but then stabs a weary shot wide of the far post. In his defence he had run 60 yards. In Brazil's defence . . . there is no defence. Their play at the back has been awful.

52 min: This game feels more clearly defined than ever: Brazil attack, Italy counter-attack. But actually it's Italy who are looking more menacing just now. Rossi falls over in the box after a shoulder charge from Luizinho and referee Klein waves him to his feet. That looks the right decision although it was a risky challenge from Luizinho.

55 min: Zoff makes a brilliant save from Cerezo! This chance came out of nothing. Cerezo set off an imperious, leggy run from midfield, into the space vacated by Serginho's clever off-the-ball run, while Zico protected the ball near the centre circle. Then Zico suddenly played a wonderful long through-pass that took four players out of the game. Zoff, sensing the danger, dragged his 40-year-old limbs kicking and screaming to the edge of his area at pace and blocked Cerezo's first-time shot. Then he delivered an impassioned bollocking to his defence.

58 min: BRAZIL SHOULD BE OUT OF THE WORLD CUP!
Both sides could have scored in the space of a minute! First
Brazil. Junior's chipped ball into the area was not far enough in
front of Cerezo for him to go for goal, so he cushioned a header
towards Serginho. He challenged for the ball with Bergomi and,
as it broke loose, improvised a backheel that was saved by the
legs of Zoff. Within 20 seconds, Rossi missed an unbelievable
chance to complete his hat-trick. Graziani swerved away from
Falcão down the left and, with defenders drawn towards him,
crossed low towards Rossi at the far post. Rossi had an entire
postal district to himself, eight yards from goal. Peres narrowed
the angle and somehow Rossi sliced wide.

59 min: A better free-kick from Eder is well held by Zoff. It was
straight at him but dipped nastily at pace just in front of him,
a difficult ball to hold, especially as Serginho and Zico were
waiting for a rebound.

63 min: Brazil have so many men forward, it's ridiculous. Junior
– the effing left-back – is the main midfield conductor at the
moment. Cerezo, on the edge of a packed area, plays the ball
back to Junior and runs in behind Tardelli for the return. Junior
lifts a golf shot over the top, but it's a fraction too firm and
Cerezo, sticking out his telescopic right leg, can only volley into
the side-netting at the near post from a tight angle. Zoff had
it covered.

67 min: Paolo Isidoro is about to come on for Brazil, presumably
for Serginho, who has been peripheral.

68 min: GOAL! Brazil 2–2 Italy (Falcão). The best player in
the 1982 World Cup may well have put Brazil into the semi-final
with an outstanding goal. Junior swaggered infield from the left,
ignoring a challenge from Conti before stabbing an outside-
of-the-foot pass to Falcão, just outside the box to the right
of centre. With Cerezo's long swerving run on the outside
distracting Tardelli, Scirea and Cabrini, Falcão had time to run
into the D and spank a left-footed shot into the net. Zoff dived to
his right but he was beaten for pace as much as anything. Falcão
bounces towards the bench, into the arms of his team-mates.
That was sheer delightful football.

70 min: Isidoro is on for Serginho as expected. It looks like

Socrates is going to play up front. Now the ball is round again, as one Brazilian journalist put it when Serginho was taken off in an earlier game. Although you can safely bet he wouldn't say it to Serginho's face.

71 min: Italy have been ragged since the goal. Brazil could put them away with another quick one here. The hitherto faultless teenager Bergomi loses the ball to Eder and for a second Brazil have two-on-one. But Eder tries to go alone and is superbly tackled by the last man Scirea, who then blocks Falcão's follow-up shot.

72 min: Zico teases Gentile on the right corner of the box, the mouse toying with the cat, before going past him and then Scirea. Bergomi comes across to make a vital clearance.

74 min: Junior finds the marauding Cerezo down the left and his clipped cross is claimed at the second attempt by Zoff, with Isidoro about to pounce.

75 min: GOAL!!! Brazil 2–3 Italy (Rossi). This is unbelievable! Italy are in front again and Rossi has a hat-trick! They had been on their knees since Brazil's equalizer and then they scored out of nothing. Antognoni's deep cross was headed behind a little needlessly by Cerezo. Conti drove it towards the edge of the area, where Bergomi, Zico and Socrates all went up for the header. It came off Socrates's head and dropped to Tardelli, who mis-hit a volley through a crowd of players that was turned in from six yards by Rossi. Junior appealed for offside – but he was the man playing Rossi onside because he couldn't be bothered to come off the near post. It's the first World Cup hat-trick by an Italian since 1934, when Angelo Schiavio put three past the USA in a 7–1 win. Before this game Rossi had been hopeless! If Italy win, this astonishing turnaround will go straight into folklore.

76 min: Tardelli injured himself in the course of the greatest miskick of his life and has been replaced by Giampiero Marini.

79 min: Oriali is booked for inflicting pain on Eder. He has won that battle emphatically today. Eder strikes the resulting free-kick just wide from 35 yards, although Zoff certainly had it covered.

80 min: SOCRATES HAS A GOAL DISALLOWED FOR OFFSIDE! He ran on to Leandro's through-pass and went round Zoff – who admittedly had stopped playing after hearing the whistle – to score. There are no real complaints from Brazil.

83 min: Scirea – the bloody sweeper – goes on a ridiculous surge upfield for Italy and almost finds Rossi. Where's he going?! There's no *catenaccio* here, no bolting of the door; everyone is caught up in the mood of an astonishing match.

84 min: Brazil are on the desperate side of urgent now. The samba beats are going at 78 rpm rather than the usual 45. Eder plays a through ball towards Junior. Zoff charges outside his box to get there first and then completely shanks his clearance. Luckily for him it goes to Oriali. Moments later Isidoro's cross flicks off the head of Gentile towards Socrates, whose goalbound half-volley from six yards is magnificently blocked by Conti!

86 min: A good couple of minutes for Italy, with Brazil struggling to get the ball. The tension is ridiculous.

88 min: ITALY HAVE A GOAL WRONGLY DISALLOWED! That should have been it. The tireless Antognoni started and finished the move. He launched another counter-attack before putting Rossi free on the right wing. Rossi ran into the area and slipped it back to Oriali, who played an angled pass across the area for Antognoni to ram home from six yards. The flag went straight up, but replays show he was being played onside, probably by Junior and certainly by Oscar. That's a terrible decision and one we'll never hear the end of if Brazil equalize in the last couple of minutes.

89 min: WHAT A SAVE BY ZOFF! They so nearly did equalize and put Italy out of the tournament! Eder was fouled on the left wing and curled the ball beyond the far post, where Oscar came round the back of a crowd of players to thump a header towards goal. Zoff plunged to his left to stop the ball and then, as it slipped from his grasp, stopped it right on the line with Brazil appealing it had gone over. It hadn't and that might just be it for Brazil.

90 min: Brazil are now playing a freestyle 1–4–5 formation. They win another corner. This is like nothing you will ever see. Falcão, in an inside-right position, plays it into Leandro, who lofts a return pass into the area. Falcão's flying volley is blocked by Graziani at the expense of a corner.

France 4–1 Kuwait (1982, group stage)
Kuwait finished bottom of their group at España 82, although they left a mark on the tournament: in their final game, they threatened to leave the field in protest.

81 min: GOAL! France 4–1 Kuwait (Giresse). OR IS IT? That's it! Platini stabs a cute pass through to Giresse, who runs into the area and smashes the ball past Ahmed Al-Tarabulsi. 'No doubt about that one,' says Martin Tyler in reference to earlier disallowed goals, but it seems there is doubt because Kuwait are very unhappy. A number of the players are down by the touchline amid a gathering scrum of photographers, officials and police. Giresse certainly was not offside although the replay shows that a number of Kuwait defenders stopped, thinking they heard a whistle. They did but not the one that matters: you're supposed to play to the *referee's* whistle, lads. This is ridiculous. In the stands, Sheikh Fahad Al-Sabah, president of the Kuwait FA, is waving the players off – and now he's coming down towards the pitch himself! Under those robes lies a serious brass neck. There are four points here: they are 3–1 down and going out anyway, Giresse was about four yards onside, they wouldn't have stopped Giresse even if they had continued playing and, well, there's a small point about independent arbiters officiating a football match. Sheikh Fahad talks to some of the players and then swaggers off imperiously, clapping rhythmically like he's in a pop video. Now he's pointing at some TV flunky. This is bedlam. The referee has gone to talk to his linesman, the two sets of players are having a full, frank and occasionally physical exchange of views. What's going on now? The goal has been disallowed and play is going to restart with a drop ball on the edge of the area! Just to clarify: France have had a goal disallowed by the president of Kuwait FA. It won't affect the result but that's not the point: that is craven, pathetic and disgraceful.

90+1 min: Eder has to move one of the advertising hoardings to make room to take the corner. He swings it right under the crossbar where Zoff, under considerable pressure, punches clear decisively.

FULL TIME: Brazil 2–3 Italy. That's it! Italy have put this astonishing Brazil side out of the World Cup! Their players are almost too exhausted to celebrate. They have given so much. Average at best in this tournament before this game, they've elevated themselves into the pantheon with a display that was staunch yet sassy. Brazil, meanwhile . . . oh Brazil! The most popular team on the planet won't be lifting the trophy but they do leave Spain with one title: the best team never to win the World Cup. A few older folk in Hungary, Holland and, yes, Brazil will be happy to have that load lifted. And while it won't make them feel any better at the moment, this brilliant Brazil side can take succour from one thing: they've just played their part in the greatest World Cup game ever.

West Germany v France

Semi-final, Estadio Ramón Sánchez Pizjuán, Seville, Spain, Thursday, 8 July 1982

It's fair to say that neither of these teams started this tournament particularly well. France found themselves a goal down within 27 seconds of kick-off in their first match, against an England team that notoriously struggles for goals. Ooh la la. From that position, the only way was up.

And so it was proven. France put away Kuwait and drew with Czechoslovakia in a game mainly notable for Antonin Panenka's last act in international football (a penalty, naturally) and Manuel Amoros clearing off the line in the last minute to keep France in the competition. In the second group stage, they lucked out, drawn with Austria and Northern Ireland, and didn't look the gift horse *dans la bouche*, beating both teams by causing death by intricate passing (although it'd have been interesting to see what would have happened if Martin O'Neill's unfairly disallowed early goal for the Irish had stood). Still, Michel Hidalgo called that performance against Northern Ireland the best of his six-year reign and here France are, in the semis, a team top-heavy with elegant talent – that midfield of Platini, Tigana, Giresse – doing just about enough to paper over the cracks of a brittle defence.

West Germany have somehow managed to be even worse, making a proper show of themselves in the group stage. First they boasted how they would beat Algeria 'without problems', with one player saying they would dedicate 'the seventh goal to our wives and the eighth to our dogs'. They went down 2–1, the first time a European side had lost to an African one at a World Cup. They breezed past a dismal Chile, then conspired with Austria to fashion a soporific 1–0 win in the final game, a result that saw both teams through at the expense of the Algerians. Boo, hiss.

The Germans needed a few friends after that, so it's questionable whether knocking out hosts Spain in the second group stage did them any favours. Still, here they are, in the semis, a team with just about enough brio and verve – Rummenigge, Fischer, Breitner, Littbarski – to make up for their collective inherent cynicism. They could do with going on a charm offensive tonight at the Pizjuán in Seville.

Who will face a resurgent Italy, who beat Poland this afternoon in the first semi-final, at the Santiago Bernabéu on Sunday? We'll know after 90 minutes. Or 120 minutes. Or approximately 130 minutes if this becomes the first match in World Cup history to go to penalties.

Kick-off: 9 p.m. in Seville, subtract an hour if you're in England.

Referee: Charles Corver (Holland).

West Germany, several of whose players have been suffering with stomach complaints this week, and whose captain Karl-Heinz Rummenigge is only fit for the bench because of the thigh injury that's been troubling him all tournament: Harald Schumacher, Manfred Kaltz, Hans-Peter Briegel, Bernd Förster, Karlheinz Förster, Uli Stielike, Felix Magath, Paul Breitner, Klaus Fischer, Wolfgang Dremmler, Pierre Littbarski.

France plump for Six instead of Soler, but otherwise this is the lot who stroked four goals past Northern Ireland: Jean-Luc Ettori, Manuel Amoros, Maxime Bossis, Gérard Janvion, Marius Trésor, Alain Giresse, Bernard Genghini, Didier Six, Jean Tigana, Michel Platini, Dominique Rocheteau.

The teams are out! There's a long delay before kick-off, with the West Germans idly kicking a ball between themselves. Nobody on either side looks remotely stressed. It's a World Cup semi-final!

1 min: The game finally gets under way with West Germany kicking off from left to right. For those listening on radio, they are in white, France are in blue.

2 min: A breakneck start from Germany. Littbarski, one of the unexpected stars of the tournament, wriggles dangerously into the box before being crowded out. France finally get a kick when Kaltz falls on his arse. Platini is caught a touch late by Dremmler and hops around theatrically in pain like a demented kangaroo.

4 min: After a superb surge by Briegel, the former decathlete, Dremmler's shot is deflected wide from 25 yards. West Germany have come out of the blocks like Alan Wells here.

8 min: A delectable example of the telepathy between – and economical brilliance of – Platini and Giresse. Platini draws two

Germans towards him and pokes a pass forward to Giresse, in space 25 yards out. He turns, draws two more defenders towards him and teases a short through-pass towards Platini, who had kept running. He would have been clear on goal but for a superb stretching block from Stielike on the edge of the area.

13 min: France are coming into the game now. A dangerous cross from Amoros is taken away from the flying Rocheteau by the head of Bernd Förster. That leads to a corner on the right, from which Giresse plays a one-two with Rocheteau before clipping in an insouciant cross with the outside of his right foot. Bossis, unmarked on the edge of the six-yard box, just couldn't leap high enough and Schumacher climbed over him to punch clear.

14 min: A truly absurd hack at Fischer from Janvion gives Germany a free-kick 35 yards out. That leads to another free-kick 20 yards out when Platini brings down Briegel. This is in a good position, just a few yards left of centre . . .

15 min: LITTBARSKI HITS THE BAR! With France still organizing their wall, Breitner touched the ball off to Littbarski, who clattered the bar with a fierce shot. Ettori was beaten and the ball hit the bar with such force that it rebounded well outside the box.

16 min: A long, angled free-kick is drilled towards Rocheteau, just inside the area and facing away from goal. It's at face-height, so he improvises delightfully: he leaps forward, twists his body in mid-air and softens his chest to steer a flying chest pass, straight into the path of Genghini, who lashes the bouncing ball over the bar from the right of the box. Schumacher administers a finger-pointing bollocking to one, possibly more, maybe all of his team-mates.

18 min: GOAL! West Germany 1–0 France (Littbarski). West Germany deservedly strike first. Breitner opened the game up with an impatient run through France's midfield before flicking a penetrative through-pass to Fischer, who had pulled cleverly away in between Trésor and Amoros. He overran the ball a fraction with an accidental second touch, allowing Ettori to come out and plunge at his feet – but the loose ball came to Littbarski, who spanked a low shot through a posse of bodies and into the net from the edge of the area.

22 min: That's eight goals in 13 internationals for Littbarski, who only made his West Germany debut last October. It was beautifully made by Breitner, who was playing at left-back in West Germany's 1974 World Cup winners but now patrols midfield like an old don. Platini heads well wide from 18 yards.

26 min: Kaltz nibbles away at Genghini, who responds with a sly kick to the back of the leg while Kaltz is being spoken to by the referee. The two men are about to start a Hegelian dialectic when the referee gets in between them.

27 min: PENALTY TO FRANCE! The free-kick that was given for Kaltz's foul on Genghini leads straight to a penalty. Giresse flicked the dead ball lazily into the area with the outside of his right foot towards Platini, who did superbly to win the header above Magath and Dremmler. He nutted it back across the face of goal, where Rocheteau went down under challenge from Bernd Förster. Förster did hook the ball clear eventually but the referee signalled that he was holding Rocheteau; replays suggest he was probably right. Stielike, unsurprisingly, does not entirely concur with this viewpoint.

28 min: GOAL! West Germany 1–1 France (Platini 28). Platini tucks the penalty away with authority, sending Schumacher the wrong way and sidefooting it low to the left. He celebrates with an instinctive, childlike leap of joy, both hands raised to the sky, before he is mobbed by teammates.

31 min: France have a bit of a strut now. Six's drilled left-wing corner goes all the way across to Bossis on the edge of the area. He kills the ball like a playmaker, never mind a defender, and arrogantly lays it back to Genghini, whose sizzling half-volley tattoos a West German thigh and deflects wide for a corner.

35 min: Amoros's low cross is flicked behind his standing leg by Six and Karlheinz Förster cushions a short-range backpass to Schumacher. As Schumacher takes the ball he rolls forward and rams into the thigh of Platini, who winces and holds the back of his right leg as he hobbles away. He should be fine.

36 min: Of all the people to get the first yellow card in this match, it's Alain Giresse, for kicking the ball away after he was penalized for handball.

39 min: Tigana's dangerous, bouncing cross is chested

nonchalantly back to Schumacher by Briegel, six yards from his own goal. Six slides in from behind on Briegel and then Schumacher's forward momentum takes him on top of Six, whereupon he pins him like a wrestler and drags his elbow a little to clarify precisely what he thinks of Six's challenge. Briegel stands over Six, looking at him almost quizzically, as a cat might look at a mouse that hasn't quite died, and then seems to give Six a little rabbit kick. As Six gets to his feet, Schumacher shoves him away angrily. Six puts his hands out in apology – he didn't actually do anything wrong – but Schumacher waves his hand in disgust. Platini motions for Schumacher to simmer down because the keeper really needs to. He's off on one.

40 min: This is getting a bit nasty now. Kaltz, marauding down the right, is clattered by Genghini, a challenge of endearing incompetence. Genghini is booked.

41 min: After five minutes of feistiness, France remind us that this is a football match with a stunning counter-attack that almost leads to one of the goals of the tournament. It starts with Giresse and Tigana riskily playing their way out of trouble inside the French area. Tigana pushes it forward to Six, who runs 30 yards and waves the ball to Rocheteau on the left with the outside of the foot. Rocheteau runs at Bernd Förster, teasing him with a series of touches and hip movements until he gets into the area on the left. Then, as Kaltz comes across, he stabs it back outside the box to Platini. He storms on to the ball, 20 yards out, and cuts across a beautiful shot that swerves and whistles just wide of the far post. That took 15 seconds from Giresse's touch in his own area to Platini's shot curving wide. You could have set that move to Beethoven. Actually you could have set it to 'Happy Talk' and it would still have stood as a work of art, it was so beautiful.

43 min: Breitner's curving pass over the top finds Briegel, almost by the right touchline in the area. He should go with his right foot, but instead he whirls his left like an arthritic ninja to send the ball towards the near post. Ettori, who had his angles right, pats it behind.

45+1 min: Karlheinz Förster wins the ball off Rocheteau down the right and sends over a superb curling cross towards the six-yard line. Litbarski gets between Janvion and Amoros but then plants his header straight at Ettori, who saves at the second attempt. Littbarski should have scored, although it might not have counted: the whistle went for something, presumably offside.

HALF TIME: West Germany 1–1 France. A brilliant game of football. More please!

46 min: Bernd Förster starts the second half with a ridiculous flying tackle on Rocheteau, for which he is booked. Rocheteau chested the ball up in the air and Förster tried to come round the side of him with a flying kung-fu kick. He didn't connect with that but his momentum knocked Rocheteau over.

49 min: It's been a scrappy start to the half, with a few fouls and a bit of residual tetchiness from the end of the first half.

50 min: The first substitution: Patrick Battiston comes on to replace the injured Genghini.

53 min: What a chance for France! Kaltz, just inside his own half, plays a lamentable square pass reminiscent of Toninho Cerezo's against Italy on Monday. Briegel gawps at it, expecting somebody else to go and get it. Tigana nips in and, with Germany's defence all over the place, slides a through-pass for Platini – but he is flagged offside. That was effectively a two-against-one break. Tigana waves his hand in disgust at Platini and mouths his frustration for the purposes of additional clarification. Platini fixes Tigana with a comically stern look in response. If Platini had waited a second longer he would have been through on goal. That said, he may well have timed it perfectly – another look suggests the linesman might have got it wrong, although it was a tough call.

54 min: ROCHETEAU HAS A GOAL DISALLOWED! The marvellous Giresse drilled a long, angled pass from the left. Rocheteau jumped for it with Bernd Förster, the last man, and when the ball broke loose he dragged it past Schumacher and into the net. But by then he had been penalized for a foul on Förster. He may have jumped into him, although it doesn't look particularly bad. We haven't seen a replay so it's hard to tell. France's lack of complaints probably tells a story.

55 min: Platini goes on a bewitching slalom from the left, past Kaltz and Stielike, but having made a decent shooting chance he wafts high over the bar from inside the D.

56 min: The French fans behind the goal take a good 30 seconds to give the ball back after that Platini shot. When they do, Schumacher runs towards them and fakes to fling the ball back into the crowd before putting the ball down to take the goal-kick.

57 min: A DISGRACEFUL ASSAULT FROM SCHUMACHER! Battiston has missed a great chance to put France ahead and, in the process, been flattened by Schumacher. Bossis, just inside the West German half on the right, won the ball and played it short to Platini. He turned, spotted Battiston haring through on goal and sprayed a nonchalant pass into the considerable space between Kaltz and Stielike. Schumacher, sensing the danger, charged out from goal. As the ball bounced up on the edge of the box Battiston took the shot first time and drifted it just wide of the far post – but as he did so he was flattened as Schumacher leapt into him. That has to be a penalty to France! It looks even worse on the replay: as Schumacher twisted his body in mid-air, his elbow smashed into the face of Battiston, who flopped sickeningly to the turf and bounced over on to his back. It was particularly horrible because both men were running at full pelt. It was also appallingly late: the ball had travelled seven or eight yards before Schumacher hit Battiston. Battiston is lying on his back and the level of French concern suggests he may be unconscious. Once he is tended to, surely Schumacher will be sent off. Never mind a red card; he could get a stretch in the clink for that.

58 min: Schumacher has left the scene of the crime and is waiting to take a goal-kick, bold as brass, chewing gum impatiently as if everyone else is holding him up, rather than attending to a man he assaulted. That's at best clueless and at worst appallingly callous. Also, surely it can't be a goal-kick? But then the referee doesn't seem to have given a penalty. There's so much going on that it's hard to tell. The referee and Platini wave for a stretcher, with a number of other players surrounding the prostrate Battiston. There is a suggestion he may have lost some teeth. Platini waves his hands to the referee as if to say: What kind of business is this? Astonishingly, the referee hasn't given a penalty. There is a chance that, because the tackle was *so* late, the referee followed the ball as it drifted past the post and missed

Schumacher's assault. It's the only explanation. Although that doesn't explain why the linesman missed it as well.

59 min: Giresse and Janvion run to the touchline to talk to their manager Hidalgo, who is waved back to his station by a stunningly pedantic FIFA official. Hidalgo pleads for a bit of sanity and humanity, realizes there will be none of that and then throws his hands over his shoulder in disgust before flouncing back to the bench, a gesture so Gallic that if you saw it in a film you'd accuse the director of excessive stereotyping.

60 min: The stretcher is finally on, almost three minutes after the collision. Battiston still doesn't seem to be moving. His right hand is draped limply over the side of the stretcher. Platini takes that hand and holds it as Battiston is carried off. This is desperate.

61 min: Lopez comes on for Battiston. Play is going to restart with a goal-kick! No penalty, no red card, nothing. That is astonishing and disgraceful.

64 min: France, who have been much the better team since half time, have picked up where they left off before Battiston's injury. Platini goes down in the area after a challenge from Briegel. It looked like a dive, and Corver waves his hands at Platini to say, no more, a hard-ass gesture that would be impressive had an unseen assault not just occurred on his watch. France get a corner anyway, from which the substitute Lopez almost scores! Schumacher came a long way to meet Giresse's corner and got nowhere near it. He was beaten to the ball by Lopez, on the six-yard line, who looped a header over the bar.

65 min: Trésor flies through the air to win the ball off Kaltz. He's penalized by the referee, presumably for showing his studs. The referee has a word with Trésor. While he's doing so, Platini rubs Trésor's head as if to say, 'Get in there!' This is in danger of boiling over. One day you'd hope players will get immediately sent off for that sort of tackle, though in the wake of the Battiston incident it's probably not fair to point the finger at France too firmly.

71 min: Briegel wins a battle of strength with Tigana, the decathlete against the athlete, and plays the ball into Dremmler. He plays a crisp one-two with Magath, back-pedalling into the area to receive the return pass before striking a good cross-shot that is well held by Ettori, plunging to his right. He had to hold that with Fischer waiting for the follow-up.

73 min: Magath, aged 81, is replaced by the hulking blond Horst Hrubesch, the man who scored both goals in the win over Belgium in the Euro 80 final and who bonded with his manager Jupp Derwall earlier in the tournament by calling him 'a coward'.

78 min: A BIG CHANCE FOR FRANCE! Amoros runs 60 yards down the left, slips past Kaltz and passes it square to Six, ten yards out just ahead of the near post. He takes a touch but then, with defenders converging, mis-hits a feeble shot that Schumacher plunges to save. There hasn't been much joy of Six for France in this game; he has been frustratingly fitful once again. The pass was slightly behind him but he should still have done better.

79 min: Germany, who have been under pressure for much of the second half, almost steal the lead. Breitner, waiting for the right option, pirouettes 270 degrees just outside the D before playing an angled through ball for the onrushing Briegel. He slips the sliding Lopez just inside the area and then smashes a shot from a tight angle that smacks off Ettori's knee and behind for a corner. Ettori has had a dodgy tournament but that was a hugely important save.

80 min: Another chance for Germany! France failed to get the ball away on a few occasions, when Dremmler burst round the outside of the defence on the right. His dipping cross towards the six-yard line somehow beat both Fischer, sliding in with Janvion at the near post, and Littbarski at the far.

81 min: ANOTHER GREAT CHANCE FOR FRANCE! Platini and Lopez combine to find Six in space on the right. He coaxes a gorgeous, teasing ball in between the defenders and keeper. Schumacher and Rocheteau go flying towards it on the six-yard line. Rocheteau gets there a split-second ahead of the keeper and his header hits the chest of Schumacher before dropping tantalizingly in front of goal. Rocheteau might have been able to get there but his collision with Schumacher knocked him away from the ball and Stielike was able to smash the ball away. Actually, it probably wouldn't have counted – it seems the referee has given a foul to Germany, which is ridiculous. Rocheteau and

Schumacher were both entitled to go for that, and Rocheteau got there first.

86 min: Tigana somehow finds the energy for yet another run. He beats Breitner on the halfway line, runs to within 30 yards and then angles over a devilish, dipping cross towards the far post – where Rocheteau and Six get in each other's way! Oh, you pair of goons. Rocheteau, who was leaping backwards on the six-yard line, didn't know Six was behind him; Six's view was impaired and he ran ahead of the ball, which hit the covering Kaltz and bounced behind for a corner.

88 min: With one of the Försters down receiving treatment, players from both sides neck a few Monte Verde chasers. They've earned them.

90 min: Germany win a corner on left. Breitner's delivery is beyond Hrubesch, but Ettori at the far post drops it and is fortunate when it comes back to him off Lopez.

90+1 min: AMOROS HITS THE BAR!!! Manuel Amoros, the young full back with Spanish parents, almost wins the match with an unbelievable effort in injury-time. He ran forward thirty yards with the ball and then, with German defenders back-pedalling, spotted immortality in the far top corner. He so nearly found it by cutting across a stunning 30-yard shot that swerved away from Schumacher and smashed off the crossbar. What an effort! The strike started well outside the line of the near post but swerved away so much that it hit the bar just inside the far post with Schumacher leaping desperately. He would not have got there. Rocheteau, on the turn, splattered the rebound over the bar from 12 yards. That was almost one of the great World Cup fairytales from a player who only won his first France cap in February.

90+3 min: NOW GERMANY ALMOST WIN IT! This is unbelievable! Tigana tried to run the ball out of trouble and was dispossessed by Breitner. He scampered to within 20 yards and then hit a low shot across goal that bounced just in front of Ettori. He couldn't hold it diving to his left, and the ball slithered tantalizingly out in front of goal. It was a race between Fischer and Ettori, who scrambled desperately to his feet. Ettori got there by a split-second, if that, throwing himself forward to punch the ball behind for a corner like a father diving in front of a car to save a baby. He got a kick in the head from Fischer for his trouble. That is a sensational recovery from Ettori. All that training goalkeepers do – every single boring drill where they make a save and bounce straight up to their feet to make another – has been justified in injury-time in a World Cup semi-final.

FULL TIME: West Germany 1–1 France. A wonderful match will go to an extra half-hour, although goodness knows how: both sides could have won it in injury-time there.

91 min: West Germany begin extra time from left to right. We might be 30 minutes away from the World Cup's first-ever penalty shoot-out.

93 min: GOAL! West Germany 1–2 France (Trésor). Or maybe not, because Trésor has given France the lead with a brilliant goal! Briegel was penalized, maybe a little harshly, for a foul on Platini just outside the area on the right wing. Giresse's clipped free-kick hit the head of Dremmler in the wall and looped invitingly towards Trésor, in a bizarre amount of space near the penalty spot. He probably had time to bring the ball down but he had a far more effective option in mind: a screaming volley on the half-turn that scorched into the net! We knew France's defenders could play but this is ridiculous: Bossis has been gallivanting around like a Beckenbauer tribute act, Amoros hit the bar from 30 yards and now Trésor has scored a stunning volley.

94 min: Littbarski nearly equalizes straight away. Amoros, with a combination of weariness and maybe a little arrogance, ignored the option of a backpass to Ettori and tried to run the ball out of defence near the touchline on the left. Littbarski won the ball with an immaculate tackle, declined to go down in the area despite a tug on the shorts from Amoros and had his shot blocked by the sprawling Ettori, who had been completely out of position after running to the left edge of the area expecting a backpass from Amoros. Ettori had to dance back across goal with Littbarski and spread himself to save.

97 min: Desperate times call for obvious measures: Rummenigge replaces the surprisingly fatigable Briegel, who doesn't drip Carling Black Label after all. It's the last throw of Germany's dice, although it's quite a throw to have.

99 min: FRANCE ARE IN THE WORLD CUP FINAL FOR THE FIRST TIME! GOAL! West Germany 1–3 France (Giresse). Alain Giresse has put France into Sunday's final with Italy with another beautiful goal! We sometimes say that players have two right feet; well Giresse's right foot has two insides, because he has been using the outside all night to great effect – but none greater than this. Rocheteau and Platini moved the ball across the face of the area, finding Six on the left. He teased Kaltz and then stabbed a gentle pass back to Giresse, lurking on the edge of the area. He stomped towards the ball and cut across a technically immaculate shot that swerved back and pinged in off the inside of the near post. Schumacher had not a solitary prayer.

100 min: Littbarski takes off his shinpads and tosses them impatiently over the touchline. Seconds later Fischer has a goal disallowed for a non-existent offside! Dremmler's cross from a narrow position was headed emphatically into the corner by Fischer, who ran off the back of Janvion and towered majestically near the penalty spot. Fischer was at least *three yards* onside when the pass was played. Rummenigge on the far side might just have been in an offside position, though I don't think he was. West Germany seem hard done by there.

102 min: Platini almost makes it 4–1 with a fierce free-kick that goes through the wall and bounces up to hit Schumacher in the chest. There was nobody following in and Schumacher claimed it at the second attempt. France then put together a patient passing move, every pass met with an *olé*.

103 min: GOAL! West Germany 2–3 France (Rummenigge). *Olé*? Oh shit more like: West Germany are back in it! That France move broke down and within seconds Rummenigge scored at the other end. Stielike got away with showing his studs to Bossis on the halfway line and worked the ball neatly out to the left with Rummenigge and Littbarski. Littbarski, on the left of the box, curled a low ball towards the near post, where Rummenigge, under considerable pressure from Janvion, twisted his body ingeniously to flick it past the advancing Ettori inside the near post. That's an expert finish indeed. The angle and height of the cross meant he had to lean backwards horizontally into Janvion, with both feet off the floor, and then, while twisting in mid-air, soften his right foot to ease the ball round the corner as Ettori spread himself.

104 min: How did that stay out? Rummenigge, who has grabbed this game by the scruff of the balls, played in Breitner on the right-hand side of the box. He could probably have gone for goal but instead whistled a cross all the way across the face. It's not often you say it about Breitner, and you'd be loath to say it to his face, but he took the wrong option there.

105 min: Another cross flashes right across the France goal! This time it was Littbarski. He received Kaltz's throw, rolled Amoros brilliantly to get into the area and then *smashed* it right across the face. There were two German players waiting in all sorts of space for a cutback. Rummenigge motions kicking the ball into the net, a nice idiot's guide to what might have happened. Another player, Stielike, charges over to give Littbarski a spectacularly heartfelt bollocking. Littbarski's cross was the last kick of a sensational first period of extra time.

EXTRA TIME, HALF TIME: West Germany 2–3 France. Are there any other directions in which this game can turn?

106 min: France start the second period of extra time – and Platini tries to score from the kick-off! It was touched off by Six and Platini's attempt to outdo Pelé struck one of the advancing German players.

108 min: GOAL! West Germany 3–3 France (Fischer). Klaus Fischer equalizes with a wonderful overhead kick! What a goal! Rummenigge, 40 yards out, waved a square pass to Bernd Förster, who moved forward and found Littbarski in a bit of space on the left. As Bossis came to meet him he stood up an excellent cross beyond the far post, where Hrubesch leapt imperiously above Janvion. He was off-balance and unable to go for goal but managed to steer the ball back across the six-yard line. Fischer fell backwards, stretched a telescopic leg away from goal and steered an overhead kick just inside the post! That was the only place he could score because Ettori, along with Trésor and Amoros on the line, had everywhere else covered. Platini responds to the goal with a brief, magnificent tantrum, waving his hands over his shoulder with such fury that he almost knocks himself off his feet. Fischer is the world leader in overhead kicks, so much so that in West Germany they call him *Herr Fallrückzieher*, or Mr Falling Kick. His overhead kick against Switzerland was voted goal of the decade – but this is on a whole new level. What a goal and what a recovery. Germany had 21 minutes to score two goals; they needed only nine of them, and in that time they had a goal wrongly disallowed. This is an outrageous comeback even by their standards. They haven't just come back from the dead; they've come back from a cremation!

111 min: Germany are all over France at the moment, the scent in their snout. Rummenigge, who has been majestic since coming on, sparks another attack by moving disdainfully past Lopez just inside the West Germany half. He flicks it to Dremmler, who moves it down the line to Rummenigge. He gives it back to Dremmler with a first-time backheel, and his cross towards Littbarski is splendidly headed away by Trésor.

114 min: Janvion, misjudging Schumacher's long throw out, leaps to deliberately handle the ball and stop Fischer breaking in behind him. The referee allows play to go on and Fischer picks up the loose ball. He runs to within 25 yards of goal before cutting infield from the right, away from Janvion, and whistling a left-footed shot fractionally wide of the far post! The referee has given a goal-kick, although Fischer seems to think it should have been a corner. If Ettori did get something on that it was an outstanding save.

115 min: Beautiful play from Littbarski, whose quick feet take the piss out of Amoros and Platini before his cross is claimed by Ettori. West Germany are playing with much the greater urgency. Maybe they don't want this to go to a penalty shoot-out after the trauma of the Euro 76 final.

118 min: NEARLY A TRAGI-COMIC OWN GOAL! Tigana plays a tired pass inside the West Germany box and the Germans break. It's fed to Rummenigge, who swaggers forward and clips a through-pass towards Fischer with the outside of the right foot. Trésor gets there first in the D and stabs it back towards Ettori – not knowing that Ettori had moved forward towards the ball himself. Thankfully for France it was close enough to Ettori that he could dive to his right and claim the ball. That would have been a crazy way to decide his match. The camera cuts to the bench, where the splendidly expressive coach Michel Hidalgo puffs out his cheeks in relief.

120 min: West Germany win one last corner, Tigana has cramp and limps back to the box. Kaltz swings it deep, Fischer finds a bit of space ten yards out to head it towards goal and the heroic Trésor heads it clear with Hrubesch flying towards the ball just behind him. France break through Rocheteau and Six, who evades Breitner splendidly near the halfway line and plays it to the right for Tigana. He ignores his cramp for a few seconds, struggles to the edge of the box and then slashes well wide under pressure from Stielike.

EXTRA TIME, FULL TIME: West Germany 3–3 France. That's it! An awesome and controversial match comes to an end, and now we will have the first ever penalty shoot-out in the World Cup. The purists won't be happy but it's a damn sight better than drawing lots. The players look unbelievably tired as they take some water. And we're off . . .

GIRESSE SCORES! West Germany 0–1 France. A confident penalty, sidefooted low to the left as Schumacher goes the other way.

KALTZ SCORES! West Germany 1–1 France. Ettori doesn't even dive, dancing a few steps to his right before realizing Kaltz has sent him the wrong way with a low sidefoot.

AMOROS SCORES! West Germany 1–2 France. For the third time the keeper goes the wrong way. Schumacher moved to his right, Amoros placed it high to *his* right.

BREITNER SCORES! West Germany 2–2 France. Breitner scores with a nonchalant clip high into the net, with Ettori again not diving – just like Jan Jongbloed when Breitner scored in the final eight years ago.

ROCHETEAU SCORES! West Germany 2–3 France. Only Giresse's penalty has been anywhere near the corner, but the keepers keep diving the wrong way. Rocheteau sidefoots to his right to put France ahead.

STIELIKE MISSES! West Germany 2–3 France. This time Ettori not only dives, he goes the right way and saves it! It was not a great penalty from Stielike, sidefooted at breast height to his left but nowhere near the corner. Ettori – who moved illegally off his line before the kick was taken – beat the shot away. Stielike's hands are glued to his face.

SIX MISSES! West Germany 2–3 France. Schumacher has saved from Six! The TV cameraman missed it; he was focusing on Littbarski hugging Stielike, when suddenly Littbarski jumped around in excitement. The camera cut to the goal, where Schumacher was picking the ball up after saving from Six! No joy for Six, who collapses to his knees! We still don't know what happened, except that Schumacher dived to his right and saved.

LITTBARSKI SCORES! West Germany 3–3 France. Littbarski, the youngster, scores with a brilliant penalty, side-footed high into the top-right corner. Ettori came out and started to move the right way but *again* he didn't dive.

PLATINI SCORES! West Germany 3–4 France. Platini scored a penalty in normal time and he scores again, going the other way this time with a calm sidefoot to the right. Schumacher went the wrong way. Rummenigge has to score or France will be in the final.

RUMMENIGGE SCORES! West Germany 4–4 France. Rummenigge scores easily, placing the ball in the bottom-right corner. And again Ettori did not dive. This really is a bizarre approach to saving penalties. So now we go to sudden death. Schumacher, waiting for the next French penalty taker, is talking to the referee Corver. Corver says something and Schumacher chuckles before moving back to his goal. The Battiston family, watching on TV, must love that scene.

BOSSIS MISSES! West Germany 4–4 France. West Germany are one kick away from the final! Schumacher has saved from Bossis! He sidefooted it low to the left, but Schumacher went the right way and made an excellent save. Schumacher definitely moved before the ball was kicked, although Ettori has been up to that as well. Schumacher raises his right arm in triumph, heroics that stick slightly in the craw.

HRUBESCH SCORES AND WEST GERMANY ARE IN THE WORLD CUP FINAL!!! West Germany 3–3 France (5–4 pens). Hrubesch scores! He rolls the ball to his right as Ettori dances the other way, again not diving. Stielike, with his top off, hugs Schumacher for dear life. Not only has the Real Madrid man avoided ignominy, he will play in a World Cup final on his home ground on Sunday. Don't expect too much home support, mind, Uli, your lads have possibly gone past the point where they can salvage this particular charm offensive.

· · · ·**MAGIC MINUTES** · · · · · · · ·**MAGIC MINUTES** · · · · ·

Italy 3–1 West Germany (1982, final)

Italy started the 1982 World Cup diabolically, yet by the end they were beating teams with ease. They missed a penalty against West Germany but still ran out comfortable 3–1 winners.

69 min: GOAL! Italy 2–0 West Germany (Tardelli).
Italy are so close their first World Cup since 1938! Marco Tardelli has put them 2–0 up! The goal came from a West Germany attack, a slow kill on the counter-attack. The imperious Gaetano Scirea led a three-on-three break, striding into the Germany half before giving it to Bruno Conti. He gave it back to Scirea, on the right of the box, who backheeled it to Giuseppe Bergomi and received the return. West Germany were hanging on desperately until more men got back (although actually half of them didn't bother; it was six on five by the time of the goal). But their defending was like the final seconds of a Pac-Man game: you know it's beyond your control, you know the kill is coming; the only issue is when and how. Soon they were put out of their misery. Scirea passed the ball to Tardelli in the D; he flicked it on to his left foot and then, as Bernd Förster came across, slid to bash the ball past Harald Schumacher. Tardelli charges towards the Italian bench, pumping his fists, crying, shaking his head furiously and shouting '*GOL! GOL!*' Now he's even shouting his own name! It was an excellent goal but it has already been overshadowed by the celebration. He has just done what every small boy dreams of, except those oddballs who are into Brahms and books rather than sports. Even if foot-ball goes on until the year 3490, nobody will ever better capture what it means to score in a World Cup final.

Brazil v France

Quarter-final, Estadio Jalisco, Guadalajara, Mexico,
Saturday, 21 June 1986

There aren't many certainties in life. Death, taxes, Wham's farewell single going to No. 1. But France v Brazil, a match almost too glamorous to function, is guaranteed to be a classic. Henri Michel, the France coach, says it is 'a privilege to meet Brazil'. Today is Michel Platini's 31st birthday. For us, it's Christmas Day. Kick back, relax, crack open a can or seven of Tinned Yellow Drink. This will be the best Saturday night of your year. The only people who might not be happy are the Brazilians: they wanted Italy and the chance for revenge for 1982.

That chance went on Tuesday, when France effortlessly dispatched the holders 2–0. Before that they came second in Group C on goal difference after drawing 1–1 with the USSR. While some have played walking football in this heat, France have played waltzing football, leading to some gorgeous goals: Luis Fernández against USSR after Alain Giresse's delightful defence-splitting chip, Jean Tigana's one-two and finish against Hungary, and Dominique Rocheteau's goal against the same opposition, which started with an 80-yard pass *from the goalkeeper.*

Brazil's memorable goals have been more about power, athleticism and particularly Josimar. An unknown, uncapped full-back ten days ago, he scored two quite ludicrous goals against Northern Ireland and Poland. He is going to be a superstar. That 4–0 win over Poland was a little deceptive – the Poles started better and hit the woodwork twice at 0–0. But it's hard to argue with Brazil's new, improved defence, whose four consecutive clean sheets are built around the solidity of the new-and-old centre-back partnership of Julio César and Edinho, and the revelatory discovery of a competent goalkeeper, Carlos.

With Denmark gone, these are the two most entertaining teams in the tournament – a fusion of philosophies and just enough of a clash of styles. It is, as David Lacey said in today's *Guardian*, 'a football purist's dream'. And their fantasy: this is the quarter-final that will give you a semi.

Team news: Brazil are unchanged. Zico remains on the bench, despite suggestions that he would come in with Junior moving to left-back. France do make a change at left-back: with William Ayache suspended, Thierry Tusseau comes in.

Kick-off: Midday in Guadalajara, 7 p.m. in Grimsby.

Referee: Ioan Igna (Romania).

Brazil: Carlos, Josimar, Julio César, Edinho, Branco, Elzo, Alemão, Socrates, Junior, Müller, Careca.

France: Joël Bats, Manuel Amoros, Patrick Battiston, Maxime Bossis, Thierry Tusseau, Luis Fernández, Jean Tigana, Alain Giresse, Michel Platini, Dominique Rocheteau, Yannick Stopyra.

1 min: Brazil kick off from right to left. They are in yellow; France are in blue.

3 min: The first taste of French wine, to borrow Barry Davies's phrase after Tigana's gorgeous goal against Hungary in the group stage. Platini plays a lovely one-two with his trusted lieutenant Giresse on the edge of the area before slithering into the box. He is blocked by a combination of Julio César and Josimar, whose attempted clearance hits Platini. He lays it off invitingly for Amoros, whose fierce low 25-yard shot whistles just past the near post. Carlos probably had it covered.

6 min: The pace is relatively slow, inevitably so in the fierce heat. Expect lots of slow-slow-quick attacks, and France to do everything in their own time. Their football is poetry in slow motion.

9 min: Carlos, the Brazil keeper, is sporting a kind of faded purple/grey top with BRASIL plastered across the breast. It looks like a 1960s P.E. kit, and one fished out from the bottom of the spares box at that.

11 min: Fernández on the left wing taps a short free-kick to Amoros. He swaggers forward and hits an excellent low drive from 25 yards that bounces awkwardly in front of Carlos, who takes it at the second attempt. France have started excellently.

14 min: Platini, receiving the ball from Giresse, eases away from Alemão and teases a gentle, almost sensual pass in between the centre-backs. Rocheteau moves on to it but Edinho gets back to clear on the edge of the box.

15 min: FINE SAVE BY BATS! Brazil have the first big chance of the match. Müller on the right plays the ball into Careca, 25 yards from goal. He sucks two defenders infield and then clips a reverse pass to Socrates, who criss-crosses with Careca by running from the centre towards the left and into space. Socrates chests the ball into the area, breaks into something resembling a jog and then, with defenders coming towards him, slaughters a left-footed half-volley that is beaten away by Bats diving to his right. Seconds later he had to intervene again, scampering to the edge of the six-yard box to dive at the feet of Branco, who was moving on to Socrates's pass from the left.

16 min: Brazil keep the ball for the best part of a minute before Socrates quickens the pace with a sharp pass into Müller on the edge of the area. He takes a touch and hits a snapshot that is too close to Bats.

17 min: GOAL! Brazil 1–0 France (Careca). Brazil take the lead with a magical team goal. This was football in a phonebox; Müller and Junior somehow created space where there was none at all. Supermen. When Josimar played a pass infield from the right towards Müller, he had his back to goal and was surrounded by three French players with another, Battiston, covering behind. He touched it a couple of yards to Junior, who played a short first-time return as Müller ran in behind Amoros and Fernández. Battiston came across but the off-balance Müller took him out of the game with another first-time touch back to Junior. He moved towards the area, waited for the last man Bossis to come across and then, with the outside of his left foot, flicked the ball square with the laziness of a femme fatale flicking fag ash out of a train window. Careca, now in heaps of space because of the work of Junior and Müller, drilled the ball gleefully and decisively into the net. The manipulation of space and the technique in such tight areas were wonderful. The first-time finish was expert as well. Frank Carson might call that a Careca cracker. We wouldn't, obviously. It was like a chess puzzle that had never previously been done in under 12 moves; Brazil solved it with seven effortless, economical touches.

19 min: Branco breaks dangerously down the left before his cross is headed away. Brazil, who started slowly, have turned it up devastatingly in the last few minutes. If France aren't careful, they will wake up in ten minutes and find themselves 2–0 or 3–0 down.

23 min: There's a seductive languor to the way both sides pass the ball, particularly France. There are no real wingers on the pitch, which means lots of easy give-and-gos in the centre of the field. And all eight midfield players are happy to receive the ball under pressure. The technical standard has been stratospheric.

25 min: Another of those lazy passing moves, the ball moved around like a spliff in a dorm, almost brings an equalizer for France. They worked it from the centre to the left, back to the right, back infield again and finally back outside to make the space when Giresse put Amoros clear on the right wing. He smashed a low cross towards the near post, where Rocheteau and the keeper Carlos got there almost simultaneously. In fact, Rocheteau's shot from barely four yards hit Carlos, who dived bravely at his feet, and the loose ball was booted behind by Julio César. Carlos has a minute of treatment on his right arm – Rocheteau's follow-through took him straight into the keeper – but he seems okay.

32 min: France almost submit Brazil to death by silk. This was a gorgeous move. Tigana, 30 yards out, played a nonchalant chipped square pass to Platini; he cushioned a sidefooted volley forward to Giresse, who with his first touch looped a clever header over the centre-back Edinho. For a second it seemed Stopyra, running infield from the left, would have a simple chance from eight yards but Josimar used all his wiry strength to hold Stopyra off.

33 min: MULLER HITS THE POST! Brazil could so easily have gone 2–0 up then. Socrates played a long crossfield pass to Careca, who roasted Bossis on the left side of the box and then squared it across the face of goal. It went all the way across to the right side of the six-yard box where Müller, getting there a fraction before the sliding Tusseau, rattled his shot off the outside of the near post. That was a devastating break.

37 min: Another great move from Brazil involving Socrates, Elzo, Alemão and Muller peaks when Careca dummies Müller's pass on the edge of the area, so nearly allowing Socrates to break beyond Amoros. In the end Amoros just does enough with a desperate sliding challenge, leaving Socrates on all fours like a dog, trying to do something with the loose ball. He still manages to look elegant.

41 min: GOAL! Brazil 1–1 France (Platini). Platini equalizes on his 31st birthday! The move was constructed down the right, where France have been such a threat, and as usual they did things at their leisure. Tigana found Giresse, who played it wide to Amoros. He drew Elzo towards him and played it back infield to the thus unmarked Giresse, who put Rocheteau clear on the right with a first-time pass. Rocheteau ran round the ball and whipped in a first-time cross that deflected off Edinho and spun awkwardly towards the six-yard line. Stopyra tried a diving header from six yards, missed, but in doing so distracted Carlos sufficiently so that, when the ball carried on to Platini beyond the far post, he had an empty net into which he could gently tap the ball. That's the second time Platini has scored on his birthday at the World Cup. It's also the first goal Brazil have conceded in the tournament, after 401 minutes.

44 min: Brazil respond to the equalizer with some fine, aggressive passing, their way of dealing with stung pride.

HALF TIME: Brazil 1–1 France. The referee blows up for half time nine seconds early. In this case less is less because that was a wonderful half of football. Brazil had the clearer chances but France had so much of the ball – and played with such charming grace – that they deserve to be level.

46 min: France kick off the second half.

48 min: Junior wheezes forward and, when nobody challenges him, swooshes a fierce 30-yarder that is punched away by Bats. It was straight at him but doing so much in the air that he decided not to try to catch it.

50 min: Careca is fouled by Battiston, just outside the box on the left. It's a tight angle but Socrates curls in a dangerous cross-shot that is flapped behind for a corner by the stretching Bats.

52 min: Elzo's attempted clearance hits Amoros and bounces back towards the Brazil area. Stopyra gets there before Julio César and almost humps it towards Rocheteau with his shins; Rocheteau spins to shoot wide of the near post from 14 yards. That was a deceptively difficult chance: he had Edinho up his backside and had to do a 180-degree turn almost in the act of shooting.

55 min: A rare bit of cynicism in this match, with Junior brazenly legging up Stopyra, who had beaten two players and was haring towards the area. The resulting free-kick is played wide right to Bossis, whose inviting chipped cross is headed over by Stopyra. He did the hard part, jumping decisively over Julio César and Josimar, but couldn't get over the ball sufficiently to direct the header.

56 min: Sound the Josimar klaxon! He goes off on his first superhero charge off the match, coming infield and galloping to within 20 yards of goal before dragging a mis-hit shot across goal and well wide. He has been one of the stars of this tournament. He didn't even make his Brazil debut until ten days ago!

59 min: Junior is a comical mix of technical brilliance and unapologetic indolence and cynicism, a pub boor who belches while dispensing obscure literary references. Here he brings down Amoros with a ludicrous hack and then rolls over as if he'd been battered himself.

62 min: Socrates beautifully frees Müller in an inside-left position. He teases a low cross towards the far post, in the no-man's-land between keeper and defenders, and Battiston gets there just before Careca. Fine defending.

65 min: Branco goes on an outrageous winding run that is more like a Benny Hill sketch than a piece of football play. Eventually his cross is cleared and moments later Tigana has a wonderful chance to put France ahead! He intercepted just past the halfway line, surged forward in the usual style and then stabbed it forward to Rocheteau. He managed to shield the ball while being dragged over by Edinho, and Tigana – who had so much momentum having already run 40 yards – was straight on the scene in support. His first touch was superb, a disguised push to the left that took him past the static last man, Julio César, and into the area. Carlos flew from goal to meet him. It was crying out for a left-footed first-time finish but instead Tigana took another touch with his right foot and then his stabbed shot hit the chest of Carlos, who spread himself superbly. It's a fine save but Tigana will feel he should have scored. He was entirely reluctant to use his left foot – even though he rattled in his first international goal with his left foot from an almost identical spot against Hungary last week. But what a run! When he retires he should give his lungs to the FIFA museum.

66 min: At the other end, Junior's vicious rising drive from 25 yards is beaten away by Bats, who is almost knocked over by the force of the shot. This is wonderful stuff. It isn't a football match, it's performance art.

70 min: An ingenious long-range one-two between Fernández and Platini is just thwarted by Branco. Some of France's football is gorgeous, as smooth as a love rat's patter.

71 min: CARECA HITS THE BAR! Brazil almost took the lead out of nothing. Careca and Socrates, just inside the France half, worked the ball wide to Josimar. He curved over a hanging cross towards the far post and Careca, arriving late in the box, leapt beautifully above Battiston to thump a header off the top of the crossbar with Bats beaten. Serginho would have scored that.

72 min: Josimar marauds forward, his legs pumping furiously, and plays a fine pass into Alemão in the D. He takes a touch and whistles a shot that is blocked crucially by the stretching Bossis at the expense of a corner. Before the corner is taken, Zico replaces the young forward, Müller. Brazil have found a player there all right.

74 min: PENALTY TO BRAZIL! This is all down to the brilliance of Branco. He steals a pass aimed towards Rocheteau, 35 yards from his own goal, and sets off. Once inside the France half he squares it to Alemão, who deferentially lets Zico take it off him. Quite right too because Zico, just past the D, stabs a stunning straight pass with the outside of his right foot that puts Branco, still running, through on goal. Branco gets there a fraction before Bats, who sends him flying. That's the clearest penalty of the tournament. What a run from Branco, the left-back, who pelted 60 yards in ten seconds to win the penalty. Imagine Kenny Sansom doing that. Alemão gives Branco an almighty hug; they may as well be celebrating a goal. Socrates and Careca scored from the spot against Poland, but it looks like Zico is going to take this . . .

75 min: BATS SAVES IT! It was a poor penalty from Zico – passed low to his right but nowhere near the corner – and the loose ball is stabbed wide by Careca, under pressure from Tigana eight yards out. That was a great chance too. Amoros jumps on Bats's back in celebration and France can't quite believe they have got away with that. Joël Bats has effectively scored an equalizer for France. Zico can't believe it either. Platini walks up and pats Zico's head in sympathy, a pretty amazing gesture in context.

77 min: Bossis miscontrols the ball past Elzo on the halfway line, reacts smartly and runs to within 25 yards before thrashing an extravagant shot, hit with the outside of the foot and both feet off the floor, towards the far post. Carlos dives sharply to his right to push it behind.

81 min: A goal now would surely be decisive. Both sides are playing with such style and joy that it's hard to believe they could be out of the World Cup in ten minutes' time. A scramble in the France box ends with Bats diving on the ball just in front of Socrates.

82 min: WHAT A CHANCE FOR CARECA! Brazil should be ahead. Careca, dropping deep again, played the ball into Zico on the edge of the D and kept running. Zico was challenged by Bossis, but his tackle returned the ball to Careca. He took it in his stride, with a majestic chipped first touch taking him between the last pair of Amoros and Battiston, but then he shot feebly at Bats from 14 yards. That must have taken a bobble or something because Careca miskicked it completely.

84 min: Giresse, who must be feeling the heat at 33, is replaced by Jean-Marc Ferreri.

85 min: BATS MAKES ANOTHER VITAL SAVE FROM ZICO! France are under almost asphyxiating pressure now. Socrates wafted an insouciant crossfield pass to Josimar on the right. He took it down on his chest and curled a sharp cross to the near post, where Zico was in a criminal amount of space on the six-yard line. He leapt almost backwards to steer his header towards goal and Bats, who had almost run too far towards the near post, dived dramatically back whence he came to palm it away. That might be a better save than the penalty.

86 min: Bossis cleans things up on the edge of his own area and then, a few seconds later, almost sets up a winner for France. The move went through the inevitable Platini and then Rocheteau. Bossis kept running all the while and was found in all kinds of space on the left of the box by Rocheteau with Brazil appealing desperately for offside. Carlos came out so Bossis tried to cut it back to Rocheteau, eight yards out, but it was a slightly tired pass, fractionally too far in front of Rocheteau, and Elzo punted it away. What a chance!

88 min: It's all Brazil now. France are hanging on for dear extra time. Amoros heads out for another corner.

89 min: Silas is about to come on in midfield for the ageing Junior.

90 min: Junior, who Brazil wanted to take off, misses a wonderful chance with the last kick of normal time! Careca's lobbed pass from the left – a nothing ball, really – clears everyone in the centre on the edge of the area and bounces to Junior, steaming up on the blind side. It bounces nicely for him, 17 yards out, but he eejits it high and wide of the near post.

FULL TIME: Brazil 1–1 France. We're afraid you're going to have to put up with another 30 minutes of this. Brazil have not been to extra time at the World Cup since their group game against Yugoslavia in 1954. Meanwhile, nobody in France needs reminding of their heart-destroying defeat by West Germany after extra time and penalties in the semis four years ago.

91 min: France kick off extra time. Silas is on for Junior. If Brazil go out, that will surely be the last kick of Junior's World Cup career. It's been quite the mixture.

94 min: Silas, the star of Brazil's win at last year's World Youth Championships, gives the match a shot of adrenaline. He comes infield from the right, past Tusseau's tackle, and plays a slick one-two with Elzo to move into the box on the right. He turns back away from Tusseau, who ends up on his arse for the second time in five seconds – but then, with bodies on both sides charging this way and that like targets in a shoot-em-up, Silas picks the wrong option and shoots the hostage in the head/finds a French defender.

95 min: ROCHETEAU ALMOST SCORES ONE OF THE GREAT WORLD CUP GOALS! This is entirely sensational; Dominique Rocheteau so nearly scored an astonishing solo goal.

He got the ball right on the edge of the centre circle and headed towards goal. Silas's tackle, 30 yards out, put him off-balance but he somehow managed to improvise, keep the ball Blu-tacked to his foot and slither between Edinho and Alemão. He staggered into the area, still off-balance, and then lashed a shot that was magnificently blocked by the sliding Julio César! The loose ball came to Stopyra, whose first-time follow-up was equally well blocked by Branco!

97 min: It's a minor miracle that these players can continue to perform with such skill in this heat, not least because eight of them are in their 30s.

99 min: Platini stuns a wonderful long pass out to Rocheteau on the left. Nothing comes of it but it's worth mentioning for the pass alone, hit first time with minimal backlift and moving both ways in the air before shimmering across the turf like a bowling ball when it lands. A few moments later, Elzo beats the weary Tigana 25 yards out and drives not far over the top, though Bats probably had it covered.

100 min: Bruno Bellone, a lively forward, is on for Rocheteau.

103 min: A meandering Brazil attack suddenly comes to life when Silas gets the ball out of his feet and explodes a 25-yarder just over the bar with Bats flying nervously through the air.

104 min: Another half-chance for Silas! Zico's clever through-pass got to him on the left side of the six-yard box. He got to the ball a fraction before the out-rushing Bats but was facing away from goal so could only help it back to Alemão on the edge of the area. His attempted cross was overhit and drifted over the bar. That had the not inconsiderable whiff of weariness.

105 min: Socrates misses another chance! He got in between Bossis and Amoros to meet Silas's cross, delivered from a narrow position on the right, but from 12 yards he planted his header straight at Bats. It was tricky in that the ball didn't have much pace on it, but even so. Branco intercepts Bats's throw-out and goes on another ludicrous solo charge that ends with a fierce low cross that Bats claims well with Socrates waiting behind him to score from approximately 0.1 yards.

EXTRA TIME, HALF TIME: Brazil 1–1 France. Again the referee blows early, three seconds this time. What's his problem?

107 min: Tusseau collapses in comic agony after a tackle with Alemão. It looks like cramp and he's rubbing his thigh furiously with his legs splayed. None of the other players seem to give a shit! They're ignoring him as he writhes around in obvious pain! After a bit of treatment and some water, he is okay to continue.

110 min: Amoros, who has had a storming game, tidies up a Brazil attack by nutmegging Socrates.

113 min: Another great chance for France! When the corner is eventually taken, after treatment for Amoros, it's only partially cleared by Brazil and Platini teases a cross back into the box from the right. Fernández misses his attempted header but in doing so puts Julio César off, which allows the ball to run to Bellone on the six-yard line. He takes a touch and then gets away a shot that is heroically blocked by Carlos. The loose ball almost drops for Fernández and then the referee gives a foul to Brazil for something or other. But it would have counted had Bellone scored.

114 min: Josimar is down with cramp.

115 min: Brazil move the ball across the field from left to right, where Alemão has room to skip into the box and thrash a fierce shot towards the near post. The diving Bats palms behind with both hands. In doing so Alemão gives himself cramp and goes down. It's easier to count the players who don't have cramp now.

117 min: ONE OF THE MOST AMAZING MINUTES IN WORLD CUP HISTORY! PART ONE! France are robbed blind – just like they were four years ago against West Germany – and then Socrates misses an open goal! This is astonishing. Brazil took a short corner after Bats's save from Alemão, and when it was eventually crossed in Bats punched it away to Ferreri on the right. He swept it infield to Platini, just short of the centre circle, and he stroked a stunning first-time pass to put Bellone through on goal. Carlos came charging outside his area to meet Bellone, who went around him and was then unashamedly man-handled by the keeper – who dived spectacularly to his right to put both hands on Bellone and try to bring him down. He didn't manage that but did leave Bellone hopelessly off-balance; although Bellone tried to continue and score, he had lost all momentum and Edinho came round to clear. The referee seemed to play the advantage, except there was no advantage. That is a warped sibling of the Battiston/Schumacher incident in 1982. Carlos did not hurt Bellone this time, he merely tried to stop him, but just as in 1982 France were bizarrely given nothing by the referee. It should have been a free-kick for France, although even that is not enough: surely FIFA must introduce red cards for professional fouls of this nature, as was trialled in England a few years ago.

117 min: ONE OF THE MOST AMAZING MINUTES IN WORLD CUP HISTORY! PART TWO! Platini shouts at the referee as play continues, and he and France would have lost the plot completely had Socrates scored 25 seconds later. Careca, one of the few players who still seems to have something left in his legs, burst beyond Battiston on the right and screamed a low ball across the six-yard line. It beat everyone at the near post, including Bats, and left Socrates with an open net. But he totally mistimed his attempted sidefoot, met only fresh air and then fell over. The ball was just behind him but, even so, it was a routine chance. That was pure fatigue. With the ball finally out of play, France have an entirely justified group flounce. Who says shite refereeing can't strike twice? And it has, a double flop, right in France's collective visage.

119 min: Platini wins the ball off Josimar – yep – and then plays it square to Fernández, who chips the ball up sweetly but then booms a volley into orbit. If that had gone any higher it would have sparked a game of Arkanoid with a series of low-flying aircraft.

EXTRA TIME, FULL TIME: Brazil 1–1 France. That's it! The referee again blows the whistle early to the consternation of Brazil, who were on the attack. A wonderful match that provided a rare fusion of class, drama, flair and technique will be decided by a penalty competition. It will be Brazil's first ever, unless you count the win over Canada at the 1984 Olympics (we don't); France, as everyone knows, lost to West Germany in the semi-finals four years ago.

SOCRATES MISSES! Brazil 0–0 France. Bats saves the first penalty! Socrates, who scored in the match against Poland on Monday with a cocky one-step run-up, tried a repeat and was denied when Bats flew to his right to beat the ball away with his right hand. It was not a great penalty: far too straight and telegraphed by what happened against Poland. If Brazil go out that could easily be Socrates's last kick in international football.

STOPYRA SCORES! Brazil 0–1 France. Stopyra takes a long run-up and hoofs the ball straight down the middle as Carlos dives to his left.

ALEMÃO SCORES! Brazil 1–1 France. Alemão gets Brazil on the board with a superb penalty, sidefooted assertively into the bottom-right corner. Bats went the right way but it was too good.

AMOROS SCORES! Brazil 1–2 France. Amoros, perhaps the man of the match, places a confident penalty to the right of Carlos, who was off his line and dived the right way but could not reach a well-placed shot. And now it will be Zico, who has already missed one in normal time . . .

ZICO SCORES! Brazil 2–2 France. It wasn't a very good penalty from Zico, driven slightly to the right of centre, but this time Bats went the wrong way.

BELLONE SCORES! Brazil 2–3 France. What a moment of fortune for France! Bellone twangs his penalty off the right post, it hits the back of Carlos – who had dived that way – and rebounds into the net. There is some debate as to whether that should count or not and Edinho runs from the halfway line to the area to discuss it with the referee, but he has given it. That probably shouldn't count under the rules. France will feel that it's karmic retribution for Carlos's foul on Bellone in extra time. What an amazing twist that is. Dame Fortune is in one frisky mood tonight. Now Branco is talking to the referee. He needs to get his mind on the job because unless he scores this penalty Brazil will be on the brink.

BRANCO SCORES! Brazil 3–3 France. He does score, hammering the ball down the middle as Bats dives to his left.

PLATINI MISSES! Brazil 3–3 France. Dame Fortune is now taking the piss: Platini, one of the safest bets in world football from a dead ball, has missed – and on his birthday too! He tried to be too precise, aiming for the top-left corner and just clearing the crossbar! This is unbelievable! With one penalty remaining per side, this is effectively sudden death.

JULIO CESAR MISSES! Brazil 3–3 France. France are one kick away from the semi-finals! Julio César absolutely creamed his penalty, which hit the left post and rebounded all the way to the halfway line! It'll be Luis Fernández to take the final penalty. The quiet man of *Le Carré Magique*, France's wonderful midfield, could steal every headline going here.

FERNANDEZ SCORES AND FRANCE GO INTO THE SEMI-FINALS!!! Brazil 1–1 France (3–4 pens). Fernández, socks round his ankles, places the ball nervously on the spot. You wonder if he can even feel his fingers or his toes. Carlos delays the taking of the kick as long as possible. Eventually Fernández steps up – and he scores, placing it carefully to his left with Carlos going the other way! Fernández and all the other players suddenly find energy in their legs where there was none before. Fernández has a long embrace with first Tigana and then Platini, his midfield mates. They will play West Germany or Mexico on Wednesday after winning the most beautiful game imaginable.

England v Argentina

*Quarter-final, Estadio Azteca, Mexico City, Mexico,
Sunday, 22 June 1986*

It was twenty years ago today . . . and the song 'Sgt. Pepper's
Lonely Hearts Club Band' had yet to be written, never
mind recorded, while England were still a month away from
becoming world champions. But let's not start pulling at
threads here. The timescale may be slightly vague, but the
parallels with 1966 are still illuminating. Back then, when
England won the World Cup, they beat Argentina along the
way in the quarter-finals. The pair run into each other at the
same stage at the Azteca today, their first World Cup meeting
since that legendary and controversial showdown at Wembley.
A welcome omen for Bobby Robson's team? Perhaps, for the
dynamic is pretty similar to 1966: Argentina are highly fancied
in some quarters to win the trophy, while England have yet
to really hit their stride but are getting better match by match
and have designs on the cup themselves. Of course, there is
one additional, crucial and unavoidable twist this time round
– the countries were at war over the Falklands/Malvinas less
than four years ago – but that extra frisson just adds to the
sense that this summit meeting between two of world football's
behemoths could be an event for the ages. It's wonderful to be
here, it's certainly a thrill.

England are certainly on the up. They began this tournament
as a rabble. Their winger-to-targetman stylings, Chris Waddle to
Mark Hateley, looked woefully anachronistic. But having lost to
Portugal then disintegrated in the draw against Morocco – when
Bryan Robson's shoulder went and so did Ray Wilkins' noggin
– Bobby Robson came up with something more in keeping with
the times. He tucked Peter Beardsley in the hole behind Gary
Lineker while also ripping up his midfield. Bang bang bang!
England blew away Poland, Lineker scoring a hat-trick that was
sadly sullied for ever by BBC analyst Jimmy Hill's pitiful, cod-
Brazilian 'gooooooooaaaaal' celebrations, which were nothing
short of cultural vandalism.

Having thus qualified for the knockout phase, England sashayed past Paraguay in the second round, Lineker and Beardsley visibly blooming on the world stage. But now they face their first big test. And let's not over-complicate things. We can tip the hat to Oscar Ruggeri and José Luis Brown at the back, to Sergio Batista and Jorge Burruchaga in midfield, to the clever Jorge Valdano up front . . . it seems ludicrous to suggest Argentina are a one-man team. And yet, by their own admission, *they kind of are.* 'He is the soul of our team,' says Valdano of the blessed Maradona. 'Diego can make a balanced team into world champions.' Bobby Robson, who knows a thing or two about one-man teams, agrees. 'Let's just say that without Maradona, Argentina would have no chance of winning the World Cup. That's how great he is.' Maradona was man of the match against South Korea, scored a high-class volley against the reigning world champions Italy, set up a goal against Bulgaria, and hit the bar and had a goal disallowed against Uruguay, when Argentina paid back their South American cousins for defeat in the 1930 final. Could he be about to settle another historical debt?

The prize, for whoever wants to reach out and grab it: A place in the final, if we accept that neither Spain nor Belgium, who face each other later in the fourth quarter, will be anything other than eminently beatable in the semi. Oh, and the small matter of pride.

Kick-off: Midday, with the sun beating down; 7 p.m. for those England fans back home who didn't have thousands of pounds to spunk on a trip to Mexico.

Referee: Ali Bin Nasser (Tunisia).

England: Peter Shilton, Gary Stevens, Terry Fenwick, Terry Butcher, Kenny Sansom, Glenn Hoddle, Trevor Steven, Peter Reid, Steve Hodge, Gary Lineker, Peter Beardsley.

Argentina: Nery Pumpido, José Luis Cuciuffo, Julio Olarticoechea, Sergio Batista, Oscar Ruggeri, José Luis Brown, Ricardo Giusti, Hector Enrique, Jorge Burruchaga, Diego Maradona, Jorge Valdano.

The teams are out! And each England player has been handed their own personal pennant by the Argentinian team. That's a classy touch ahead of a game that has been predictably overshadowed by the Falklands/Malvinas conflict. 'The spirit between the two teams could not be better,' says Barry Davies on the BBC. Meanwhile, a worldwide audience of many millions is treated to the picture of a topless man in the stand draining a plastic cup of lager while sucking back a cheroot. It's what top-level professional sport is all about.

Maradona is *pumped*. He's wandering around screaming at his team-mates, shaking a fist, giving it the full come-on. Before the game starts, as the players literally warm up under the blistering sun, the referee and his assistants take refuge in the spiral shadow in the centre circle caused by the stadium's speaker system. Both teams will be wishing the PA went one louder, big enough to cast the entire pitch in a cooling shade.

England kick off! It's a shimmering scene, England in their famous white shirts and less renowned powder-blue pants, Argentina in their away strip of dark-blue shirts and black shorts. Reid goes on a scamper down the left but is crowded out before he can reach the area. He wins a throw, which is launched into the box – the English notoriously pay no heed to the territorial claims of Argentina – but Butcher is all over Brown and it's a free-kick. Still, a lively enough start to the match from Bobby Robson's side.

3 min: Steven comes through the back of Maradona, who makes sure the referee knows he's been fouled by elaborately throwing himself forward while thrusting his nipples into the air. Saucy boy.

5 min: Reid whips the ball off Maradona's toe as Argentina look to build something down the right. He's here, there and everywhere at the moment. He was PFA Player of the Year in 1985 and has arguably got better since – even if he was beaten into last season's PFA Team of the Year by *Stewart Robson*. Will this be the match that defines the Everton star's international career?

7 min: The ball lands at the feet of Fenwick, 30 yards out. He lumps an idiotic shot 40 yards into the air and out for three rugby points. The crowd express their derision very loudly indeed; they've paid to see top-level international football, not this Sunday-league nonsense.

9 min: Maradona embarks on his first serious run of the match, cutting past Sansom on the outside down the right before immediately switching inside again. Fenwick, having already showcased his credentials, slides in to cut the Argentinian captain off at the knees. Within milliseconds of the impact, he's shown a yellow card and can have no complaints whatsoever. What a hoodlum.

10 min: Maradona takes the free-kick, 25 yards out, just to the right of goal. He's looking for the top right but only smacks the wall. The ball balloons in the other direction, looping on a dangerous arc towards the top left. Valdano rushes in to challenge Shilton, who does extremely well to tip the ball over the bar under severe pressure. The corner comes to naught.

12 min: This is all Argentina at the moment, with England looking slightly panicked at the back.

13 min: And after all that, England so nearly take the lead! Hoddle, on the centre spot, rakes a pass down the right channel for Beardsley to chase. There's too much weight on it but Pumpido makes a holy mess of collecting a simple ball, slipping as he steps in to gather. The ball clanks off his shin and out of the area to the right. Beardsley, ever the scamp, is first to it. Pumpido chases but is sent sailing towards the byline by an outrageous wiggle of the hips. Beardsley, having feinted to turn left, takes a step back up the pitch, turns again and whips a shot towards the unguarded net. Unfortunately for England, it billows the side-netting. So, so close. Maradona himself would have been proud of Beardsley's bustling brilliance.

16 min: A magical atmosphere in the ground, no doubt everyone's high on booze and fags if that pre-match sweep of the stands was anything to go by. Many of the spectators are holding one note, creating an atmospheric drone that makes 'Venus in Furs' by the Velvet Underground sound like Paul McCartney and the Frog Chorus.

20 min: Giusti clips Hoddle in the middle of the park, a common or garden foul. On the BBC, analyst Jimmy Hill argues, in schoolboy tones, that Fenwick's earlier booking was less offensive because 'you see, that foul was much more premeditated . . . Fenwick made a strike for the ball and the skill of Maradona beat him, he was only fractionally away from it, but that one, the player knew he was bringing him down and the referee never even looked for a yellow card.' It's this sort of myopic denial that's keeping English football in the dark ages. Fenwick nearly sent Maradona's kneecaps whirling like Catherine wheels towards Guadalajara! Meanwhile, millions watching at home will be retuning their television sets, concerned about the long whine emanating from the speaker. It doesn't sound good, does it?

23 min: Argentina are enjoying the lion's share of possession but doing very little with it. On the BBC, commentators Davies and Hill are using the spare time to criticize the appointment of a referee from Tunisia – 'an emerging nation', says Davies, which would have been news to those who founded the city of Tunis in the fourth century BC. To precis: it's seen as a political sop offered by the expansionists at FIFA to those with world-views different to folk employed by the sports department at the BBC. Did these same people question the appointment, ability and impartiality of, say, the linesman from notable football hotbed Azerbaijan at the 1966 World Cup final? If they did, it's not down on record. Beardsley knocks over Maradona and is penalized. 'For nothing!' chirrups Hill, warming to a theme. Oh, for goodness' sake.

29 min: Steven makes his way to the corner flag down the right but his cross flies straight out of play. Time for the Mexican television cameras to take another sweep of the crowd. What service on offer at the Azteca! An usherette carrying a tray of 15 ready-poured lagers is ambling through the stand with a view to vending them to thirsty punters. One chap, a young gentleman with a fashionable Zapata moustache, sits behind a big bass drum. 'Well, he doesn't seem to have too much to say, does he, the Argentine drummer?' sniffs the BBC's Davies, although it's not clear what he's expecting from the percussionist, one-third of the way through with the scoreline goalless. A coruscating, Gene Krupa-style, ten-minute big-band solo?

30 min: Enrique flicks an exquisite pass with the outside of his boot down the inside left for Valdano, who would have been clear on goal were it not for the covering Sansom. Valdano's forced out to the wing, where he backheels down the touchline to Maradona. Sheer brilliance from the wee man, who returns with a backheel of his own. It's a perfectly weighted pass that gives Valdano time to scoop a ball into the area for Batista and Burruchaga to chase. Shilton is out well to smother. For a second, it looks as though things may kick off but everyone was within their rights to challenge for the through ball and soon enough handshakes are exchanged. There's nice.

32 min: The crowd are occupying themselves with a Mexican wave, which goes to show how dull this game is becoming. Maradona attempts to lift them with a full-speed slalom down the inside right. Picking the ball up just inside the centre circle, he zips past Hoddle and Fenwick, then is clipped from behind by Hodge. Maradona accidentally headbutts Sansom in the stomach as he falls. Sansom springs up in anger but simmers down quickly enough as Maradona has clearly come off the worse. Free-kick to Argentina, just to the right of the D.

33 min: Maradona flips the ball over the wall and out of play on the right. Shilton was across in time, though if Maradona had hit the target while finding a little more height on the ball, the keeper might have been struggling.

34 min: Another free-kick to Argentina in a dangerous position, just to the right of the box. England bring it on themselves, Hoddle ducking out of a 50–50 with Hector Enrique in the middle, Giusti flying up the right before being upended by Hodge. The Aston Villa player is incensed with Giusti, angrily miming gestures for GET UP and DIVE! that travel across all borders. The Argentina midfielder did indeed go down in a very artistic manner, but he was clipped and there can be no complaints. England's players really need to get over this, their self-righteous fury does them no favours. Maradona looks for the top right but the free-kick pings off the wall. Corner.

36 min: A ludicrous hold-up as Maradona shapes to take the corner but finds some photographers blocking his run-up. He takes the corner flag out, so he can approach the ball from another angle. The Costa Rican linesman Berny Ulloa Morera demands he replace it. Maradona replants the pole. But the flag has fallen off. Pick that up too, demands the linesman, who really should have been telling the cameramen to move their fat arses instead of faffing around with this muscle-flexing nonsense. Maradona drapes the flag over the top of the pole. Not good enough, says the linesman, put it on properly. Maradona, taking all of this in a better humour than most of us could muster in the face of such pedantic jobsworthery, re-sheathes the pole – and then gets the photographer who should have moved in the first place to shift. What a roundabout business! After all that, the corner, with grim predictability, sails straight into the hands of Shilton. The linesman might like to consider that people have paid to watch Maradona and not him.

37 min: What a run by Maradona! He picks up possession inside his own half and burns off Hoddle as he tears through the centre circle, showing him the ball awhile just because he can. He then skates past Fenwick with such ease that the defender is sent spinning and scrabbling on all fours in the hope of bouncing back upright. Entering the box to the left of the D, Maradona shoots low but his effort is deflected off Stevens. The ball drops to Hodge on the penalty spot. The England midfielder looks to hoof clear, but slices in impotent panic and the ball spins out to the left of goal for a corner. Hodge will need to stop that. Butcher thumps Burruchaga's setpiece upfield with a forceful header.

40 min: FENWICK ASSAULTS MARADONA!!! Maradona is beginning to cause a lot of trouble. He skitters down the inside left, drawing three white shirts towards him, then lays off to the right for Cuciuffo, who sends a scuffo over the bar. But that's not the story here. The closest man to Maradona was Fenwick, who planted his left elbow into his mouth! Maradona's down receiving a spot of treatment, a sponge to the lips. Fenwick should walk for that, regardless of his booking earlier. What abject thuggery, totally missed by the referee, who was following the ball. To Maradona's eternal credit, he doesn't lose his rag when he finally picks himself off the turf, instead simply wagging his finger at the clumpish defender before miming an elbow. It's a disgraceful situation and yet here's how it's dissected for viewers back home in England: 'He actually ran into the back of a player who's showing no interest in him whatsoever,' begins arch-jingoist Jimmy Hill. 'And feigning the injury to get sympathy! He's the best player in the world and by no means the worst actor . . . You can't foul a man who's behind you.' Yes, Jimmy, that's right.

43 min: England are hanging on a bit here. Maradona goes on a run across the face of the England area, right to left, but can't spot a passage through. He backflicks for Batista, whose shot is blocked. Burruchaga tries to split the English last line with a backheel but Butcher blooters it clear.

44 min: Lineker has touched the ball! Yes, he really has managed it! He toe-pokes it out of play down the right. It's not much but it's something. Occasional flashes from Beardsley apart, England have shown nothing up front.

45 min: Cuciuffo bundles Reid off the ball down the England left. A chance for Hoddle to wave his wand with the free-kick. He lifts a clever ball down the flank to release Sansom into space but Hodge foolishly scuttles across to get involved, forcing the linesman to put his flag up. Sansom whacks the ball right through the Argentinian area in frustration. That was a well-worked training-ground routine. Hodge clearly wasn't paying attention in class.

HALF TIME: England 0–0 Argentina. Well, that could have been better from England's point of view. They offered little in the way of attack, while Maradona shone for Argentina. But at least the referee didn't send Fenwick off, eh, so he'll be good to continue his duel with Maradona into the second half.

And we're off again! As Argentina kick off the second period, news filters through that Telê Santana has resigned as manager of Brazil, who were knocked out by France yesterday. As a result of that defeat, Argentina are the only South American team left standing, the only men who can stop a European side winning on this continent for the first time. Within seconds of the restart, Steven clatters into Maradona as the pair contest a high ball in the middle of the English half. The free-kick's chipped into the area, but the offside flag is immediately raised.

50 min: Maradona goes up with Fenwick in the centre circle and takes another clatter to the head. He's really testing his luck, the butcher of Shepherd's Bush.

51 min: GOAL! MARADONA SCORES!!! BUT HOW??? AND WITH WHAT?!?!? England 0–1 Argentina. This is outrageous play from Maradona, in more than one sense. Cutting in from the left, having picked up a pass from Olarticoechea, he dances down the channel, slipping past Hoddle and Reid, then ghosting past Fenwick. At the edge of the D, he draws Butcher and Sansom towards him, then clips a pass to the right for Valdano, who attempts to flick and turn outside Hodge. But Hodge sticks a boot out and slices – again! – a looping ball into the middle of his own area. It's dropping just in front of the penalty spot. Shilton comes out to claim, but he must have swapped his boots for sandbags at half time because he doesn't get any elevation on his leap. Maradona, who has continued forward, rushes towards him and gets there first, dinking the ball over the flapping keeper and into the unguarded net. Maradona tears off to celebrate in front of the stand on the right but not before glancing back briefly, sheepishly. That'll be a goal! But should it stand? No, it damn well shouldn't! He's tipped it over Shilton with his left fist! Shilton waves his hands in the air in despair; Butcher is theatrically hammering away at his own mitt to illustrate what's just occurred; while Fenwick gets right up in the referee's grille, wafting his pinkies in a mixture of mime and seething frustration. England have been robbed in plain sight here, though whether Fenwick should be the man clambering on to that lofty steed, his high horse, is another matter altogether. As for Shilton, eight inches taller than the goalscorer? Ah, let's not go there.

52 min: England restart the game. The referee's made a horrendous error there, though it's got bugger all to do with him being Tunisian, so Jimmy Hill can pipe down. There's no justification for the linesman missing it either, though it's probably fair and instructive to note the reaction of BBC commentator Davies, who is never slow to wrap himself in the Union Jack. 'They're appealing for offside but the ball came back off the boot of Steve Hodge' is his initial commentary, and it takes him another 32 seconds and two replays before he mutters, 'Now at what point was he offside . . . or was it a use of the hand that England are complaining about?' And still he's not certain enough to make a definitive call on live television. Which if nothing else shows how the referee can be excused, if not necessarily forgiven, for missing the handball in real time. Legality aside, Maradona displayed genuine sleight of hand there. He's really done a number on England! And it looks like Argentina have payback for the Rattin incident all those years ago.

53 min: England attempt an immediate comeback, Hodge making good ground down the left and whipping a cross through the area. Cuciuffo miskicks wildly, allowing Lineker to sweep a shot on the turn from 12 yards. It hits Ruggeri at close range. The striker appeals for a penalty but he's not getting anything there.

54 min: The view from the press box is unequivocal, at least among those sitting nearer England's goal. 'They have little doubt that it was a hand that put the ball past the England goalkeeper,' reports Davies. On the England bench, Bobby Robson looks reasonably calm and collected, all things considered. What a gentleman he is. You'd not blame him for descending into a blind fury but he's a credit to his nation.

55 min: AND NOW MARADONA'S SCORED ONE OF THE GREATEST GOALS IN WORLD CUP HISTORY!!! England 0–2 Argentina. Haw, well, there are no doubts about this one. Hoddle, who has been hopeless today, gives away possession cheaply in the middle of the Argentinian half. The ball's shuttled up to Maradona, facing his own goal just to the right of the centre circle. He spins around, past Beardsley and Reid, and makes his way down the right. Drawing Butcher, he nips inside as the defender lunges. Picking up pace, he accelerates towards the box with extreme prejudice, sashaying past the goonish Fenwick. He teases Shilton off his line, rounds the keeper on the right as he holds off the returning Butcher and slides the ball into the right-hand side of the goal. He hugged the ball with his left foot all the way, even taking the shot with that peg, an almost reckless decision as it gave Butcher the chance of getting back in. He races off to celebrate in front of the same stand on the right but there's no need to look back this time. And in fairness to Barry Davies, who we've given some stick this afternoon but is a class act when on top of his game, his instantaneous, magnanimous response is: 'You have to say that's magnificent . . . Pure football genius.' And then some, Barry. And then some.

56 min: England restart again and a long ball sends Beardsley scuttling around the left wing. He cuts back for Sansom, who thinks about a cross, then takes a whack instead. It's a decent daisy-cutter, but Ruggeri hacks it away before it can get through to keeper Pumpido.

58 min: Hodge needlessly runs the ball out of play on the left, with plenty of grass in front of him. He's one of several England players – Fenwick, Shilton, Hoddle – having a personal crisis this afternoon, for one reason or another.

60 min: Batista takes a wild hack at Reid as the pair go in for a loose ball. That nearly took the England midfielder's foot off! Batista's booked. A long free-kick sent into the area glances off Brown's head. Hoddle's delivery is poor, but he's granted a second chance to put the ball into the mixer and fires a low cross, which is met adroitly by Beardsley, England's Tesco Maradona. He flicks a first-time shot towards the bottom left from the edge of the area. There's no real speed in the effort and Pumpido gathers, but that's decent from Beardsley and better from Hoddle.

63 min: Chris Waddle has been standing on the touchline waiting to replace Reid for a couple of minutes. The ball finally goes out of play but the referee doesn't notice the board go up. Argentina get on with it and Reid is given a momentary reprieve.

65 min: Waddle finally comes on for Reid.

66 min: Maradona chases after Pumpido's long clearance down the left. Fenwick fells him with another clump to the back of the head. This is getting ridiculous now. He could easily have been sent off three times, a hat-trick of straight reds! Maradona clutches the back of his neep in some distress. 'There's no question about it, he wasn't touched, he's an actor,' spits Hill on the BBC, who unlike Davies is still on the naughty step.

67 min: Maradona is still off the field looking fairly groggy, it has to be said. Oh, Jimmy!

68 min: Maradona is back on, just in time to defend a free-kick, Giusti having brought down Hoddle 25 yards out, just to the right of goal.

69 min: Hoddle takes, his shot starting outside the right post but curling back in. Pumpido is forced to use a strong hand to turn it out for a corner. This is much better now from Hoddle, who was anonymous in the first half.

72 min: England are enjoying more possession, pushing Argentina back. Brown is forced to concede another corner down the right, albeit as a result of the fairly basic tactic of Stevens launching a long throw into the area. From the corner, Fenwick powers in from the left but slaps his header well over the bar. Maybe he should visualize the goal as Maradona's face: he'd never miss.

75 min: A final throw of the dice by Robson, who exchanges Steven for John Barnes. The Watford winger will go out on the left, with Waddle stationed on the right. The two wide men should in theory cause Argentina some problems, as they're only playing three at the back. Which does beg the question why the manager's left it until the final 15 minutes to stretch the game, but let's see how it pans out.

76 min: Burruchaga is replaced by Carlos Tapia.

77 min: Beardsley is bundled over by Cuciuffo down the right. Hoddle curls the free-kick to the far post. Hodge attempts a diving header but doesn't connect properly. The ball squirts to the right for Butcher, but the big man can only direct his header from close range straight at Pumpido.

80 min: England have been the better team since Maradona's second goal, without creating much. Another free-kick, this time to the left of the box. Barnes runs over it and makes off down the left. Hoddle tries to find him but Argentina are wise to the grift and charge his pass down.

81 min: HELLO! ENGLAND ARE BACK IN IT!!! England 1–2 Argentina (Lineker). The brilliance of Barnes! On the left-hand corner of the Argentinian area, he nudges the ball past Enrique, then swishes past Giusti. Just before he reaches the byline, he clips a cross into the middle, where Lineker heads down and into the right-hand corner from six yards! Stunning! Lineker's done absolutely nothing whatsoever but suddenly he's brought England right back into this game with one confident nod! The sign of a great goalscorer. Mind you, that was all about Barnes because, if Lineker wasn't there, Waddle and Fenwick were both *in situ* to bundle home. England rush back upfield celebrating, desirous of a quick restart. The hapless Hodge ensures the game won't begin again quickly by trying to wrest the ball from Pumpido's grasp, a demand that only succeeds in causing much stubbornness on the goalkeeper's part, slowing things up. What a comprehensive shocker Hodge is having.

82 min: STRAIGHT FROM THE RESTART, ARGENTINA HIT THE POST! Maradona spins past three challenges and feeds Tapia down the left. Tapia cuts inside, rides a challenge from Sansom and from the left-hand corner of the D wallops a low shot off the base of England's left-hand post! The ball twangs across the face of goal and away! England were so lucky to escape there. Argentina were an inch away from the semis.

84 min: Maradona is happy to waste time now, faffing around down by the right-hand corner flag near England's goal. A few party tricks, tick tock, tick tock.

85 min: Valdano bombs down the inside-right channel. He's about to break past the last man, so the last man takes him down with an appalling slide tackle. The name of that last man? You've already guessed, but just to confirm: it's Terry Fenwick! He could easily have been sent off on *four* separate occasions this afternoon. What a galoot!

87 min: Hoddle rakes a long pass towards Sansom on the edge of the box down the left. Ruggeri should intercept but misjudges and lets it fly through. But Sansom hesitates, allowing Brown to clatter him with a clean tackle. That's a risky gambit in Brown's own box with time running out.

88 min: LINEKER FAILS TO CONVERT FROM AN INCH OUT! Oh me, oh my. Maradona races down the right channel but is robbed by a brilliant slide from behind by Hodge, who pokes back to Hoddle. Beardsley takes charge and strokes a pass out to the left for Barnes, who keeps going towards the byline until he manages to get a step ahead of Enrique. The minute there's a gap, he whips another stupendous cross to the far post for Lineker. The ball's arcing over Pumpido, inches in front of the goal-line. The striker surely must score but though he ends up in the net, the ball doesn't. He's denied by some stunning last-ditch heroics from Olarticoechea, who gets in first and glances the ball out for a corner. That's an astonishing clearance, one of the greatest in football history. He's got under the ball, with Lineker up his jacksie, and bumped it away with the back of his head. On the BBC, Hill started off with that disingenuous GOALLLLLLLLLLL nonsense again and had to pipe down in doublequick time. And look how that ball's spinning

Argentina 3–2 West Germany (1986, final)

Having scored twice in the quarter-final against England, and another two in the semi against Belgium, Diego Maradona was expected to be the difference between these two teams at the Azteca. He did indeed make a telling contribution, but not the scoring one everyone envisaged . . .

GOAL!!! Argentina 3–2 West Germany (Burruchaga 85). Maradona's already set up Burruchaga for one spectacular goal in this World Cup, dinking a ball down the left in the first round and wedging a cross to the far post for the midfielder to nut home. But this one will have a bit more cultural capital, you'd reckon. Argentina should be reeling from Germany's eight-minute, two-goal comeback, but here's the initiative regained and surely a killer blow. A loose ball in the centre circle. Maradona has three green shirts converging on him – Karl-Heinz Rummenigge, Lothar Matthäus and Ditmar Jakobs – but he magic-wands an instant poke down the inside right, allowing Burruchaga to burst clear. He takes two touches, the second a bit heavy as he enters the area. But Harald Schumacher is slow off his line, and Burruchaga pokes past the advancing keeper and into the far corner! All that German effort to claw back into the match and it looks like the jig is up!

off! A physics lesson arcing through the air. Butcher can't meet the resulting setpiece with his head. That may well have been England's last chance.

90 min: Butcher wafts his boot near Maradona's head near the centre circle, allowing Argentina to waste some time over a free-kick. Plenty of whistles from the crowd, who either want full time or for Argentina to get on with it in the hope of seeing some extra time.

FULL TIME: England 1–2 Argentina. Enrique holds the ball adroitly near the left hand corner. Eventually it's given back to Shilton, who pumps long. England win a throw down the right but when Waddle flings the ball back into play, the final whistle goes. That's it! It's a controversial win for sure, though in all honesty the better team won, regardless of how it came about. As a wonderful footnote that doubles as a callback to events after the quarter-final in 1966, Hodge, whose wild miskick set up Maradona's saucy opener, swaps shirts with the man himself. I wonder what Sir Alf Ramsey thinks about that?

The 1990 Finals

Argentina 0–1 Cameroon (1990, group stage)

Cameroon's victory over the defending champions is the most sensational start to any World Cup. André Kana-Biyik was sent off, his brother François Omam-Biyik scored; then, with a few minutes remaining, came one of the most famous fouls of all time.

89 min: MASSING SENT OFF! Cameroon are down to nine men after an astonishing triple-team assault on Claudio Caniggia. He broke upfield from a Cameroon corner, trying to run 80 yards straight for goal, but Cameroon had a few ideas to stop him, all variations on one central theme: maim him. OOF! Near the halfway line, Emmanuel Kundé runs across Caniggia, who had to hurdle his challenge. BLAM! Caniggia, at full speed, jumps over another tackle from Victor N'Dip, who pays no attention to the ball and, upon realizing Caniggia is away, tries unsuccessfully to boot him up the jacksie. He partially succeeds and the off-balance Caniggia staggers seven or eight steps towards the ball on the right wing, 35 yards from goal. When . . . KAPOW! Benjamin Massing ends the argument in a style that might be called decisive, flattening Caniggia with a preposterous tackle. He hared across at full pelt, every stride betraying confused determination and, in his head, imminent heroism. Caniggia pushed the ball further down the line; a split-second later Massing came right across his line, sending him up in the air like a stuntcar. Massing has already been booked and won't be of this match much longer. He loses a boot in the challenge, so ridiculous and overzealous was it. Burruchaga sidles across, has a sly look both ways to make sure none of the officials are watching and eases his studs on top of Massing's bare foot! Massing instinctively kicks out at Burruchaga and misses. He considers continuing the argument in the traditional style as Burruchaga flees the scene of the crime, realizes he hasn't yet been sent off and might just have got away with the original tackle and so starts to innocently replace his boot, hoping he can kid the referee. He can't. The referee checks Caniggia still has the use of both legs and then the red card comes out, although actually Massing has only been given a second yellow card. Still, it evens out in the end: Kana-Biyik's red card earlier in the match was ridiculous but Massing's tackle was worth two red cards. Actually, the referee could have shown two red cards there: N'Dip, who studded Maradona just below the neck in the first half, deserved a second yellow for his tackle. After that assault, the word Massing should be used as a verb to describe inept violations of opposing players all over the world of football.

West Germany 2–1 Holland (1990, last 16)

West Germany v Holland needs no introduction as a football rivalry but there was a particular edge in 1990. Holland had beaten West Germany in the semi-finals of Euro 88 – in West Germany – and this World Cup meeting was scheduled for Milan. AC Milan had the three Dutchmen, Internazionale the three West Germans. It was a home derby – in a World Cup knockout match. West Germany won emphatically with Jürgen Klinsmann, giving the performance of his career, on his own up front. The reason he was alone was because of early cards for Frank Rijkaard and Rudi Völler.

22 min: RIJKAARD AND VOLLER ARE SENT OFF!
Völler moves smoothly down the left and is scythed down by Rijkaard. That's a poor tackle and a clear yellow card. The referee shows the card to Rijkaard, who sniggers as if to say: 'Oops, naughty me.' As the pair make towards the area for the free-kick, Völler starts feeling his perm. 'Did he

spit at Völler as he ran past?' asks BBC commentator Tony Gubba. 'Was that my imagination? Let's hope so.' We know Germany and Holland hate each other, but they don't hate each other that much. Now Völler and Rikjaard are mouthing off at each other, with Rijkaard making a mouth signal with his hands and then waving jazz hands at Völler. He couldn't care less! Völler goes to complain to the referee and now he has been booked! It's hard to know why. He's still showing his hair to the referee. Eventually the free-kick is taken by Brehme. He curls it towards the far post where Berry van Aerle, under challenge from Völler, loops a header back towards Hans van Breukelen. Völler challenges for the ball with van Breukelen, with both men sort of clicking heels as they jump out the way of each other. Then van Breukelen and Rijkaard gang up on Völler while he's on the floor! Rijkaard tries to pull him by the ear, so Völler springs to his feet to continue the argument. Klinsmann gets in between them, and Völler stumbles and falls over. Then, just as a loud bang goes off round the ground, the referee whips out the red card for both Völler and Rijkaard! Völler bursts out laughing at possibly the most ridiculous red card in football history. Rijkaard runs past and nonchalantly spits in his hair, like a jogger aiming for a lamppost! Völler does a wide-eyed, wild-eyed double-take, probably trying to process the fact that, in the space of 60 seconds, he has been spat at twice, kicked up in the air and given two yellow cards! He must feel like he's Edward Woodward in *The Wicker Man*, the entire world conspiring against him. In a perverse way, Rijkaard was almost hard done by: the referee did not see him spit the first time and the second came after the red card. So what was he sent off for? The referee seemed to get bored of the pantomime. Mind you, by then Rijkaard's noggin had completely gone. Replays show that, while Klinsmann was helping Völler to his feet – this was before the red cards, remember – Rikjaard was horking furiously, like a schoolboy, trying to summon up every last speck of phlegm from the deepest recesses of his sinuses, with a view to sharing it with Völler. It's disgusting and highly unpleasant but there's also something highly amusing about it. Rijkaard had totally lost it. A World Cup knockout game against his fiercest rival, one of the biggest games of his life and all he cared about was pettiness and greenies. That is one of the most spectacular examples of plot-loss in the history of football and, in Völler's case, one of the most staggering injustices.

Republic of Ireland 0–0 Romania (5–4 pens; 1990, last 16)

Ireland's first ever World Cup campaign was imbued with a strange kind of glory: they didn't win a game and scored only two goals in five matches, yet they charmed Italy and reached the quarter-finals before losing 1–0 to the hosts.

O'LEARY SCORES AND IRELAND ARE INTO THE WORLD CUP QUARTER-FINALS! The substitute David O'Leary walks forward from the centre spot. Has he ever taken a penalty in his life? Surely you would want Niall Quinn to take one rather than O'Leary? Anyway, here he comes. He places the ball once, then places it again, taking an age, the collective pulse rate rising exponentially. Finally, he retreats a few steps, strolls forward and scores! Silviu Lung went the wrong way and O'Leary passed it high into the right side of the net. 'It defies belief!' says Alan Parry on ITV. O'Leary goes down on all fours for a second, trying to take it all in, then assumes a messianic pose before being buried under an avalanche of team-mates and backroom staff. The real messiah, Jack Charlton, walks calmly on to the pitch – which might as well be made of water – before shaking hands with some of the Romanian players.

England v Cameroon

Quarter-final, Stadio San Paolo, Naples, Italy,
Sunday, 1 July 1990

Once more unto the altar of pain, dear friends, once more.
England's World Cup so far has been a kind of exquisite torture:
'No Football Please, We're English', that infamous headline
after the draw with Ireland; Bryan Robson's latest heartbreak;
the threat of lots before Mark Wright's winner against Egypt; the
threat of penalties before David Platt's feelgood swivel against
Belgium. But there is a general sense that things should be different tonight. As brilliant as Cameroon have been, this is one
of the easiest quarter-finals you could wish for in a World Cup.
England's biggest concern is finding goals: just three in four
games so far, only one of those from open play, and with Gary
Lineker's troublesome toe various shades of black and blue.
England should be thankful for their excellent defence: if you
combine the qualification for the World Cup and the four games
in Italy, they have conceded just one goal in 15 hours 10 minutes.
The bookmaker's odds of 6/1 against Cameroon feel a fraction
excessive, but England will surely go through here and win the
prize of certain defeat against the brilliant West Germans in
Turin on Wednesday.

**Not least because Cameroon have four players suspended, an
inevitable consequence of their, ahem, zesty approach:** André
Kana-Biyik, Jules Denis Onana, Victor N'Dip and Emile
M'Bouh are all unavailable. They have five more players who
are a yellow card away from missing the semi-final, including,
of course, Benjamin Massing. Cameroon have been one of the
joys of the tournament, some of their football unforgettably
exotic and exciting, but they have the worst disciplinary record
in the tournament. 'I hope they knock us down all afternoon,
particularly in the box,' said Bobby Robson of the 9 p.m. kick-
off. In short, Cameroon have 11 Stuart Pearces. That has made
theirs a slightly awkward fairytale but we shouldn't lose sight of
the good stuff – not least the astonishing story of Roger Milla,
this remarkable 38-year-old who was happily retired, living on

Réunion, before getting a call from the Cameroon president asking him to help out at the World Cup. A few weeks later, Milla has four goals to his name, all scored from the bench. Despite an injury scare, the man whom the *Daily Mirror* reckon is nicknamed 'The Witch Doctor of Woe' is fit to take his place as a substitute again.

England bring in David Platt, making only his second start at international level, for Steve McMahon. Cameroon make those four aforementioned changes, with Massing, Emmanuel Kundé, Thomas Libiih and Jean-Claude Pagal replacing the missing quartet.

Kick-off: 9 p.m. in Naples, 8 p.m. at home.

Referee: Edgardo Codesal (Mexico).

England: Peter Shilton, Paul Parker, Des Walker, Mark Wright, Terry Butcher, Stuart Pearce, Chris Waddle, David Platt, Paul Gascoigne, John Barnes, Gary Lineker.

Cameroon: Thomas N'Kono, Jean-Claude Pagal, Benjamin Massing, Emmanuel Kundé, Bertin Ebwellé, Cyrille Makanaky, Louis-Paul M'Fédé, Stephen Tataw, Thomas Libiih, Emmanuel Maboang, François Omam-Biyik.

Let's hope England start the game better than the usually immaculate Des Lynam began the BBC's coverage. After the continuity announcer apologized for the rescheduling of Agatha Christie's *The Mirror Crack'd* – now on BBC2 at 8.05 p.m., folks – it was over to Naples where Lynam, ordinarily so smooth, lost his way completely with his intro. 'Good evening, welcome to Naples on a hot and sultry night for England against Cameroon. The last semi-final place is at stake. And of course [looks down at notes] England now know who they'd have to meet at the next stage of this, er, [looks at notes again] of this match. England trying to go of course tonight, er, as far as they, nearl— Well, I'm so sorry I'm forgetting what I'm saying but they're endeavouring to go nearly as far as they did in 1966.' And then, his composure regained, he leads into a ludicrously uplifting three-minute montage of England's tournament thus far, soundtracked by the Stone Roses's 'Elephant Stone'. It includes Terry Butcher and Chris Waddle's infectiously naff dance after the Belgium game, Bobby Robson's jig of delight and, of course, umpteen clips of

Gazza, the boy who made us all fall in love with football again. And we're soon falling back in love with hapless old Des, too, who pulls a self-deprecating 'See Naples and dry' line out of the gagbag. What a star. And to think ITV have been making do this month with Elton Welsby, very much the Steve Bull to Lynam's Lineker.

There are few nerves in the tunnel. Both teams are smiling and joking with each other. Someone is singing. Everybody seems to be smiling apart from the captain Butcher, who, as if you needed telling, has his Business Face on. The BBC's Barry Davies sums it up best: 'Four years ago, when they played Argentina in the quarter-final, England hoped. This time, England expects.'

1 min: Cameroon kick-off from left to right. They are wearing their highly cool strip of green-and-white tops, blood red shorts and light yellow socks. England are in white.

3 min: An early example of England's new continental style: Chris Waddle hits a booming 80-yard long ball – sorry, long *pass* – towards Lineker, whose loses out to Kundé.

5 min: Pearce, on the touchline, is whistled up in the air by a truly appalling tackle from Pagal – almost identical, in fact, to the Pearce tackle against Yugoslavia that caused such a brouhaha last December.

6 min: There have been loads of long balls from both sides early on. It's like a less sophisticated version of Wimbledon v Aston Villa. A long punt from Tataw leads to *six* consecutive headers: England win that game-within-a-game 4–2. Somewhere in England, Charles Hughes is sporting a big grin.

11 min: A round-up of the incident and excitement thus far would run to a whopping zero words. Action, please!

13 min: Ah, thanks! The first chance goes to Cameroon, with Peter Shilton, aged 94, making a brilliant save from Omam-Biyik. Cameroon broke through midfield, with Makanaky finding M'Fédé on the right. He flipped an insouciant pass with the outside of the left foot towards the D, where Walker was left two against one. He challenged the first man, Pagal, who ingeniously hurdled the ball to allow it to reach Omam-Biyik on the edge of the area. Omam-Biyik took a fractionally heavy touch and then, with Shilton roaring towards him, absolutely welted the bouncing ball towards goal. It hit Shilton, who was out beyond the penalty spot by this stage, and bounced back to M'Fédé, 30 yards out. He took another swipe with the outside of his left foot, this time sending the ball spinning towards goal as Shilton, just back on his line, dived desperately to his right. It beat both him and the post before slapping into the advertising hoarding.

17 min: An entirely pathetic Stuart Pearce shot goes out for a throw-in. England might want to consider revising those aforementioned expectations because Cameroon are bossing this.

21 min: M'Fédé's mis-hit cross from the right dribbles towards Makanaky, who goes flying after a tackle from Butcher. There's no appeal for a penalty, although replays suggest Butcher didn't touch the ball. The more you see that, the more it looks a certain penalty.

26 min: GOAL! England 1–0 Cameroon (Platt). England take the lead with their first decent attack. After 26 minutes. It's David Platt again, continuing the greatest week of his life. It was a patient attack that quickened when Butcher played a good pass down the left for Pearce, who ran behind Libiih and whipped an excellent cross to the far post. Platt, arriving late and unmarked on the six-yard line, thumped a downward header through the legs of N'Kono and into the net. Platt's huge, cheesy, boyish smile is seen again. What a season/month/week he's had.

29 min: Massing 'Massings' Lineker near the halfway line, booting him right up in the air in a style that is generally described as 'unceremonious'. The referee plays the advantage but books Massing when the ball goes dead. If Cameroon reach the semi-finals, Massing will be suspended. If shinbones could breathe, those of the West German players would be panting with relief just now. Some of Cameroon's tackles have been on the dangerous side of roughhouse. At times they seem determined to win by foul means or fouler, and the persistent offending is one of the reasons England can't get going. The other – far more important – is that they are playing abysmally.

33 min: Gascoigne plays a neat one-two with Lineker before being crowded out. He has been England's most purposeful player so far.

37 min: How are England ahead? Cameroon have been much the better team and now Libiih has missed a great chance. After a patient move, the excellent M'Fédé pulled left to find space. Wright was drawn out to meet him, which left a big hole in the middle. M'Fédé curled over a fine cross towards the near post, where Libiih ran into the considerable space between Gascoigne and Walker only to head a great chance over the bar from 12 yards.

39 min: Libiih misses another chance! He made an excellent run off the back of Gascoigne to meet Maboang's golf chip over the top. Gascoigne ran into Wright and fell over. Libiih got to the ball before Wright on the edge of the area but his first touch was a minor disgrace: he clodhopped it straight through to Shilton and the chance was gone.

HALF TIME: England 1–0 Cameroon. Cameroon have been faster, stronger and more skilful than England. That aside it's an even contest – except on the scoreboard, where England lead.

Now the game really begins: Roger Milla is coming on for Cameroon, replacing Maboang. The official World Cup graphic is still showing his name as 'Miller'. What's in a name? A fair bit in this case. Roger Miller is an old country and western star who once sang 'Eng-er-land swings like a pendulum do'. Roger Milla is an ageless superhero hoping to disrupt Eng-er-land's rhythm like a pendulum don't. Like bobbies on bicycles, the changes are being made two by two, the rosy red cheeks of Peter Beardsley coming on for the sadly peripheral John Barnes.

46 min: England pick up where they didn't leave off: with the ball in their possession, as it's their turn to kick off.

51 min: Cameroon *have* picked up where they left off. A majestic touch from Milla, who chests N'Kono's half-volleyed goal-kick around his marker, Butcher, on the halfway line. He sparks an attack that ends with Pagal shooting well wide from long range.

54 min: Butcher makes a great block from Massing. Cameroon are battering England. They moved the ball smoothly through midfield to Milla, who dropped off the defence, turned and then played a simple through-ball down the side of the defence. It found Massing, of all people, who had sauntered inquisitively upfield in open play, and his first-time shot from the right of the box was blocked by the sliding Butcher.

56 min: The official television clock, beamed to hundreds of millions around the world, flashes up and tells us we are in the 127th minute of the match. What's the Italian for P45?

60 min: Gascoigne goes past Massing and lives to tell the tale. He gives it to Waddle, who gives it to Pearce on the left. He struggles past Makanaky and hits a low cross towards the near post. Platt gets there a fraction before the keeper N'Kono on the left side of the six-yard box and goes down, but the referee waves play on. N'Kono went feet first and although Platt was going nowhere, the keeper seemed to bring him down. The referee has given a goal-kick and seems to be suggesting that N'Kono kicked the ball on to Platt and out of play. That definitely didn't happen but Platt may have dived or slipped. Either way, this is nothing new: England, bizarrely, have not had a penalty for four years.

61 min: PENALTY TO CAMEROON! This is amazing. Forty-three seconds after Platt went down, Cameroon are given a penalty at the other end. Milla was inevitably involved. He dropped into the space, played the ball off to Omam-Biyik and then darted into the area. Omam-Biyik played a nice return pass down the side of the defence and Milla was sent tumbling by Gascoigne. That's a clear penalty and a thoroughly inept tackle from Gascoigne, who simply needed to track Milla's run.

61 min: GOAL! England 1–1 Cameroon (Kundé pen). Kundé scores an emphatic penalty, a booming sidefoot high into the right-hand side of the net. Shilton went the right way but it was just too high for him to reach.

62 min: Cameroon made a change straight after the goal, with Eugène Ekéké on for the excellent M'Fédé. This is Ekéké's first appearance in the tournament. It's quite a step up: he usually plays in the French second division for Valenciennes.

64 min: The way things are going England will be out of the World Cup in half an hour. Cameroon have just missed another chance. Omam-Biyik led a three-on-three break, running 40 yards to the edge of the area. Walker held him up well but Omam-Biyik laid it off to Makanaky, whose shot took a big deflection off Wright and looped over the bar.

65 min: GOAL! England 1–2 Cameroon (Ekéké). Cameroon have taken the lead! They are taking England apart and fully deserve this. It was made by the two substitutes, Ekéké and you-know-who. Ekéké sauntered infield from the left near the halfway line and played a sharp pass into Milla, who had again dropped off the centre-backs. Makanaky baulked Butcher, which allowed Milla to turn daintily, a movement that had everything but the heel-click, and run at the defence. Wright prepared to challenge Milla, who was two moves ahead and slipped a lazy, arrogant pass to the side to put Ekéké through on goal; and as Shilton came out Ekéké flipped it beautifully into the corner of the net. What a goal! Milla and Ekéké cavort across the turf in celebration; then Omam-Biyik leaps on top of both of them, his trouser arrangement precariously balanced on their necks for a couple of seconds before he falls off and inadvertently drags Ekéké to the floor. That sparks an impromptu bundle by the corner flag, with even the keeper N'Kono joining in. This is outrageous. They are without four players, they were massive underdogs, yet they are slaughtering England.

68 min: Cameroon have been sensational but England, you have to say, have been awful tonight. We will never be able to compete at this level unless we start playing with a sweeper syste— oh.

69 min: Pearce is booked for a frankly ridiculous hack at Makanaky. Milla walks up to Pearce and uses his hands to make the shape of a football, reminding Pearce of the essential purpose of this particular sport.

72 min: Trevor Steven is coming on for England – and it's the captain Terry Butcher who's coming off. That's a brave call from Bobby Robson for two reasons: he is taking off Butcher, who has been a kind of son to him during his managerial career, and it means the abandonment of the nation's beloved sweeper system and a return to the very occasionally unmaligned 4–4–2.

73 min: STUART PEARCE KEEPS ENGLAND IN THE WORLD CUP! That should have been it. Ekéké – where have Cameroon been hiding him – plays a good pass infield to Pagal, who helps it on first time towards Makanaky. He slips Walker's ill-judged attempt to win the ball 30 yards out and runs into the area. Shilton stays on his six-yard line as Makanaky shoots but Pearce hares all the way across the area from left-back to make a sensational block at the expense of a corner. It's taken short to

Milla, who almost dupes Gascoigne with a beautifully disguised flick over his own head. He is streets ahead of anyone else on the field.

76 min: WHAT A CHANCE FOR ENGLAND! David Platt should have made it 2–2. Gascoigne turned Pagal quite magnificently in the centre circle and threaded an immaculately weighted through ball to Platt 20 yards from goal, taking three defenders out of the game in the process. Platt's first touch was perfect, taking him into the area, but as N'Kono came out he dragged his left-footed shot just wide of the far post. A few seconds before that, Gascoigne had taken a corner from the left, with a banner draped behind him reading 'John 3:16'. That verse is all about eternal life; the Bible's own tribute to Milla?

77 min: Is there anything Milla doesn't do? He has just announced to the referee that the pressure of the ball is wrong. The referee agrees and it's going to be changed.

79 min: ANOTHER ESCAPE FOR ENGLAND! This is getting ridiculous. How are England still in the World Cup? Omam-Biyik started the move by using his indecent strength to ignore a tackle from Gascoigne just past the centre circle. His short square pass was slightly behind Milla, who improvised brilliantly to drag an ungainly return pass into the area, which came to Omam-Biyik when a shattered Pearce simply missed the ball. Omam-Biyik, facing towards the right wing while on the penalty spot, improvised with a brilliant backheel that was blocked yet again by the outrushing Shilton.

82 min: PENALTY TO ENGLAND!!! England have got a lifeline from the most improbable source – a penalty, their first in four years. Gascoigne's inswinging free-kick from the left was headed away by Massing, but Parker nipped in front of Milla to head it back towards the area. Wright, still forward, flicked it neatly towards Lineker, who had taken up a brilliant position just inside the box, and he went down under challenge from Massing and Kundé. Cameroon aren't happy with that at all. The referee, who looks like he has been practising his signals in front of a mirror for 20 years, stands dramatically on the spot and points both hands theatrically towards the goal. Then he jogs purposefully to the left side of the area and puts both hands behind his back. What a clown! Far more important is that England have a penalty. Replays aren't conclusive either way as to whether it was the right decision. Massing came in from the side with a high foot and Kundé from behind. If anyone caught him it was Massing, grazing the leg as Lineker moved the ball towards goal. On balance you would say it's a penalty although there's a suspicion that Lineker started to go down in anticipation of being hit, an understandable flinch given Cameroon's record in this tournament.

84 min: GOAL! England 2–2 Cameroon (Lineker pen). Lineker scores! He had to wait over a minute after the award of the penalty and looked nervous as hell, but he sidefooted it calmly to the right as N'Kono went the other way. England are still in the World Cup! Butcher appears on the touchline, whirling his hands around, a gesture which loosely translates as: if you come into the dressing-room having lost this game I'm going to put the head on every single one of you.

87 min: Makanaky nutmegs Pearce on the left of the box before the covering Steven concedes a corner with a vital tackle. Before it is taken there is treatment for Wright, who has blood pouring from his left eye after a clash of heads with Milla. That looks pretty nasty. He will have to go off for the time being, at least, and that's a big problem as England have used both subs. For now Parker moves to centre-back and Steven to right-back in a 4–3–2 formation.

88 min: Shilton makes a fine save from Omam-Biyik! Milla, dropping off the defence yet again, picked up the ball in space and ran to the edge of the area before teeing up Omam-Biyik. He swept a first-time left-footer from 20 yards towards the near post and Shilton plunged to his right to make a fine save. It wasn't right in the corner, but still, there are two minutes to go in a bloody World Cup quarter-final so that goes down as an excellent stop.

90+1 min: Wright is coming back on. He might not even be able to see out of his left eye, so heavily is the bandaging, and he is clearly only back on because England have no substitutes left.

FULL TIME: England 2–2 Cameroon. This weirdly self-important little referee signals theatrically for the end of 90 minutes. England have been excruciatingly outplayed by a brilliant Cameroon side, yet they are still in the World Cup. There is a long break before the start of extra time, with the captains tossing for choice of ends. It's such a long break that it almost feels like a new game is about to start. England will hope it is a whole new ball game. 'What a fright we've had, eh?' says Bobby Charlton on BBC1 with a mixture of admiration, relief and confusion.

91 min: Cameroon kick off from left to right.

92 min: Mark Wright is playing on the right of midfield, with Steven at right-back and Parker in the centre. That must be because he can't risk opening up the wound with regular headers, so England are effectively down to ten-and-a-half men. The sweeper is playing wide right: it's Total Football! (Okay, it's Total Desperation.)

94 min: Shilton makes another vital save! Makanaky turned Pearce one way and then the other on the right before swinging over a dangerous low cross towards the six-yard line. The stretching Steven did magnificently to take the ball off the head of Ekéké, who had flown into a diving header, but he could only kick it straight up in the air. It seemed to hang in the air for ages – and so did Omam-Biyik, who soared towards the ball from well outside the box with an almost comic majesty. He couldn't quite get over the top of Walker for a clean header and instead shouldered the ball towards goal, where Shilton saved. That was the definition of a towering jump: Omam-Biyik hit Walker with such force (legitimately so) that, as Shilton was saving the ball, Walker's momentum had him stumbling towards the goal before falling over the line in the comedy style. England are not just living dangerously; they're on the bloody lam.

96 min: Omam-Biyik accidentally lets the ball run past his body but saunters back towards the half line to collect it, brushing Beardsley aside with ease. Then he's off again, past first Platt and then Gascoigne before welting a sizzling left-footed drive just over the bar from 25 yards. He is a monster of a player.

97 min: Yet another chance for Cameroon! Milla sucks Walker in on the halfway line and finds Omam-Biyik, and from that moment England's besieged defence are always playing catch-up. Omam-Biyik plays it wide right to Makanaky, whose first cross is half cleared by Parker. It loops towards the right touchline, where Makanaky heads it towards the near post. Shilton lunges towards it but Omam-Biyik gets there first, acrobatically flicking it right across the face of goal. Luckily for England it goes not to a forward but to Steven, who desperately kicks it clear from almost under the crossbar. He is having a vital game but, dear God, England are all over the place. Moments later Milla lobs a bouncing ball over his own head, away from Parker and Gascoigne, before smashing it over the bar from a tight angle.

98 min: It gets worse: now Des Walker is limping. If England were a horse . . .

102 min: Milla, back to goal, plays a reverse pass into Tataw in the D, spins behind Walker to meet the instant return and is only denied a clear shot on goal by the presence of the covering Pearce. Where has Milla been since 1982? He is *magnificent*.

104 min: PENALTY TO ENGLAND! It's the third penalty of the match, and England – battered, bruised and hopelessly outplayed – have a chance to take the lead! Gascoigne picked up the ball deep inside his own half, ran forward to the centre circle and then threaded a wonderful long through-pass to Lineker, sidefooted with real pace. Kundé tried to intercept and failed, allowing Lineker to take it in his stride with a flick of the ankle and run through on goal. 'And here's Linekerrrrrrrrrrrrrrrrrrrrrrr,' purred the marvellous Barry Davies, rolling the name around his tongue almost as long as he held Claudio Caniggia's when he scored against Brazil. Lineker got inside the area, tried to go round N'Kono and went down under a combined challenge from N'Kono and Massing, coming in from the back. That looks a definite penalty.

105 min: GOAL! England 3–2 Cameroon (Lineker pen). Lineker scores again! There was a long wait, almost two minutes, with Lineker receiving treatment and N'Kono booked for something or other (he'll be out of the semi if Cameroon get there). Then Lineker eventually strode up and slammed his penalty straight down the middle. Is it possible to love Gary Lineker any more?

EXTRA TIME, HALF TIME: England 3–2 Cameroon. This bizarre little referee – who has had an excellent game but can't stop the theatrical gestures – waves his hands all over the place to signal the end of the first period. Some England fans in the stadium are doing the conga.

106 min: England kick off the second period of extra time

107 min: Lineker misses a great chance of a hat-trick! He started the move by dummying Waddle's pass near the halfway line, allowing it to reach Gascoigne. He surged thrillingly past Massing and Pagal, beat Kundé with beautiful touch and balance, and then stabbed it square to Lineker, who had followed up the play and reached the edge of the area. Lineker took it in his stride and then drove a fraction wide of the near post from 15 yards with N'Kono beaten. It pinged off the pole behind the goal. Gascoigne has been England's best player, admittedly in the face of seriously flaccid competition.

111 min: Lineker receives a pass from Steven with his back to goal, is forced back into his own half and eventually passes it back to Shilton from 50 yards.

112 min: This has probably crossed your mind too: *BUT HOW THE HELL ARE ENGLAND WINNING THIS GAME?*

113 min: Pagal's long-range shot is comfortably held by the sprawling Shilton. For the first time in this heroic performance, Cameroon are starting to look a little resigned to their fate.

114 min: Wright, on the right wing, is caught late by the sliding Ebwellé and the two have a quick wrestle on the floor before realizing they are grown men.

117 min: Milla drops off the defence to receive possession yet again, turns and hits a fierce shot from 20 yards that is blocked by Steven at the expense of a corner. The corner comes to nothing. England are so nearly there.

119 min: Milla is booked, either for handball or more probably for dissent. He is in a proper funk now as the dream finally dies. He's shouting right in the referee's face. His noggin has gone.

120+1 min: England almost add a fourth in added time! Steven, who has been outstanding since coming on and must be a serious contender for the semi-final, beats a couple of defenders down the right and puts over an excellent bouncing cross. Platt misses his attempted flick header at the near post, and Lineker at the far post just runs ahead of the ball. Platt's was the big chance.

EXTRA TIME, FULL TIME: England 3–2 Cameroon. And that's that! England reach only the second World Cup semi-final in their history! Bobby Robson and Paul Gascoigne have a big daft hug on the touchline. Africa, meanwhile, are still awaiting their first semi-finalist. They've never come closer than this, they've never passed up a better chance than this and they've never worried one of the big names in world football on the biggest stage quite like this. A sickener. Cameroon are doing a lap of honour around the ground and all of Africa should be celebrating the breaking of new ground, but the prize has slipped their grasp. They lived by the clog and eventually they died by it, conceding two penalties that cost them. England, meanwhile, have never been luckier than this. 'I've had 17 heart attacks, I feel 92, but I'm absolutely elated,' says Bobby Robson. 'I'm so pleased for everybody. I wish I was home, because they tell me everybody's dancing in the streets.' They might not be dancing on Wednesday. England will not get away with this sort of carry-on against the Germans. It could be carnage. Gulp.

England v West Germany

Semi-final, Stadio delle Alpi, Turin, Italy,
Wednesday, 4 July 1990

Are you sitting uncomfortably? Then we'll begin. This is England's biggest match for 24 years, since the day some people were on the pitch thinking it was all over. You might want to lie down as you contemplate this, but when England step on to the field to face West Germany tonight, *they will be 90 minutes away from a World Cup final.*

In real terms, they are arguably already in one. 'If we can win tonight, we're in the final, with a great chance of beating Argentina,' says Bobby Robson. 'Great chance. This is the big one. Germany's the big one.' Although Diego Maradona's side played well to lubricate Italian eyes last night, they have otherwise been poor in this tournament and will be without four suspended players for the final, including the superb but very stupid basketball star Claudio Caniggia.

That said, England haven't exactly been pulling up trees all over Italy this last month. They were incredibly lucky to beat Cameroon in the quarter-final and only really excelled in the 0–0 draw against Holland. West Germany, by contrast, have been immense: they are the modern power team *par excellence.* Having already wiped the floor with two very good European sides in Yugoslavia and Holland, and eased past another in Czechoslovakia, they must be strong favourites tonight. England will not so much have to raise their game as redefine it.

That's the logical viewpoint, anyway. But balls to logic. As has been mentioned before, England are in a World Cup semi-final!!!

Team news: Bobby Robson said that '4–4–2 saved us' against Cameroon on Sunday but while that formation will always be his beloved wife, he was always likely to return to his sexy foreign bit on the side against such formidable opposition. That means the extra defensive cover of a sweeper system and just one change from the side that started against Cameroon: Peter Beardsley for the injured John Barnes. Des Walker and Mark Wright have been passed fit, although Wright has six stitches above his left eye. England's five substitutes include Trevor Steven, so impressive when he came on against Cameroon, and Steve Bull of the Second Division.

West Germany bring in two impish schemers, Thomas Hässler and Olaf Thon, for Pierre Littbarski and Uwe Bein. Rudi Völler also returns, having served his one-match suspension for being used as a hankie by Frank Rijkaard; Karl-Heinz Riedle drops to the bench.

Kick-off: 7 p.m. English time, 8 p.m. in Turin.

Referee: José Roberto Wright (Brazil).

England: Peter Shilton, Paul Parker, Terry Butcher, Mark Wright, Des Walker, Stuart Pearce, Chris Waddle, Paul Gascoigne, David Platt, Gary Lineker, Peter Beardsley.

West Germany: Bodo Illgner, Guido Buchwald, Klaus Augenthaler, Jürgen Kohler, Thomas Berthold, Thomas Hässler, Lothar Matthäus, Olaf Thon, Andreas Brehme, Jürgen Klinsmann, Rudi Völler.

Build-up: The BBC – don't say you're watching it on ITV, you'll have missed Pavarotti for a start – begin their coverage with an obvious but neat montage contrasting the classes of 1966 and 1990. The highlight is Bobby Robson shaking his head back and forth in utter confusion, like a man contemplating the promise of a night of unbridled lust with Cindy Crawford, as he considers the possibility of winning the World Cup: 'Well . . . I've been in the game now 40 years . . . it would be lovely to . . . To win the . . . the biggest prize the game had to offer, the world championship.' What a lovely man he is.

Back in the studio, homoerotic comedy duo Terry Venables and Jimmy Hill shake hands before saying a word. Let's give it two minutes before they disagree over something. They make for great TV. Alongside them, Bryan Robson exudes the impotent frustration of a man looking in on his own party. Hill says he is 'frightened out of my life'. He's not the only one.

The players are in the tunnel. Wright has a big plaster on his left eye; it's a right mess, like someone applied it while blindfolded and high on Hofmeister. Waddle has chopped off his mullet (insert your own Samson joke here). Gascoigne gives Beardsley a kiss on the right cheek. This is just another game in the park to him, isn't it? He has spent the last month taking the piss out of everyone, from Ronald Koeman to Mark Goodier on *Top of the Pops*, so why should this faze him? West Germany look calm, businesslike and other German clichés. This really *is* just another game for them, their eighth semi-final out of nine attempts in the last 20 years. You probably don't need me to tell you how many England have been in during that time. Clue: it's less than one.

Anthemwatch: The England fans boo the West German anthem. For heaven's *sake*, you bastards. Gascoigne, who has had some absurd criticism from humourless clowns for sticking his tongue out during the anthem, settles for just easing the tip out and smiling gently.

1 min: England kick off from right to left. They are in white; West Germany are in their funky epilepsy-inducing green away kit.

2 min: WHAT A START FROM ENGLAND! England come storming out of the traps and Lineker wins a corner on the right inside 15 seconds. It's taken by Beardsley and half-cleared to the edge of the box, where Gascoigne hooks the bouncing ball back whence it came with his left foot. It's a beautiful effort and, although it's swerving just wide of the near post, Illgner leaps to his left to palm it behind. That leads to a second corner, which leads to a third. That leads to nothing but England almost get in again thirty seconds later when Beardsley, played onside by Buchwald, breaks into the box from the left. He has Lineker and Waddle in support but tries to take on Buchwald, who dispossesses him well. Rousing stuff from England.

3 min: Butcher, rather than Wright, is playing as the spare man at the back. Perhaps they don't trust his legs in a one-on-one against these two quick West German forwards. Walker is taking Völler and Wright is on Klinsmann.

5 min: Difficult to know how to break this to you, but England have started brilliantly. Lineker lays a loose ball off to Gascoigne, who shimmies smartly inside Augenthaler on the edge of the box before his thumping left-footed shot is well blocked by Kohler.

10 min: Another decent opening for England. Beardsley breaks the offside trap on the right wing but, with only Lineker in support, he shanks his cross wide of the near post.

11 min: 'England are playing some tidy football,' exclaims the BBC's John Motson, shocked by a display of incontrovertible Anglo-competence.

12 min: West Germany have their first half-chance. Hässler, a mischievous little player, dupes Butcher on the edge of the box before hitting a left-footed shot that spins off Pearce and not too far wide of the far post.

15 min: Gazza cockily Cruyff-turns away from Klinsmann on the halfway line. He has been very confident and influential so far, more so than Matthäus. This really is his stage.

17 min: A delightful move from England. Platt, with six West German defenders surrounding him, waits and waits and then plays a smart pass in behind the defence for the onrushing Pearce. He hits a first-time cross towards Lineker at the near post and Kohler slides in desperately to concede a corner. A great tackle, and lovely stuff from England.

19 min: Lineker's movement and link play have been really smart. He shifts the ball away from Kohler on the left and hammers over a deep cross towards Parker of all people, and he heads wide under pressure. The BBC co-commentator Trevor Brooking says this is 'easily England's best start' of the tournament.

24 min: Another good effort from Gascoigne. Waddle's free-kick from the right is headed clear by Klinsmann; it comes to Gascoigne, who controls the ball on his chest 22 yards from goal and then lashes the bouncing ball towards goal. It was a sweet strike but straight at Illgner, who held on.

27 min: Terry Butcher does a backheel! We've seen everything now. Butcher, in the centre circle, backheels the ball to Gascoigne and then swans off back to his position with the studied indifference of a man who has just saved the world but, honestly, it's no biggie.

28 min: Platt and Gascoigne play a classy one-two on the halfway line, and Platt keeps running into the space down the left wing, all the way into the area before trying and failing to take on Augenthaler. He should have looked for Waddle or Lineker but that was a rare bit of immaturity from a player who has been one of the surprise joys of this tournament.

30 min: That was a bit of a scare for England. Völler ran down the right-hand side of the box on to an angled pass from the sweeper Augenthaler. Shilton came to meet him unnecessarily and Völler moved away from him before Gascoigne came round to block his cross. That was an important interception because Shilton was out of the game.

34 min: CHRIS WADDLE HITS THE BAR FROM 45 YARDS! It wouldn't have counted, as the referee had blown for a foul by Platt a split-second earlier, but that was an incredible effort. The ball broke loose off Augenthaler and Waddle lofted it first time towards goal, a golf shot really, and Illgner had to jump backwards to tip it on to the bar. That was reminiscent of Pelé in 1970 but this time it was a bloody *Englishman* doing it.

39 min: Karl-Heinz Riedle replaces Völler, who is being helped down the touchline. He must be doubtful for Sunday's final when, sorry, *if* West Germany get there. What a tournament he has had: sent off for being flobbed on in the second round, suspended for the quarter-final, now injured in the semi.

41 min: West Germany's best chance yet. They win a free-kick 25 yards out, left of centre, and while everyone is expecting a shot Brehme instead lays it square to Augenthaler. He cuts across a very good, swooshing right-footed strike and Shilton has to move smartly to his right to tip it over two-handed, falling off his feet in the process.

42 min: GET BEHIND THE SOFA. IT'S HAPPENING! West Germany are suddenly all over England, having their best spell of the game by a mile. A sustained spell of high-tempo possession in the England half ends with Buchwald failing to win a free-kick on the edge of the area. England are hanging on and could really do with half time.

HALF TIME: England 0–0 West Germany. After a few hairy minutes, England get the breather they need and deserve for a superb first-half performance: controlled, mature and rousing. There weren't any clear-cut chances for either side but it's been a very good game.

Half-time chit-chat. The BBC boys are full of praise for Walker, with Terry Venables describing him as 'unbeatable'. That's what they sing. Jimmy Hill, channelling William Morris, says it's 'a pleasure to see an England team give such a display in the arts and crafts of the game'.

46 min: West Germany kick off from right to left.

47 min: Matthäus plays a dangerous one-two with Riedle before breaking into the box but four England defenders manage to crowd him out.

48 min: West Germany have started this half as they finished the first and are having a lot of the ball.

53 min: England win a corner – and almost concede a goal within 20 seconds. After Pearce miscontrolled the ball 35 yards from goal, West Germany broke in a flash. Walker tackled Klinsmann but the ball came to Thon, who ran 25 yards into the box before shifting the ball to the left of the last man Parker and hitting a shot that Shilton had to beat away to his left.

54 min: This game is extremely open at the moment – too open – and Wright makes a really important block from Riedle on the edge of the box.

56 min: Lineker is flattened by Kohler, who then picks him up and pats his sweaty head. There's been a lot of that in a match that has been played in a really good spirit.

58 min: A lucky escape for England. Matthäus goes on a trade-mark robotic charge down the left wing, away from Waddle, Gascoigne and Walker, but when he gets into the box he slips over just as he is about to pick out a cross. 'England are under siege now,' says John Motson.

59 min: GOAL! England 0–1 West Germany (Brehme). It had been coming but England are desperately unlucky with the manner of this goal. Pearce fouled Hässler 22 yards from goal, to the right of centre. The free-kick was touched off to Brehme, whose shot took a vicious deflection off Parker before looping high in the air and agonizingly over the stranded Shilton, who couldn't back-pedal quickly enough and ended up helping it into the net as he fell backwards.

61 min: Is Shilton at fault for the goal? Difficult to know. His feet didn't move quite as quickly as they might but it was a horrible and unexpected deflection.

62 min: Matthäus moves away from Butcher far too easily and charges to within 25 yards of Shilton before shooting across goal and well wide. England just need to keep their nerve and make sure they don't go two down because if they do it's over.

63 min: WHAT A CHANCE FOR ENGLAND! That was desperately close to an equalizer. After he was fouled on the left, Gascoigne swung in a superb free-kick and Pearce, getting in front of Riedle at the near post, flicked a backheader across goal and just wide of the far post with Illgner motionless.

65 min: You have to admire the spirit England have shown since going behind. No sulking or feeling sorry for themselves after such an unfortunate goal; just a quiet determination to get an equalizer. Gascoigne swerves away from Augenthaler on the edge of the area and is baulked. He is so good at taking defenders out of the game in the middle of the pitch, a rare quality indeed among midfield players. The free-kick hits the wall and moments later Parker clatters Buchwald, bringing the first yellow card of the game.

67 min: West Germany make their second substitution: Stefan Reuter replaces Hässler, who hasn't recovered from the tackle from Pearce that led to Brehme's goal. Reuter is normally a right wing-back but he has gone straight into midfield.

69 min: HOW IS THAT NOT A PENALTY? England are desperately unlucky here. Waddle, on the left of the box, draws the tackle from Augenthaler with a swing of the hips and then shifts the ball to his left just before Augenthaler takes him down. That is a clear penalty but the referee waves play on. In his defence, nobody appealed – Waddle just got straight up with that hangdog gait – and on first viewing it was hard to be certain it was a penalty. But when you see the replays there is no doubt whatsoever.

71 min: Pearce goes on a barnstorming, leggy surge from the halfway line, all the way to the edge of the box where he falls over after a double challenge from Berthold and Augenthaler. It looked like Berthold got something on the ball but the referee gives the free-kick, 20 yards from goal. This is a great opportunity for Gascoigne – but in fact Waddle lays it square to Beardsley, whose shot is blocked desperately by Matthäus. Before the kick was taken, Trevor Steven came on to replace Butcher.

75 min: The game is meandering a bit. England are doing okay but West Germany look reasonably comfortable.

79 min: The tireless Parker runs Brehme down the right to win a corner. It's tossed deep by Beardsley and Wright's looping header is comfortably saved by Illgner. Bobby Robson is about to roll the dice for the last time: Steve Bull is coming on, presumably for Beardsley.

81 min: GOAL! England 1–1 West Germany (Lineker). England have saved themselves in the last ten minutes again! Parker swung over a long cross towards Lineker from near the halfway line on the right. It hit the thigh of Kohler, who was running towards his own goal, and as it bounced up Lineker kneed it away from Augenthaler and Berthold before cracking an excellent left-footed shot across goal and into the far corner. The Germans had too many cooks in the box but it was clinical finishing. On the bench Bobby Robson reclines in his seat while wearing the most beautiful smile: warm, benign and extremely proud.

83 min: That's Lineker's tenth World Cup goal: four this year and six in 1986. What a gem. He started this tournament slowly but has looked really sharp tonight and he took that beautifully. It was a more difficult chance than it looked.

84 min: Gascoigne nails a glorious 60-yard crossfield pass to Lineker, who is just about to put the ball back in the box when Platt is penalized for some off-the-ball tomfoolery.

85 min: Beardsley is still on, the plan to introduce Bull having been aborted after the goal.

87 min: A little bit of West German pressure, with an extended series of throw-ins on the right wing, but England defend them comfortably enough. Walker and Wright have been outstanding.

89 min: England are passing the ball around at the back and both sides look happy to take extra time now. That's all well and good for them but some of us planned to watch *M*A*S*H* on BBC2 at nine.

FULL TIME: England 1–1 West Germany. How's your ticker? For the third game in a row, England are going to extra time – the first time that has ever happened in any World Cup. It's the least they deserve after a fine, sophisticated performance, their best of the tournament by a mile. Bobby Robson is wandering round rallying the troops and giving tactical instructions to Parker; Waddle and Bull are having a laugh about something. England look pretty relaxed. 'We've got another half-hour and we might have penalties,' says Des Lynam. 'Are you ready for this?'

91 min: West Germany kick off from left to right. England haven't used their final substitution.

92 min: A bit of danger for England as West Germany break two on two. Klinsmann runs into the box but is superbly tackled by Walker. He really is imperious.

95 min: GREAT SAVE FROM SHILTON! Shilton has had scarcely anything to do all night but now produces a superb save from Klinsmann. West Germany moved the ball slowly, all the way across the field from right to left, with Thon eventually shifting it down the line to Brehme. He curled over a wonderful first-time cross and Klinsmann, towering above Walker on the six-yard line, thumped a downward header towards goal. Shilton plunged to his right to make a superb reaction stop with both hands. It wasn't right in the corner, and someone as good in the air as Klinsmann might feel he should have done better, but it was a brilliant save. That mistake against Uruguay just before the tournament seems a long, long time ago.

96 min: KLINSMANN MISSES ANOTHER CHANCE! West Germany could easily be ahead. Wright came deep with Klinsmann to try to win possession and, as he followed the ball, Klinsmann kept running into the space behind. The ball came to the sweeper Augenthaler, who flipped an inviting angled pass over the top. Klinsmann was free, 12 yards from goal and in line with the left-hand post, but he screwed his left-footed volley across goal and just wide. It was a harder chance than it looked because the pass was coming almost over his shoulder and there was no pace on the ball, but again a player of his class should surely have done better.

97 min: England are rocking. Beardsley gives the ball away cheaply on the halfway line and, seconds later, Walker just gets in front of Riedle at the near post to put Brehme's cross out for a corner.

99 min: HOLD ON . . . THERE COULD BE TROUBLE HERE . . . Gascoigne overruns the ball in midfield and then lunges with typically naive enthusiasm at Berthold. It's a clear foul but does not merit Berthold's reaction – 77 rollovers – or that of the rest of the German camp, who are all at the referee, both on the field and from the bench. Gascoigne, realizing the implications, put both hands up in apology like a kid who has used that whoopee cushion on his teacher once too often and will never do it again I promise but please don't punish me this time. He immediately goes to apologize to Berthold. It looks like he's got away with it, for ten seconds at least, but then, with Hitchcockian suddenness, out comes the card . . .

100 min: . . . AND GAZZA MISSES THE FINAL. England have to get there first, of course, but if they do, Gascoigne will not feature against Argentina on Sunday. This is horrible. He is on the cusp of tears and the proud English tradition of the stiff upper lip is taking a serious hit: Gazza's is wobbling all over the place. Lineker says something to Gascoigne and then pulls his Grave Face before saying 'Have a word with him' to the bench. That is just too cruel. It does rather seem that the West Germans got him booked, which is a desperate shame because this game has otherwise been played in an incredibly good spirit. Poor old Gazza. He has been the star of England's tournament and now his whole world has collapsed. It's not just Gazza, either; English football has just had its heart broken into a million tiny pieces.

101 min: Thon, 25 yards out, swooshes a very good shot not too far wide of the near post. West Germany have been much the better side in this half.

103 min: After that initial wobble, Gascoigne has managed to refocus and is doing some diligent defensive work.

105 min: WADDLE HITS THE POST! England come within an inch of going ahead with the last kick of the half. When Steven's cross from the left was partially cleared, the same man leapt above Berthold to head it back towards the area. It came to Waddle, 12 yards out on the left side of the box, and he smacked a brilliant first-time shot across Illgner and flush off the inside of the far post. That's desperately unlucky – not least because Platt was within a whisker of putting the rebound in, but it flew off the post so quickly that he couldn't react in time.

EXTRA TIME, HALF TIME: England 1–1 West Germany. Who needs a drink?

106 min: England kick off the second period of extra time. Fifteen minutes without a goal and England will be involved in their first-ever penalty shoot-out. West Germany have had three: they lost in the final of Euro 76 but won matches at the World Cup in 1982 and 1986.

107 min: England have switched their wingers so that they are playing on the 'wrong' side: Steven on the left and Waddle on the right. Steven plays a beautiful pass on the turn down the left but Pearce is fractionally offside.

109 min: Riedle nutmegs Walker down the left and toe-bungs a dangerous cross towards Klinsmann. Gascoigne, running towards his own goal at the near post, just manages to divert the ball away from Klinsmann.

110 min: Gascoigne shields the ball down the right wing and Brehme simply boots him up in the air from behind. That's an appalling tackle – much worse than Gascoigne's on Berthold – and he is rightly booked. Brehme and Gascoigne shake hands and pat each other on the head. There's been a huge amount of goodwill in this game. You have to admire Gascoigne's response to that yellow card. If anything it's given him a second wind.

111 min: PLATT HAS A GOAL DISALLOWED! From the resulting free-kick, swung in by Waddle, Platt flicked a smart header past Illgner but he had been flagged offside a split-second earlier. There are no complaints but that was seriously tight. The Germans pushed up but Berthold stayed a bit deeper and was so close to playing Platt onside. He was level at worst, as was Gascoigne further across the line. Platt was fractionally onside and Gascoigne fractionally off. So it's the right decision but it was painfully close.

113 min: It's credit to Platt and Gascoigne in particular that Matthäus has been so quiet as an attacking force tonight. He has had his hands full defensively.

114 min: GOOD SAVE FROM SHILTON! Thon has far too much space to take possession on the edge of the D and shape a lovely right-footed curler towards the far post. Shilton springs a long way to his left to catch the ball – a slightly showy save but still a good one.

115 min: England are starting to look tired now. Brehme, a man with two right feet, zips infield from the left and plays a one-two with Riedle before spanking a vicious right-footed shot just over the bar from 20 yards. Shilton had it covered but it came right off the sweet spot.

116 min: John Motson says that Bobby Robson told him this afternoon that the five penalty takers, if needed, would be Lineker, Beardsley, Gascoigne, Pearce and Platt. We almost didn't need them because Illgner fumbled Steven's cross from the left awkwardly over his own bar for a corner.

117 min: The corner comes to nothing and Germany break dangerously. Augenthaler drills a superb 40-yard pass to Klinsmann, who heads it beyond the last man Walker and, for a moment, looks like he has him beaten for pace. Don't be silly. Walker catches him up on the right of the box, stays on his feet and makes a superb interception. He has been simply majestic.

118 min: NOW BUCHWALD HITS THE POST! Can you take any more of this? Germany were so close to winning the match there. Riedle broke forward from the halfway line and played the ball to the right of the box for Matthäus, who came inside and had his left-footed shot blocked by Pearce. It broke to Buchwald – the bloody centre-back – who controlled it calmly 20 yards from goal and then, using Steven as a screen, placed a lovely curler to the left of Shilton that bounced up on to the outside of the post! Unbelievable stuff.

EXTRA TIME, FULL TIME: England 1–1 West Germany. With England hanging on for dear life, the referee blows five seconds early. So England are into virgin territory: a penalty shoot-out. Both sets of players embrace warmly. This has been a cracking game and there's a general recognition that neither side deserves to lose. The mutual respect is quite moving.

Before Sunday's game against Cameroon, England had not had a penalty for four years. Now they will have taken at least seven in four days. There are 17 years between the goalkeepers: Peter Shilton, 40, and Bodo Illgner, 23. Illgner will be first in action because England are going to kick first. It'll be Lineker, in fact.

LINEKER SCORES! England 1–0 West Germany. Did you expect anything else? Lineker drills it confidently into the left side of the net as Illgner dives the other way.

BREHME SCORES! England 1–1 West Germany. An even better penalty, placed carefully into the bottom-left corner with his right foot. Shilton dived the right way but it was a wonderfully accurate penalty, right into the side-netting. When Brehme took a penalty at the 1986 World Cup he used his left foot. You can't get much more two-footed than that.

BEARDSLEY SCORES! England 2–1 West Germany. Beardsley shuffles forward a little nervously then takes another excellent penalty, high to his right. Illgner went the right way but couldn't get near it.

MATTHAUS SCORES! England 2–2 West Germany. You don't save those. Matthäus booms a frighteningly certain penalty low to Shilton's right. Shilton went the right way again but was getting nowhere near that.

PLATT SCORES! England 3–2 West Germany. That was a bit close for comfort. Platt sidefooted it to his left but it was at a saveable height and Illgner managed to get fingertips on it. Thankfully for England it was far enough out of his reach that he couldn't get a full hand on it and he could only help it into the net. Platt trots back to the halfway line with the nervous smile of a man who has avoided a firing squad.

RIEDLE SCORES! England 3–3 West Germany. Again Shilton goes the right way and again he's nowhere near saving it. In fact, it seems he's waiting to see where the kick is going before he dives. That's a dodgy tactic because the German penalties are so accurate. That one, from Riedle, was whipped high into the right of the net.

PEARCE MISSES! England 3–3 West Germany. Oh no. Stuart Pearce, so reliable from the spot for Nottingham Forest, has had his kick saved by Illgner. In truth it wasn't a great penalty, blasted almost straight down the middle but low enough so that, even though Illgner had dived to his right, he was able to save it with his feet.

THON SCORES! England 3–4 West Germany. England are on the brink now. Thon places another accurate penalty into the bottom-right corner. Shilton went the right way yet again but, again, got nowhere near it. It'll be Chris Waddle rather than Paul Gascoigne, who is presumably too much of an emotional wreck to take a penalty, and if he doesn't score England are out.

WADDLE MISSES AND ENGLAND ARE OUT! England 1–1 West Germany (3–4 pens). Waddle smashes his penalty inches over the bar – although such is its dramatic trajectory it soon looks like he's missed by yards – and England's dream is over. It's the cruellest way to go out, particularly after such a wonderful performance. Many of us have never seen them play better. Waddle sinks to his knees, crestfallen. Matthäus breaks away from the German celebrations to help him to his feet, which is a nice touch from a truly world-class player. Bobby Robson smiles ruefully but also proudly, gently punching the air as if to say, 'Bugger our luck.' He knows how desperately close England were – not just to reaching the final but to winning the World Cup. Their campaign started farcically and ended gloriously. Yes, okay, gloriously and farcically.

It's not too trite to say that neither side really deserved to go out. England were the better side in normal time and West Germany in extra time. The Germans will go on to their third consecutive final, hoping to avenge their defeats in 1982 and 1986. England go into a third-place play-off with Italy on Saturday after a night of raw emotion and proud heartbreak that will live with us all for ever. Gazza has tears streaming down his reddened face as he salutes the England fans. Time to listen to 'World in Motion' on loop while drowning a million sweet sorrows.

Romania v Argentina

Second round, Rose Bowl, Pasadena, USA,
Sunday, 3 July 1994

Here's a weird thing. We're going into a World Cup match involving Argentina – yet for once it's their opponents who hope we will be talking about Maradona in two hours' time. If we are, it will mean that Romania have put Argentina out and that we will be focusing on the absence of the disgraced Diego, banned for a 'cocktail of drugs' in his system. The Romanians also hope that some of the post-match chitchat will be about the excellence of Gheorghe Hagi. Described as the 'Maradona of the Carpathians', he is finally starting to show that not all comparisons are odious. It's ludicrous to think he spent last season in Serie B with Brescia – and that Romania might not even have qualified for the World Cup had Welshman Paul Bodin scored from the spot last November!

Romania were excellent and clinical against highly fancied Colombia, when Hagi scored outrageously from the touchline (and yes, he did mean it); shambolic while losing 4–1 against Roy Hodgson's Switzerland; and comfortable in dispatching the hosts USA 1–0 to finish top of Group A. A game against Argentina isn't exactly a reward for finishing top, although the alternatives (Spain and Brazil) weren't much better. And Romania do have one big advantage: they have had seven days' rest since their last game, Argentina just three.

Still, you've about as much chance of winning the new National Lottery when it starts in November than you have of predicting this game. While Romania topped their group, Argentina finished third in theirs despite winning their first two games by an aggregate of 6–1. They lost their third game 2–0 to Bulgaria, though were obviously distracted by Maradona's positive urine sample. They need to get that out of their system today and remind us why everyone was raving about them in the first two games, when their fast, aggressive football was hailed as an antidote to the hilarious negativity and misanthropy of the team that somehow reached the final in 1990 (annoying the hell out of the self-righteous but amusing to those who enjoy watching born troublemakers insouciantly swing the wrecking ball). Whoever prevails will play Sweden in the quarter-final.

Florin Răducioiu, who scored two excellent goals in beating the pre-tournament darlings Colombia, is suspended after being booked for kicking the ball away against the USA. He is replaced by Gheorghe Mihali, which suggests Romania will push Ilie Dumitrescu or Gheorghe Hagi up front. Either that or they are going to give Andy Gray something new to talk about in the Boot Room by going all Malcolm Allison and playing without strikers. (It'll never catch on.) Argentina have plenty of front-men, though: Ariel Ortega is in for the injured Claudio Caniggia and will play behind Gabriel Batistuta and Abel Balbo. Roberto Sensini, fit again, is in for Hernán Díaz and José Basualdo replaces Leonardo Rodríguez.

Kick-off: 9.30 p.m. on Sunday night in England, 1.30 p.m. on Sunday afternoon in Pasadena.

Referee: Pierluigi Pairetto (Italy).

Romania: Florian Prunea; Dan Petrescu, Daniel Prodan, Miodrag Belodedici, Tibor Selymes, Gheorghe Mihali, Ionuţ Lupescu, Gheorghe Popescu, Dorinel Munteanu, Gheorghe Hagi, Ilie Dumitrescu.

Argentina: Luis Islas, Roberto Sensini, Fernando Cáceres, Oscar Ruggeri, José Chamot, Diego Simeone, Fernando Redondo, José Basualdo, Ariel Ortega, Gabriel Batistuta, Abel Balbo.

It's relatively cool in Dallas: a mere 100 degrees, around 15 lower than it was for this afternoon's Wimbledon final between Pete Sampras and Goran Ivanišević, according to John Motson on the BBC.

1 min: Argentina kick off from right to left. The newfangled BBC clock at the top left of the screen starts four seconds late. Wake up lads! It's the World Cup! Argentina get off to a fast start, with Balbo picking up a loose ball and hitting a long-range shot straight at Prunea after 42 or 46 seconds, depending which clock you're using.

3 min: Diego Maradona, never a man to flick one V-sign at authority when both hands are available, has arrived at the stadium to work for Argentina radio or TV. He's wearing sunglasses, stubble and an entirely ludicrous T-shirt that seems to depict a marching band in a field, with a blue sky above them. It also has orange arms and a zebra sleeve. He looks like a henchman from *Carlito's Way*. He really couldn't care less what anyone at FIFA thinks. What he apparently lacks in marbles, he more than makes up for in stones.

4 min: The slippery Ortega wins a corner on the right. He takes it himself, hitting an outswinger towards Batistuta near the penalty spot. He heads it up in the air, beyond the far post, and Balbo hooks a volley on the turn over the bar from eight yards. That was a pretty difficult chance.

8 min: This has been a really sharp start from Argentina, who seem to have left the Maradona business and the defeat to Bulgaria behind. A lazy pass from Hagi is intercepted by Sensini, who pushes it urgently forward to Batistuta, just outside the box on the right wing. It's a preposterous angle from which to go for goal so that's precisely what he does, smashing a fierce low shot towards the near post that is beaten away by Prunea, plunging to his left.

10 min: Argentina should be in front. Simeone, receiving possession in a tight area 35 yards from goal, suddenly shredded the Romania defence with a run to create a big chance for Balbo. He ignored a tackle from behind and burst between two Romanian players before swerving past another just outside the D. Then he stabbed a superb short through-pass to put Balbo clear on goal. He took a touch and by the time he shot the sliding Prunea was right on top of him and blocked. That was great goalkeeping, so alert, although Balbo should have done better.

11 min: GOAL! Romania 1–0 Argentina (Dumitrescu). Romania take the lead with a memorable goal! This comes almost offensively against the run of play. Munteanu won a soft free-kick on the left wing after running into Cáceres. It was almost in line with the penalty spot, halfway between the edge of the area and the left touchline. Everyone lined up in the area for a cross – and Dumitrescu bent it straight into the far corner! That's a ridiculous goal, from a not dissimular position to Hagi's against Colombia on this ground. That said, the goalkeeping was dreadful. Islas was far too close to the near post and got nowhere near the ball with a showy, desperate dive as it dipped over him and into the far corner.

15 min: PENALTY TO ARGENTINA! Batistuta wins a soft penalty to give Argentina the chance of an equalizer. He was running away from goal on the left, by the touchline, when he suddenly changed direction with a slick Cruyff Turn. Prodan put his hands across the chest of Batistuta, who went down as if molested by a cattle prod. You can see why the referee gave it, although that contact surely wasn't strong enough to knock Batistuta over.

16 min: GOAL! Romania 1–1 Argentina (Batistuta pen). Batistuta is one of world football's more decisive penalty takers and he hammers this into the bottom-left corner with Prunea going the other way. Argentina deserve to be level, although Romania will be justly aggrieved by the manner of the goal.

18 min: GOAL! Romania 2–1 Argentina (Dumitrescu). Romania are back in front barely a minute after the kick-off! It's another beautiful goal, this time following a smooth, unusually unhurried counter-attack. After Redondo was well tackled on the edge of the Romania area, Petrescu pushed the loose ball crisply forward to Hagi on the halfway line. He made 40 yards with a simple one-two with Lupescu, taking four players out of the game with one pass. Then he teased Cáceres on the right corner of the box while waiting for support, before slipping a delicious angled pass into the space between keeper and defenders that took another three Argentinians out of the game. Dumitrescu – who seconds earlier had been on the edge of his area helping out defensively – met it first time eight yards from goal, opening his body up ingeniously to sidefoot past Islas at the near post so disdainfully that you wonder if he did it just to take the piss. The timing and weight of Hagi's pass were immaculate; Dumitrescu's technique equally so. That is a magnificent goal.

20 min: This is insane in the membrane; we've just had four chances in 40 seconds! This is one of the most dramatic minutes in any World Cup match ever. Romania are destroying Argentina on the counter and could easily be 3–1 up. Then again it could also be 2–2. Romania's first chance came far too easily. Munteanu curved a long ball down the left to Dumitrescu, who slipped

Cáceres with laughable ease and ran into the area as Cáceres went down holding his snout. The angle was too tight for the shot so he laid it back for the onrushing Popescu, whose first-time shot from 15 yards was blocked by the legs of Islas. Redondo probably did just enough to put Popescu off. It rebounded to Mihali, 40 yards from goal, who was dispossessed by Balbo. He charged straight down the left wing before squaring it to Ortega, unmarked 12 yards out. He should have shot first time but took a touch and was brilliantly tackled by Prodan. Romania exploded again on the counter-counter-counter-attack and could have scored twice more. Selymes sliced Argentina open with a simple, straight through ball to Hagi, running infield from the left. He held off Basualdo, who fell over like Cáceres a moment ago, and got into the area before driving a shot that was blocked by the body of Islas. A few seconds of scrambling later, Petrescu laid the ball back for Popescu to spank a fierce 25-yard shot that was palmed away by Islas diving to his right. All the while Cáceres was lying down holding his face after the original incident with Dumitrescu, which only happened 60 seconds ago but now feels as relevant as Lucien Laurent's opener for France against Mexico in 1930.

21 min: Phew. Cripes. Lummee.

26 min: After an understandable lull, an excellent chance for Batistuta! Ortega pulled left and played a flat chip into the area. Balbo flicked it a couple of yards to Batistuta. He chested it away from Prodan, who lunged forward to try to intercept the pass, but then dragged a left-footed volley wide from 12 yards. He was under a fair bit of pressure from Hagi, sliding in from behind, although he will probably feel he should have scored.

27 min: Another chance for Argentina! This game is taking a shortcut straight to classic status. This impressive youngster Ortega went on a fine run from the right, slipping away from one man and nutmegging Munteanu before sidefooting a cross towards the penalty spot from a deepish position. Balbo got there just in front of Mihali, flew forward and sent a diving header just wide with Prunea watching.

33 min: At the moment every Argentina attack is crackling with menace – for Argentina, such is the speed and decisiveness with which Romania break. When Redondo miscontrols the ball a fraction, a couple of quick passes free Dumitrescu on the halfway line. He runs straight at and past Ruggeri, who takes him down and is booked.

36 min: Selymes and Munteanu seem to have modelled their running styles on Hagi. Single White Midfielders. So if we mix the three up – and it's easy to do because they are all left-footed and all tearing Argentina some new apertures – that's why.

39 min: There's not much happening just now. This has been an unusual game of quiet periods and explosions of almost overwhelming incident: three goals in eight minutes, four chances in 40 seconds.

44 min: Islas bursts superbly from his line to claim Selmyes's through-ball a fraction before Munteanu.

45+1 min: CACERES CLEARS OFF THE LINE TO DENY DUMITRESCU A FIRST-HALF HAT-TRICK! Yet another stunning break from Romania. They had eight men within a ten-yard radius of the ball when Simeone's pass to Balbo on the edge of the box was intercepted; the other two, Munteanu and Dumitrescu, were loitering with palpable intent upfield and that was all they needed. One pass from Lupescu, played wide left to Munteanu on the halfway line, left Argentina two against two at the back. He strode forward 20 yards and then curved an outrageously good pass, shaped almost like a walking stick, behind Ruggeri and Cáceres to put Dumitrescu through. His first touch was just slightly too soft, which meant the ball ran away from him, and with his second he lobbed it over the advancing Islas, but it was a slightly unconvincing finish and Cáceres had just enough time to run back and boot it behind for a corner. Another awesome counter-attack from Romania.

HALF TIME: Romania 2–1 Argentina. So sad to hear the whistle. If only that could have gone on for ever.

46 min: Romania begin the second half – and Batistuta almost equalizes within 15 seconds! It was a double cock-up from Romania. First Mihali drove a crossfield pass straight to Batistuta. Then, when Popescu intercepted Ortega's subsequent backheel on the edge of the box, he dawdled and allowed Batistuta to nick the ball off him. He roared into the box and struck a rising shot that was too close to Prunea and beaten away.

47 min: Romania have their left their minds in the dressing-room. Another dismal pass out of defence – we know they like playing on the counter-attack but that's no reason to keep giving Argentina the ball – goes straight to Balbo. He runs to the edge of the box on the left and moves it all the way across with the help of first Ortega and then Batistuta, who sets up Basualdo to slash a shot wide from 12 yards.

49 min: Popescu is booked for a foul from behind on Ortega.

52 min: Another chance for Argentina! They are battering Romania even more than they did at the start of the first half. Basualdo opened up the defence with a simple straight pass, stabbed down the inside-left channel to Balbo, who ran off Mihali and past the flat-footed Belodedici to receive it near the byline. He drew the keeper and tried to pull it back to Batistuta six yards out; it was blocked by Belodedici, who passed it back towards the keeper Prunea and turned nonchalantly on his heels as if to say: Not my problem any more, lads! In fact, it was almost Romania's problem: Balbo, whose momentum had taken him off the field, ran back on and got to the ball before Prunea. He tried to stab it back towards the centre and this time it hit the lunging Mihali before deflecting to safety.

53 min: The hitherto disappointing Redondo plays a fine one-two with Ortega, taking the return pass beautifully in his stride before going down under a challenge from Hagi right on the edge or possibly just inside the box. The referee gives nothing and waves his hands to suggest Redondo dived. There are no real complaints from Argentina. Replays suggest it was a dive, although it was a risky tackle from Hagi. Against that, Hagi's willingness to get his hands (well, knees) dirty reflects very well on him and the all-for-one spirit within this side.

56 min: Redondo and Chamot are both booked in the space of a minute for fouls on Hagi/Selymes/Munteanu. Actually they were definitely both on Hagi.

58 min: GOAL! Romania 3–1 Argentina (Hagi). Romania go two goals clear with another breathtaking counter-attack! This was the best of the lot. It started with an Argentina corner on the left, taken by Ortega. It was headed to within 35 yards of the Romania goal, where Basualdo slipped under challenge from Dumitrescu. The moment he did so, it was if as if a starting gun had gone off and Romania had 20 seconds to score. They needed just 13. Dumitrescu charged straight down the field, with Selymes deliberately curling his off-the-ball run to drag Cáceres to the left. Dumitrescu used Selymes by not using him and instead teased Sensini, winding his foot back and forth like a dial while he waited for Hagi to appear on the right – and for the covering Chamot to run beyond the line of the pass he wanted to play. Dumitrescu's pass was so well timed that Hagi did not have to break stride. He marauded on to the ball and, with his weaker right foot, rammed it into the net with numbing certainty. John Motson – a brilliant commentator who really doesn't need to use these silly rhymes that have started popping up in his work – partially ruins a perfect moment by telling us 'there wasn't a defender in sight, when he broke on the right'.

59 min: Argentina almost get back into it straightaway. Ortega runs round the outside of the defence and stabs a cross-shot that is blocked by Mihali. It comes back to Ortega, who lobs it towards Batistuta on the penalty box. He controls the ball on his chest but it won't sit down as he wishes and his shot deflects over off Petrescu. Actually Batistuta was penalized for controlling it with his arm – replays aren't conclusive – so it would not have counted anyway.

63 min: The Argentina coach Alfio Basile is not going to die wondering: he has replaced the defender Sensini with the forward Ramón Medina Bello.

67 min: Ortega has a penalty appeal turned down when his cross hits Belodedici. It seemed to hit the arm although there were only a few yards between the players.

68 min: Selymes is booked for fouling Simeone right on the edge of the area. Or was it inside? It wasn't a red card as Simeone was running away from goal on to Ortega's pass. That's such a tight decision, although the first contact was probably a fraction outside the box. The free-kick will be taken by Batistuta . . .

69 min: . . . and it's comfortably held by Prunea.

73 min: It's all Argentina now but Romania seem comfortable enough: they haven't quite declared at three but it's not far off that. They have a two-goal lead, Prunea hasn't had a difficult save to make for nearly half an hour and they seem content to say to Argentina: let's see what you've got. In that case, not much. Batistuta belabours one into orbit from a ludicrous angle.

75 min: GOAL! Romania 3–2 Argentina (Balbo). Romania aren't comfortable any more! Argentina are back in it! Cáceres takes a second off from being driven doolally by Dumitrescu to join the attack, picking up a clearance 45 yards from goal. He moves forward ten yards and then hits an awkward, wobbling shot that is fumbled by Prunea diving to his left, and Balbo is first to the rebound to stab it over Prunea and in off the underside of the bar. Prunea should have done better. It was an awkward ball to catch but at the very least he had to palm it away from goal rather than back out to Balbo. He dived too far across and the ball ended up hitting him on the chest.

79 min: Those with a crick in the right side of their neck are able to enjoy this match without pain for a second: Romania have entered the final third of the field for the first time in almost five minutes.

80 min: Bello is allowed to turn in the box by Popescu. He runs at him, towards the byline, and cuts the ball back dangerously towards the six-yard line – where there are no Argentina forwards and Petrescu is allowed to clear.

82 min: Romania are attacking with urgency again after their 20-minute siesta, realizing they may need a fourth. Hagi, on the right wing inside his own half, runs around the ball and slashes an unbelievable 60-yard pass to put Dumitrescu clear on the left side of the box. Basualdo catches up but Dumitrescu wriggles past him and then, as Cáceres closes in, hammers a left-footed shot from a tight angle that is wonderfully saved by Islas, diving to his left with scarcely any reaction time. What a game Dumitrescu has had. Moments later, Cáceres is booked for dissent after fouling Dumitrescu. He is in a rare old funk! He pats his heart angrily at Dumitrescu, who pats him patronizingly on the head; Cáceres shoves his arm away. Dumitrescu has slaughtered Cáceres today.

84 min: A good chance at each end! It started with a Romania corner on the left. Hagi took it short to Dumitrescu and the pair decided to take the piss. He flicked it behind his standing leg to

Hagi, ran on to a nonchalantly chipped return pass and lobbed a cross towards Petrescu on the six-yard line. He would have had a simple volleyed finish but for a fine interception from Redondo, who came round the side to get the ball. From there Argentina broke, with six Romanian players caught forward for almost the first time all half. It was a cavalry charge, four on three, led by Balbo. He had Simeone one side and Batistuta the other but overran it fractionally near the halfway line and Belodedici made a vital tackle. He was 50 yards from his own goal yet that was almost a goal-saving tackle because Argentina would have been four on two.

85 min: Dumitrescu has been booked for time-wasting and Romania are taking off Hagi. What a bizarre risk. He is going to be replaced by the more prosaic midfielder Constantin Gâlcă. That would be fine if this was a league game but not in knockout football: if Argentina equalize, Romania will be without Hagi for extra time. You hope that isn't the last we see of him at this World Cup because he has been simply magnificent. The word is overused in sport but by God he's a genius.

87 min: Romania certainly aren't hanging on. They've attacked with much more menace at 3–2 than they did at 3–1, with Balbo's goal waking them up as an attacking force. Lupescu receives a return pass inside his own half, runs 40 yards into the open spaces but then totally mis-hits a weary through ball to Dumitrescu.

89 min: Now Dumitrescu has been taken off, replaced by the youngster Corneliu Papură. Anghel Iordănescu has taken an unbelievable risk. If this goes to extra time, Romania will be playing 5–5–0 with their two best players on the bench. Dumitrescu has had the game of his life. He scored two brilliant goals, could easily have had two more and gave Cáceres the chasing of his lifetime.

90 min: Ruggeri, playing up front now, wins a corner for Argentina. Ortega swings it out from the right and Batistuta, under pressure, heads well wide from 15 yards. That could be it.

FULL TIME: Romania 3–2 Argentina. It's all over! You don't need to feel it in your fingers, or your toes, to know that this was a true World Cup classic, the best since Brazil–France eight years ago. Romania go through to the quarter-finals of this tournament for the first time. Argentina played a full part, yet ultimately they were undone by one of the all-time great counter-attacking performances from Romania, with Gheorghe Hagi unplayable and Ilie Dumitrescu even better. Eastern Europe's first world champions? You never know.

The 1994 Finals

USA 2–1 Colombia (1994, group stage)

After their astonishing 5–0 win in Buenos Aires during qualification, Colombia were the hipsters' choice for USA 94. They were also Pelé's: he said they were the best team in the tournament. But their campaign was disastrous and tragic. They lost their first game 3–1 to Romania and another defeat to USA cost them their place at the World Cup. It also cost Andrés Escobar his life. He was shot dead in Medellín two weeks later. There are a number of theories as to why he was killed; the most common is that a drug cartel who had wagered a significant sum of money on Colombia blamed him for the team's World Cup exit.

35 min: OWN GOAL! USA 1–0 Colombia (Escobar). Colombia's World Cup has gone from bad to worse: Andrés Escobar has given the USA the lead! The goal came out of nothing. Mike Sorber clipped a nice pass to John Harkes in an inside-left position. He ran at Luis Fernando Herrera and then, spotting Earnie Stewart at the far post, curled a low pass into the space between keeper and defenders. Escobar got there first, stretching out a leg and inadvertently sliding the ball past the wrongfooted Oscar Cordóba from 15 yards. That's horrible luck for Colombia. Escobar probably had to go for it; had he not got there, Stewart would have scored. 'A tragedy for the Colombia defence,' says the ITV commentator John Helm. Escobar's name is on the scoresheet, although so many things go into a goal like that: Paul Caligiuri's off-the-ball run, which distracted Herrera, Hernán Gaviria being slow to close Harkes down, Cordóba going too far across his line.

Germany 1–2 Bulgaria (1994, quarter-final)

Bulgaria went into USA 94 having never won a game at the World Cup final in 16 attempts. A Hristo Stoichkov-inspired side righted that wrong by making it all the way to the semi-finals before they lost 2–1 to Italy. They would take one particular memory home with them: a sensational 2–1 win over the defending champions.

78 min: GOAL! Germany 1–2 Bulgaria (Letchkov). Bulgaria are in front! Yordan Letchkov has made it two goals in four minutes with a spectacular diving header! After some sustained pressure from Bulgaria, Zlatko Yankov moved neatly away from Thomas Berthold on the right and floated an inviting ball towards the penalty spot. Everyone had been drawn beyond the near post except Thomas Hässler and Letchkov, who came on the blind side of Hässler and soared spectacularly through the air to drift a header past Illgner from 15 yards. That came right off the sweet spot – which is the big bald bit just above the monk spot. In one moment, he's done more for baldness than anybody since Kojak! Bulgaria are 12 minutes away from the World Cup semi-final and the football world is having roast *Schadenfreude* for Sunday dinner.

Brazil 0–0 Italy (4–3 pens) (1994, final)

The 1994 World Cup final was the first without a goal and the first to go to penalties. Four men failed to score in the shoot-out, but few people recall the misses of Franco Baresi, Marcio Santos and Daniele Massaro, whose miss was probably the most crucial. All they remember is Roberto Baggio, who got Italy to the final almost single-footedly, played against Brazil despite injury and had the final kick of the tournament.

· · · · ·MAGIC MINUTES · · · · · · · ·MAGIC MINUTES · · · · ·

BAGGIO MISSES AND BRAZIL ARE WORLD CHAMPIONS!!! Baggio sidefoots his penalty over the bar! Brazil have won the World Cup! It was a couple of inches away from being a perfect penalty; instead it sailed into Waddle territory. Baggio stands on the spot, hands on his hips, before eventually bowing his head slightly. The camera cuts to the stands, where Pelé, in his stars and stripes tie, is dancing around on the spot. Baresi is lying on his back in tears. It seems to have hit him harder than anyone else. He deserves so much more for an immense performance. So does Baggio, who was one of the stars of the tournament, along with Romario, Hagi and Stoichkov. On an individual level it was a World Cup for the little people; on a collective level it belonged to the biggest football nation of all: Brazil, who claim the trophy for the fourth time.

Argentina v England

Second round, Stade Geoffroy-Guichard, Saint-Etienne, France, Tuesday, 30 June 1998

Don't mention the war. Or the Hand of God. Some chance. In the build-up to this game, most of the world has been about as adept as Basil Fawlty when it comes to not mentioning skirmishes of the past. The entire game has been framed in the context of 1982 and particularly 1986. There's been plenty of jingoism hot off the press. '8 p.m. tonight: payback time' was the *Daily Mirror* headline today, with a big picture of the Hand of God goal. Mind you, the thing that stood out the most was the use of a colon in a headline, in a tabloid. Is it wrong to be fascinated by that? Probably. 'England will come to a halt at 8 p.m. tonight as the Band of Hod set out to take World Cup revenge on Argentina for the Hand of God', punned the paper. The *Sun*, meanwhile, offered a rewritten version of 'Don't Cry for Me Argentina', penned by showbiz editor and News International librettist Dominic Mohan. If we tell you the first line is 'We Hod to make it happen, it Hod to change', you'll probably not need to hear much more, and might even want to run a hot bath with some friends from Gillette for company. But just in case, you can apparently hear *Sun* staff sing this 'World Cup classic' by calling 0660 111 184. Calls cost 50p a minute. In other news, a pack of three razors costs £2.

The jingoism partially reflects the significance of the game, which is far too big for the second round of a World Cup – not just because of the history but because of the quality of the teams. The Argentina manager Daniel Passarella says it is 'a classical international, especially at this stage of the tournament'. His team come into the match in better shape. They have not conceded a goal in eight games and breezed through an admittedly weak group, beating Croatia and Japan 1–0 and slapping Jamaica 5–0.

England's group performance was a mixed bag. A comfortable 2–0 win over Tunisia, a worryingly shambolic 2–1 defeat to Romania and then an emphatic, exhilarating 2–0 win over a decent Colombia side. The upshot of that Romania defeat is that England are in a disgustingly hard half of the draw: Argentina tonight, then potentially Holland in the quarter-finals, Brazil in the semis and France, Italy or Germany in the final. But Glenn Hoddle – like Sir Alf Ramsey in 1966 and Bobby Robson in both 1986 and 1990 – seems to have stumbled upon a decent system during a World Cup. The terrifyingly precocious teenager Michael Owen is on fire up front and David Beckham – whose World Cup started miserably when he was dropped and publicly criticized by Hoddle, being told when practising setpieces that 'you are not good enough to do that skill' – is back in the side and back on track after scoring that wonderful free-kick against Colombia. Adidas certainly think so: Beckham, with his poster-boy looks, adorned one of their posters this morning that promised that 'After tonight, England v Argentina will be remembered for what a player did with his feet.' Now wouldn't that be nice?

Kick-off: 9 p.m. in Saint-Etienne, 8 p.m. in bars up and down England.

Referee: Kim Milton Nielsen (Denmark).

Argentina replace the injured Nestor Sensini with José Chamot, who on Sunday was restrained by police after a row with a journalist, with Chamot promising: 'I am going to kill you': Carlos Roa, Nelson Vivas, Roberto Ayala, José Chamot, Javier Zanetti, Matías Almeyda, Juan Verón, Diego Simeone, Ariel Ortega, Gabriel Batistuta, Claudio López.

England are unchanged and, like Argentina, are in the trendy 3–4–1–2 formation: David Seaman, Gary Neville, Tony Adams, Sol Campbell, Darren Anderton, David Beckham, Paul Ince, Graeme Le Saux, Paul Scholes, Alan Shearer, Michael Owen.

There's a buzzing atmosphere at the ground, almost menacing in fact. Tony Adams, in his nasal style, is belting out the national anthem like his life depends on it. On ITV, Kevin Keegan picks out David Beckham as England's key man. The players are ready for kick-off a couple of minutes too early, which leads to some awkward standing around.

1 min: Argentina kick off from left to right. They are in their dark-blue away kit; England are in white.

3 min: Batistuta miscontrols the ball straight to Owen, who eschews niceties and hares straight for goal. The last man, Ayala, on the edge of the area, takes man, ball and huge dollops of fresh air with a brusque and important tackle. The loose ball comes to Le Saux, whose mis-hit cross-shot bobbles across goal and just evades Shearer, sliding in beyond the far post. Meanwhile, Anderton is off the field receiving treatment because – and you'll like this – he's lost a contact lens.

4 min: It's been an almost comically fast start, with none of the usual dancing around the ring during the opening exchanges. The pace is demented, probably because of the pride that comes with the history between these sides. Both sides have got the battle fever on all right.

5 min: PENALTY TO ARGENTINA! A nightmare start for England. Ortega played in a nothing cross from the right, which was helped on by the head of Batistuta on the edge of the box. Simeone ran on to it but was moving away from goal, on the left corner of the six-yard box, and had Anderton stalking him. Yet Seaman was drawn towards the ball as well. Simeone got there a fraction before Seaman and as soon as he felt the slightest touch he was down. Adams motions desperately that it was a dive – he's waving his hands around ridiculously, like a lunatic monkey. Seaman's protests are more muted, which suggests he knows. It may be soft, and there's no doubt Simeone made the most of it, but it was a penalty. Simeone motions for the referee to show a card to Seaman, which he does – only a yellow, as Simeone was going away from goal and there's no way it was a clear goalscoring opportunity. There's a sense of shock around the ground, both that we have a penalty so soon and also that it came from such an innocuous incident.

6 min: GOAL! Argentina 1–0 England (Batistuta pen). Batistuta smashes the penalty through Seaman. It was leathered low to the keeper's right. Seaman went the right way, as he so often does, but he was beaten for pace and could only push it into the side-netting. Batistuta, a new father, celebrates with the worst celebration in football: the Bebeto baby-rock. If you're going to inform the world of the successful working of your genitalia, at least do so with something imaginative, an elaborate nappy-changing routine, perhaps, or a mime about trying it on with the au pair.

8 min: There's a strut about Argentina at the moment, particularly the waspish Ortega. England haven't started playing.

9 min: PENALTY TO ENGLAND! It's another soft penalty but not one person in England will give a solitary one about that. It was won by the scarily decisive running of Owen. Le Saux, just inside the Argentina half, won a loose ball against Zanetti and lobbed it infield to Scholes. With four players drawn towards him, Scholes looped a clever first-time header over the top to Owen, who had taken up an excellent position in the space between the other defenders and the last man Ayala. He went straight for goal again, knocked it past Ayala inside the area and went down as soon as Ayala brushed against him. The referee had to give that as well. Owen did make the most of it but there was certainly contact. At times like that, Owen looks unplayable. He's 18! Ayala has not been booked, which is a bit odd. Some referees might have sent him off, although a yellow would have sufficed as the covering Vivas was close enough to Owen. Ince has been booked for some kind of protest.

10 min: GOAL! Argentina 1–1 England (Shearer pen). Shearer equalizes with a majestic penalty. That was utterly unsaveable, sidefooted at pace and into the top-left corner. Shearer wheels away in the usual style. That's the first goal Argentina have conceded in nine games.

15 min: The back-pedalling Adams makes a vital and slightly desperate headed clearance to stop López's cross reaching Batistuta or Ortega. England are having to defend on the seat of their grundies.

16 min: GOAL! Argentina 1–2 England (Owen). Michael Owen has just scored one of the greatest goals in England's history! When you consider the context – the World Cup, Argentina, a bloody 18-year-old – this is almost too much to comprehend. *What an effing goal.* England had been defending for three minutes solid when suddenly they scored from nowhere. The already overworked Ince put out another fire on the edge of the area and found Beckham. He clipped a pass into Owen, who was in the centre circle with Chamot alongside him. It was slightly behind Owen, who improvised a superb first touch to ankle-flick the ball into the space ahead of him. From there he just ran straight for goal, ignoring Chamot's challenge around 30 yards from goal even though Chamot got a toe on the ball. Ayala took up position on the edge of the box with a posture that was half thou-shalt-not-pass and half what-the-hell-do-I-do-now. Owen simply ran straight past him to the right and then, despite Scholes potentially putting him off, clipped a wonderfully accomplished shot across Roa and into the far top corner. That is a ridiculous goal. The entire England party are off the bench, going mad. Paul Merson looks almost orgasmic with joy. In fact, the only man who hasn't lost it is Owen, who celebrates as if it's just another goal in the park. The defending wasn't great – the gap between Ayala and Chamot was scandalous, and then Ayala just stood gawping at Owen on the edge of the area, allowing Owen to build up all that momentum – but even so. It was boy against men and the boy tore them umpteen new ones. That's the kind of moment that makes men thrice his age lose it all: plot, voice, dignity. And quite possibly pint, as all around England plastic glasses will surely have been Begbied through the air with joy. 'You just don't do this at 28 years of age, never mind 18,' says Keegan. How good will Michael Owen be at 28?

17 min: It's hard to know what's more outrageous: that goal or the scoreline. Argentina have played all the football and they are 2–1 down.

18 min: Argentina haven't a clue how to deal with Owen's pace. He skins Chamot on the right wing and is fouled. Beckham's free-kick is headed out by Batistuta to Ince, who lashes a dipping strike just over the bar from 25 yards. That was beautifully struck, although the keeper probably had it covered.

22 min: Passarella hunches forward as he sucks down a fag on the bench. A callback, perhaps, to the man he helped to win the World Cup back in 1978, César Luis Menotti. If he smokes another ten before half time, we'll know it's an allusion to the great man for sure.

24 min: The dangerous Ortega runs infield from the right, away from Ince, before nutmegging the outrushing Adams contemptuously, but then he overhits his through-ball to Simeone.

Holland 2–1 Argentina (1998, quarter-final)

Holland and Argentina were both serious contenders in a strong field at the 1998 World Cup. After fine goals from Patrick Kluivert and Claudio López, and red cards for Arthur Numan and Ariel Ortega, an outstanding game was heading to extra time when Dennis Bergkamp defined his career. 'It is,' he later said, 'like your whole life is building up to this.'

89 min: GOAL! Holland 2–1 Argentina (Bergkamp).
Bergkamp has put Holland into the semi-finals YET THAT ALMOST SEEMS PIDDLING with one of the greatest goals of all time! Take Michael Owen's goal against Argentina, multiply it by 1,000 and you're still nowhere near. Frank de Boer, sauntering towards the halfway line on the left, drove a wonderful 60-yard reacher, left to right, into the Argentina area. Bergkamp, running at full pelt with Ayala, jumped towards the ball and cushioned it with a telescopic leg while in mid-air, his boots a mixture of velvet and velcro. Then, as he landed, he slipped it through Ayala's legs; finally, as Roa closed in, he flicked it imperiously into the far top corner with the outside of his right foot. 'Beautifully pulled down by Bergkamp – OH WHAT A GOAL!!!' screams Barry Davies on the BBC. Three quickfire touches, all with no margin for error, all measured perfectly, a level of brilliance almost beyond comprehension. Even Bergkamp, football's great aesthete, can't believe he has done this: he puts his hands to his face, a neat sibling to Rinus Michels's reaction when Marco van Basten scored his volley against the USSR in the Euro 88 final. This, ten years and nine days later, is a perfect companion piece to that. Bergkamp raises his hands in the air, to a backdrop of the most perfect orange in the stands, and then lies on his back.

27 min: Ortega loses Ince with another beautiful nutmeg and hares for goal. Adams steps out to tell danger to sling its hook.

32 min: Owen turns Vivas thrillingly on the halfway line and sets off on another charge towards goal. He gets to within 35 yards, with a terrified Chamot back-pedalling, before hitting a shot that deflects wide off Chamot for a corner. This is a complete joke. He is running through a rugged group of defenders almost at will.

37 min: Lovely play from Beckham, who keeps an errant cross-field pass from Adams in play with a deft first touch and then runs past Chamot and Batistuta before being clattered.

39 min: What a chance for Paul Scholes! That should have been 3–1 to England. Shearer on the right towered majestically above Chamot to meet Seaman's long kick forward and send an angled header into the area. It went over Owen, Ayala and Vivas, but Scholes had run off the back of Almeyda and got to it first, only to slip a left-foot shot just wide from ten yards. He normally takes those chances in his sleep. If anything he tried to be too precise, clipping it with the side of the foot when he could have belted it.

41 min: Batistuta misses a good chance to make it 2–2. The move was sparked, inevitably, by Ortega. He moved away from Ince through sleight of hip, nutmegged Scholes – England need to close their legs around Ortega – and then played the ball to Batistuta, lurking in the D. As many as five England defenders converged on Batistuta, with Campbell getting there first. His attempted sliding clearance hit Batistuta, who then thrashed it high and wide on the half-volley from 16 yards. He was under pressure, with bodies charging around all over the place and Neville throwing himself towards the ball, but a finisher as merciless as Batistuta might feel he should have scored. The aggrieved look on his coupon suggests that's precisely what he thinks.

42 min: Campbell makes a brilliant saving tackle! England really need half time here. Again Argentina went right through the eye of England's needle, this time after an intrepid run from the right-back Zanetti. He ran at Le Saux and Shearer, who half-stopped him with a double-team tackle. But Zanetti took the resulting rebound off Scholes to swerve past Adams before playing a short pass behind Beckham to Simeone. He eased it through to López, who had run off Neville and would have had a clear chance but for a desperate and brilliant sliding challenge from the last man Campbell.

43 min: After a ten-minute nap, Argentina are wide awake again. Ortega exchanges passes with López down the right, gets into the area and comes back inside Campbell. He might have gone for goal but instead played a square pass that was just behind the onrushing Simeone. England have the best seat on the precipice at the moment.

44 min: Verón is booked for a foul on Owen.

45 min: Another dangerous attack from Argentina. Ortega finds Zanetti on the right, just inside the England half, and he chips a dangerous straight pass behind Campbell to free López round the back. Seaman starts to come, then changes his mind, and for a second it seems López might be able to get a shot in from a tight angle. But Campbell does enough to make the angle not so much tight as impossible, and Seaman easily claims López's drive.

45+1 min: GOAL! Argentina 2–2 England (Zanetti). Argentina are level with a wonderful free-kick! This was straight from the training ground. The free-kick was 22 yards out, fractionally to the right of centre, after a foul by Campbell on López. Batistuta and Verón both lined up as if they were going to leather it. Batistuta ran over the ball and then Verón, who ran towards the ball with an intensity that suggested he wanted to kill it, instead played a short pass to Zanetti, who was hiding behind the England wall and ran to the right of the area to receive the pass. He controlled the ball on the half-turn with his right foot and then, as the England wall closed in, thrashed a superb rising shot across Seaman with his left foot. That is such a fine goal, both in its conception and execution: Zanetti had scarcely any margin for error in the timing of his movement away from the wall, the weight of his touch while his body did a 180-degree turn, and then the speed with which he got his shot away with his weaker left foot. The Argentina bench are going doolally on the sidelines. Verón jumps into the manager Passarella's arms; Simeone jumps on top of them both. Ayala jumps on top of Zanetti for a good 10–15 seconds and they hold a pose that was last seen in the

Kama Sutra. England didn't do much wrong there. That was just an outstanding goal.

HALF TIME: Argentina 2–2 England. In the ITV studio Bobby Robson, who could barely look more proud if his own son had scored England's second goal, says this is the 'best game of the tournament. Owen is a genius, and Ortega has touches of Maradona.'

46 min: IT'S RESTARTED! AND IMMEDIATELY, IT'S ON! England kick off the second half from left to right. A loose ball is headed forward by Adams towards Beckham, who is shoved over aggressively by Simeone near the halfway line. Now Simeone is down as well. What's happened here? A few players from both sides are around the scene and the referee is going to book someone, presumably Simeone. We didn't see how Simeone went down because the camera was focusing on a close-up of Beckham's face. Nobody looks particularly animated apart from Shearer, who pushes Batistuta away, with Scholes, Almeyda and Verón also involved. On ITV, Kevin Keegan, whose voice suddenly sounds very grave, has just suggested Beckham might be sent off for retaliation. What?

47 min: BECKHAM IS SENT OFF!!! Oh no. Simeone is indeed booked but as soon as Kim Milton Nielsen goes back to his pocket for a different card you know England are in trouble. Beckham walks straight off. He looks in shock. Batistuta nods his head almost patronizingly in approval. We still don't know what he actually did. Here's the replay. Ah, Beckham, who was lying on his front, flicked out with his right leg and kicked Simeone on the calf. The referee was a couple of yards away. Football is getting a little softer but is that really worth a red card? On ITV, Brian Moore suggests the referee has 'overreacted quite violently'. Keegan, perhaps mindful of defending Leonardo's inexcusable elbow on Tab Ramos four years ago, said he has to go and Moore concurs after seeing another replay. But should it have been red? It was stupid and naive – he was suckered by Simeone – but it was a flick rather than a full-blown kick. Either way, England are in big trouble and Beckham, who seemed to have left all his early tournament woes behind, now has another trauma to deal with.

48 min: We see another shot of the sending off and, as referee Nielsen brandishes the card, he's staring up at it intently, almost as though he's having an out-of-body experience, watching himself making a little bit of history. It does make you wonder where his ego's at.

49 min: Shearer, burning with vengeance and the mistaken perception that he is Roy Race, tries to score with a free-kick from 35 yards. He wallops it miles over the bar.

50 min: Scholes loses the ball to Verón, who gallops forward on a three-against-three break. Adams and Campbell half clear but Argentina come back through Ortega, who bursts into the box, dummies Le Saux and Campbell beautifully and then chips a cross just behind Batistuta. Fifteen seconds later an Ortega cross does find the head of Batistuta, who flashes a good chance wide of the post. He was on the penalty spot and seemed offside, with England's defence all pushing out, but the flag didn't go up and replays showed Neville played him on. It was not an easy header to get power into because the cross came from a narrow, deep position, but again he will probably feel he should have made Seaman do something.

52 min: Batistuta brings down Ince, 25 yards out. Batistuta could easily have been booked on a couple of occasions. This time, Shearer hits a much better free-kick that is palmed spectacularly behind by Roa, moving to his left. It wasn't right in the corner and as such was a relatively comfortable save, but it was beautifully struck.

55 min: England have done really well so far with ten men. In fact, they have been more comfortable defensively than in the first half. They have switched to a 4–4–1, with Scholes playing on the left of midfield, Anderton alongside Ince and Owen on the right wing.

59 min: David Seaman makes a deceptively brilliant save. The inevitable Ortega picked up the ball just past the centre circle and ran straight at England's back-pedalling defence before playing an angled pass to the right to find López in the box. He had Campbell and Le Saux with him but managed to manufacture enough space to strike a left-footed shot towards the near post that deflected off Le Saux and drifted just wide of the far post. Replays showed Seaman got down superbly to his right to brush it with his fingertips. It's hard to say whether it was going in or not, so faint was Seaman's touch. Either way, it was a fine piece of goalkeeping.

61 min: Alan Shearer saves a certain goal for England. In open play! This is ridiculous. Shearer has swapped with Owen to do that shift on the right wing and England will be thankful he did. Verón came infield from the right, past Le Saux, and then stabbed a nice pass down the side of the box for López. He rolled Campbell, who was too tight, and knocked it past Seaman across the face of goal. There would have been an easy tap-in for Vivas had Shearer not got there first to lump it clear. He got a rare old boot on the back of the calf from Vivas for it as well.

64 min: Set pieces could be England's biggest chance of a goal – but they could also be Argentina's, so devastatingly do they break when England have a corner. When Anderton's corner from the left is cleared, Argentina charge forward in numbers again. López plays a dangerous through-pass to Chamot of all people, and only the discipline and tirelessness of Anderton get England out of trouble.

69 min: England's defence have achieved the moral victory of getting Gabriel Batistuta and Claudio López substituted. Their reward? The fresh legs of Hernán Crespo and Marcelo Gallardo to torment them. Batistuta hasn't had his best night, although it's still a huge call to take him off, not least as he's the captain and joint leading scorer in the tournament.

71 min: England are in their bunker for the first time since the red card, defending dangerously but understandably deep. Gareth Southgate comes on to replace Le Saux.

72 min: Campbell, now at left-back, bulldozes comically past Vivas and then swings over a cross well beyond the far post. Anderton, running away from goal, takes it down superbly with a telescopic leg and then hits a snapshot that is well blocked by Simeone six yards out.

73 min: Ince picks Gallardo's pocket superbly from the side, finding Anderton at the same time. He charges forward and is brought down by Almeyda, who is booked.

74 min: The England fans have been great tonight, although you do worry that it's all denial and that this will end first in impotent rage, and then in violence.

75 min: Owen almost scores another wondrous goal. Seaman's kick was won in the air by Shearer and Owen ran off the back of Almeyda to collect the ball 40 yards out. He had the usual complex ploy in mind – head down and straight for goal, with only Ayala in his way and Vivas coming round from the side. Owen went away from Ayala, to the left this time, and into the area before slicing his shot high and wide from a tightish angle and under pressure from Ayala. There was a significant bobble, which did Owen no favours either. Shearer, from a combination of tiredness and pragmatism, didn't even bother to support the play once Owen picked up the ball. He had the popcorn out! He knew what was coming and it was almost another famous goal.

77 min: This, as the saying doesn't go, has been a game of two distinctive 45-minute segments: a boxing match before half time and a chess match since.

78 min: Argentina appeal for a penalty when Chamot's cross hits the hand of Adams. His arm was away from his body but he was only a couple of yards away from the ball at most. Some referees would have given it, although after everything else an England player might have chinned Nielsen if he had done.

79 min: Paul Merson is coming on for Scholes. Glenn Hoddle is not afraid to think outside the box. Merson has only played 13 minutes of competitive football for England since 1993, and of course he spent last season in the second tier with Middlesbrough. But he has plenty of experience of playing on the left and carries the ball well on the counter-attack. Seconds after the substitution, Crespo beats the offside trap and just can't reach Simeone's angled through-ball. Had he done so he would have been clear on Seaman.

81 min: ENGLAND HAVE A GOAL DISALLOWED AND ARGENTINA NEARLY SCORE! Both sides almost score in an astonishing see-saw minute. First England thought they had gone 3–2 ahead. Anderton dumped over a high corner from the left towards the far post. A posse of players went up for it, and Campbell got there to head it down and into the net. He set off wildly, punching the air, not realizing it had been disallowed because Shearer, just in front of Campbell, fouled the keeper Roa with a leading elbow. Argentina took a quick free-kick and broke four on four – with most of the England players still on the touchline celebrating! Verón ran 60 yards with the ball, and eventually Ortega's through-pass to Crespo was heroically intercepted by . . . Anderton, the man who took the corner on the other side of the pitch! Crespo was actually offside, although Anderton didn't know that. That was a heroic, almost absurd level of commitment from him. England are still asking about the goal, with Ince waving his hand in disgust. When they see the replay they will realize: Shearer definitely caught Roa, who missed his attempted punch as a result.

83 min: With Anderton lining up a free-kick on the right wing, the camera shows Merson laughing. *How can you stand there guffawing at a time like this, man?! Don't you know what we're going through?*

88 min: Seaman watches Gallardo's long-range effort go a few yards wide. England seem relatively comfortable – relatively – and this is surely going to extra time.

FULL TIME: Argentina 2–2 England. England defended outstandingly after David Beckham's dubious red card, and now we go into extra time and golden-goal territory. Then, perhaps, penalties. For the next hour, the best seat in the house might be the one behind the sofa.

91 min: Brian Moore says Darren Anderton had a 'terrific massage' during the break in play. There's no sign yet of Anderton being replaced, although Argentina have just made their final substitution: Sergio Berti is on for Simeone. Why make a change after 40 seconds of extra time?

92 min: That should have been a penalty to England! Merson hoofed a long, angled free-kick from the halfway line towards Shearer. His marker Chamot mistimed his jump and the ball struck his outstretched fist. It bounced through to Roa but the referee waved play on. He might have been unsighted, with Shearer jumping across his line of vision, and England's appeals were relatively muted – mainly because play went on so they all had to charge back into defence. But the more replays you see the more you realize that was a penalty. He might feasibly have penalized Shearer for jumping into Chamot; either way, play shouldn't have continued. Had the penalty been given, England would have been one sweep of Shearer's right foot away from the quarter-finals.

94 min: We are told that, as is customary in such situations, the *News at Ten* will follow this programme. The news *is* this programme. Ortega twists Southgate's blood on the right of the box and puts in a dangerous cross that is booted clear by Campbell.

97 min: Anderton off, David Batty on.

99 min: Ince – who has played preposterously well, with a rare combination of desire and intelligence – slips Almeyda inside his own half and sets off on a solo run. He goes past Verón, loses the ball to a combination of Chamot and the recovering Almeyda but then wins it back again before slashing a slightly weary shot not far wide from 25 yards.

100 min: Argentina break four on four for the umpteenth time tonight. Gallardo slips it through to Crespo, who is wrongly flagged offside just before sidefooting a fraction wide of the far post.

101 min: The otherwise excellent Neville gets away with a two-footed tackle on Berti. You can't do that any more and he should probably have been booked, even though he didn't really come into contact with Berti. Berti did him a favour by not going down, a shattering blow to jingoistic self-styled experts on the history of diving up and down the country.

103 min: Ortega slips Adams and plays a pass to Berti in a coronary-inducing amount of space on the left of the box. Ince, the wonderful Ince, Pac-Mans up that space to deflect Berti's cross safely into the hands of Seaman.

105 min: There are three Argentina defenders who, when they grow older, will treat the words 'Michael Owen' as others do 'Macbeth'. He has driven them to distraction and now he sets off on another solo run, going outside Chamot before driving an optimistic shot wide of the near post from a prohibitive angle.

EXTRA TIME, HALF TIME: Argentina 2–2 England. What's left to say? Other than: aieeeeeeeeeeeeee.

106 min: It's going to penalties, isn't it? Argentina's shoot-out record is much better than England's. In 1990 their heroically dastardly side tried to become the first side to win the World Cup after three consecutive penalty shoot-outs and overall their record is four wins in five.

108 min: England are down to nine men, with Owen off the field receiving some stitches after Vivas accidentally kicked him in the back of the head. And they could have been down to eight because Ince was really lucky not to get a second yellow after ploughing through the back of Verón. The Argentina bench are all up, with Batistuta being told to get back in his box by a comically aggressive FIFA official.

113 min: All the England bench on their feet now in a show of solidarity and the inability to sit still.

115 min: It increasingly looks like England's defence have broken the will of Argentina. They are still busy and technically excellent but they simply cannot get behind England. They're like confused kids who have been fiddling with a Rubik's Cube for hours without doing anything: what the hell do we do now? Seaman has had only one difficult save to make since Beckham's sending off, from López, and even that might have been drifting wide.

117 min: Verón opens up the game with a fine first-time pass infield from the left to Gallardo. Crespo's run takes Campbell out of the way so that Gallardo can swerve round Southgate into the space on the edge of the area – but then Merson arrives with an excellent sliding challenge in the D. Paul Merson, centre-half. It's been that kind of evening. Moments later Verón's well struck but straight shot is easily held by Seaman.

118 min: Tony Adams almost steals it for England! Batty was fouled, 40 yards from goal to the left of centre. Merson curled it flat and deep towards the far post, where Adams dived all over Ayala before curling his header wide of the far post. He couldn't quite get around the ball enough because of the presence of Ayala.

EXTRA TIME, FULL TIME: Argentina 2–2 England. For the fourth consecutive knockout match at a major tournament, England are going to penalties. It's a minor miracle they got that far after Beckham's red card. Some of England's defending has been exceptional. There has been an over-my-dead-body defiance, for sure, but they have also defended with wonderful intelligence and skill. Ince, Campbell and Adams were particularly outstanding, while Owen is on a fast-track to immortality. Seaman has an excellent record in penalty shoot-outs, most obviously against Sampdoria and Spain, but England have lost two out of three. It'll be Argentina to go first.

BERTI SCORES! Argentina 1–0 England. A textbook penalty, low and dragged into the side-netting to the right. Seaman went the right way but you can't save those.

SHEARER SCORES! Argentina 1–1 England. Alan Shearer's penalty is even better than the one he scored during the match! Berti hit the side-netting; Shearer hit the top-netting with a fierce blast to Roa's right.

SEAMAN SAVES FROM CRESPO! Argentina 1–1 England. England have the advantage! It wasn't the best penalty from Crespo, passed at saveable height to the keeper's left. Seaman saved with both hands.

ROA SAVES FROM INCE! Argentina 1–1 England. That was almost a repeat of Crespo – struck with pace but at a good height for the keeper, who went to his left and beat it away. Ince of all people did not deserve that. He sat out the shoot-outs in 1996, not even watching the other penalties as they were taken. How he'll be wishing he'd chosen the same course of action tonight.

VERÓN SCORES! Argentina 2–1 England. A stonking penalty from this outstanding young playmaker, smashed into the top of the net to Seaman's right. That was almost identical to Shearer's.

MERSON SCORES! Argentina 2–2 England. But only just. There was an almighty delay before the penalty. First Merson had to move the ball, then Roa was booked for moaning that the ball wasn't on the spot. Every additional second doubled Merson's heartbeat – but he scored with a sidefoot to his left that went through Roa's hand.

GALLARDO SCORES! Argentina 3–2 England. An excellent penalty, swept into the bottom-left corner. Seaman has gone the right way for all four penalties.

OWEN SCORES! Argentina 3–3 England. Of course he scores. That was either, depending on your view, a stunning penalty or dangerously close to heartbreak. He pinged it high to the left and in off the inside of the post as Roa went the other way. The

* * * *MAGIC MINUTES* * * * * * * *MAGIC MINUTES* * * * *

Brazil 2–0 Germany (2002, final)

Probably the worst World Cup of all was partially saved by the story of Ronaldo, who achieved redemption after missing the 1998 final in mysterious circumstances. He hardly played in the intervening four years, but returned to score eight goals (well, seven; FIFA disgracefully gave him a goal against Costa Rica that was a clear own goal) in Brazil's triumph, including both in the final.

67 min: GOAL! Brazil 1–0 Germany (Ronaldo). Brazil are ahead! No surprise about the goalscorer, although there's plenty of surprise about the man who made it: Oliver Kahn. He has arguably been the player of the tournament, yet when it mattered most he was badly at fault. Ronaldo won the ball off the dawdling Hamann 25 yards out and gave it to Rivaldo. His shot was fiercely struck but straight at Kahn, who spilled it to his left. Ronaldo was on to it first, getting there before Ramelow to sidefoot in from six yards. He runs away, wagging his finger in celebration before embracing Kleberson. That is almost inhumanely cruel on Kahn, without whom Germany would be nowhere near this final.

nerveless youngster guffaws and makes the angle of post and crossbar with his arms. Everything's easy when you're a teenager. **AYALA SCORES! Argentina 4–3 England.** The centre-back Ayala teases an almost piss-taking penalty into the bottom-right corner. Seaman waited to see which side it was going. Had he moved earlier he might have got there as it wasn't right in the corner. It's now sudden death. David Batty has to score or England are on the plane with the flight number DO 1. **ROA SAVES FROM BATTY AND ENGLAND ARE OUT OF THE WORLD CUP! Argentina 2–2 England (4–3 pens).** On ITV, Brian Moore asks Kevin Keegan if Batty will score, yes or no. It's a daft thing for such an experienced commentator to do, and Keegan's in a hole. He can only say 'Yes', and it can only end one way for Batty, who has never taken a spotkick before in his pro career. There's planning for you. It was a poor penalty and easily saved by Roa to his right. 'Oh *no*,' growls Keegan. Ah well, there goes the dream. Hoddle and England will never be able to say 'we'll always have Paris', but at least they'll retain bittersweet memories of Saint-Etienne, where they played so bravely only to come up short at the death. They have some brilliant young players – most notably the astonishing Owen – and a generation that we might even call golden are clearly going places under their excellent young manager. For now England's miserable penalty record continues, although look on the bright side: the law of averages suggests they'll win the next two shoot-outs, whenever they might be.

Germany v Italy

Semi-final, Westfalenstadion, Dortmund, Germany,
Tuesday, 4 July 2006

Germany have already done something far more remarkable than win football's World Cup: they've made the world love German football. Their intrepid, effervescent, F.U.N. football has led to the weird sight of many fans from their traditional bogey countries (i.e. almost all of FIFA's other 208 member states) rooting for them. Their 4–2 win over Costa Rica in the opening match set the tone and their penalties victory over the tournament sensations Argentina means they are the most popular team left in the pot. They've come a long way since they were slaughtered 4–1 by Italy in March, after which questions were asked in the German parliament.

Italian football has regressed dramatically since then – but that's because of the ongoing match-fixing scandal rather than events on the field. It's hard to know what to make of their progress in this tournament. On the one hand they got out of a tricky group – the Czech Republic, Ghana and the USA – with scarcely a scare and have conceded only once in five games, and that a slightly weird own goal. But they needed a dodgy penalty to beat Australia in the last 16 (albeit with ten men) and their 3–0 win over Ukraine in the quarter-final was rendered inscrutable by the feebleness of opposition who, if they were in a film, would be played by William H. Macy. We will know a lot more about Italy in two hours' time.

Team news: Germany are without Torsten Frings, suspended for touching Julio Cruz in the pud-em-up aftermath of that match against Argentina – an indiscretion helpfully pointed out to FIFA by Italian TV executives. He's replaced by Sebastian Kehl, who gets to play a World Cup semi-final on his home ground. Tim Borowski comes in for the brilliant but erratic winger Bastian Schweinsteiger. Italy make one change: Everton alumnus Marco Materazzi, available again after suspension, replaces Andrea Barzagli.

Kick-off: 9 p.m. in Dortmund, 8 p.m. on ITV.

Referee: Benito Archundia (Mexico).

Germany: Jens Lehmann; Arne Friedrich, Christoph Metzelder, Per Mertesacker, Philipp Lahm; Bernd Schneider, Michael Ballack, Sebastian Kehl, Tim Borowski; Miroslav Klose, Lukas Podolski.

Italy: Gianluigi Buffon; Gianluca Zambrotta, Fabio Cannavaro, Marco Materazzi, Fabio Grosso; Mauro Camoranesi, Andrea Pirlo, Gennaro Gattuso, Simone Perrotta; Francesco Totti; Luca Toni.

Fashion news: Jürgen Klinsmann and his assistant Joachim Löw are, as usual, dressed like the greatest love interests Sarah Jessica Parker never had, with His & His challengingly tight white shirts – both of which look like they've been ironed for at least four hours – and no tie, tucked neatly into black trousers. On the opposite bench is Marcello Lippi, once described as a 'good-looking bastard' by Sir Alex Ferguson. The Paul Newman lookalike may be good-looking but this isn't such a good look: he is in a polo shirt and tracksuit bottoms, with his ground pass fetchingly hanging over his neck. He looks like a man shuffling from settee to kitchen to get a new tube of Pringles and can of pop in time for kick-off. If Italy get to the final, what next? An egg-stained string vest and Y-fronts combo?

Pre-match tunefulness: Gennaro Gattuso squeezes his eyes tight as he bellows out the Italian anthem. He looks like he's about to cry. An experienced Italy side – nobody under 27 – look ready for this. But then so do Germany, packed full of young players.

1 min: Germany kick off from right to left. They are in white; Italy are in blue. A classic look to this match. The whole scene is imbued with a deliciously naive hope: in two hours' time, one of these groups of players will have lost their best chance to win a World Cup.

2 min: The atmosphere in Dortmund is just wonderful, as it has been all tournament. Not so much a wall of sound as an entire building. German teams may be utterly hopeless in the Champions League but off the field their fans are the best in Europe.

3 min: Podolski picks the pocket of Gattuso, who boots him in the shin for his impertinence. It was a clear foul, although

Podolski's dive was somewhere between theatric and pathetic. Gattuso, a man who could stare out a corpse, fixes him with a look that says: what kind of man are you? Shudder.

8 min: Michael Ballack wangs a shot high and wide from long range. It's been a fast start – almost breezy, given the importance of the game – although there have been no chances yet.

11 min: A lovely move from Italy. Totti sprays a fine pass out to Perrotta on the left. He moves it down the line to Grosso, who sweeps a dangerous cross along the line of the six-yard box. Lahm is in what Ron Atkinson used to call the wide-awake club before he was bundled off the telly in disgrace, and gets to it a fraction before the lurking Camoranesi.

15 min: And now a fine move from Germany. Borowski's pass/cross from deep on the left finds Klose just inside the box. He cushions an ingenious volley into the space behind Materazzi, inviting Podolski to run on to it. Cannavaro covers excellently from the side and just gets there first to clear. That was another example of the almost telepathic understanding between the Poland-born pair of Klose and Podolski.

16 min: Germany have an appeal for a penalty turned down, and moments later Perrotta misses the first big chance of the game. First the penalty. Ballack's header certainly hit the arm of Pirlo and replays suggest he instinctively moved his arm towards the ball. Against that, he was only a couple of yards from Ballack. A quick glance in the Ginormous Book of Football Clichés tells us that, yes, yes, we have seen them given. But play continued and a few seconds later Totti, running infield from the left on the halfway line, clipped an outstanding pass over the top of the defence that took four German players out of the game. Perrotta ran between Mertesacker and Metzelder through on goal in the inside-left channel, but his first touch was a fraction too heavy and that allowed Lehmann to come out and block his shot. 'Best chance yet for the Italian No. 20, Simone Perrotta, born in Ashton-under-Lyme,' says ITV's usually excellent Clive Tyldesley with endearingly confused pride.

24 min: Zambrotta is fouled by Borowski, 40 yards from goal on the right wing. Pirlo's wicked, outswinging free-kick dips over the head of Toni, before hitting Mertesacker and bouncing over the bar. The unsighted Materazzi was just in front of Mertesacker, six yards from goal, but missed his attempted header. It wasn't that great a chance.

26 min: An ITV graphic confirms what the eyes have seen: that Italy have dominated the game thus far. They have had 57 per cent of the possession, a reflection of a cool, authoritative and fearless performance.

30 min: Camoranesi is fouled by Lahm just outside the box on the right. As a pack of players charges towards the six-yard box, Totti comes the other way to meet a sharp cut-back from Pirlo with a 15-yard shot that is blocked by a combination of Klose and Mertesacker. He didn't quite hit it cleanly, probably because he ran into Materazzi on his way to meet the ball and was off-balance as a result. Totti gives Materazzi a look as he jogs back to the halfway line.

31 min: Italy deserve to be ahead. Grosso, Palermo's late-blooming left-back who has had such a fine tournament, receives a reverse pass from Perrotta on the left, nutmegs Schneider with his first touch and powers into the box. Then he drives a low cross towards Toni, whose first-time flick from six yards is blocked crucially by the sliding Metzelder.

34 min: Italy may deserve to be ahead but Germany should be ahead. Schneider has just missed the best chance of the match. Germany broke quickly after a lazy square pass from Pirlo on the halfway line. Kehl pushed it forward to Klose, who played a quick one-two with Podolski and then dragged the ball cleverly away from Gattuso. That allowed him to run at the two centre-backs, and with Grosso stranded upfield there was an indecent amount of space for Schneider on the right. Klose pushed it into that space, allowing Schneider to run into the box and hammer a shot from 15 yards that whooshed just over the bar. His first touch wasn't quite right – a touch too soft, which meant the ball was running away slightly as he struck it.

40 min: Borowski is booked for a foul on Totti. He got the ball but came through Totti to get there. Klinsmann waves his hands around in disgust. It was a fair decision. The Mexican referee has been brilliant so far, allowing play to continue wherever possible. He has contributed enormously to the openness of this match.

45 min: Ballack and Totti go for a 50/50 ball, with Totti jumping spectacularly over the back of Ballack. The referee tells Totti to get up and gives the foul to Germany. He has been great. It's like *Life on Mars* in reverse: this referee could easily have come from the mid-1970s, such is the physical contact that he is allowing on both sides. (And don't say we never do anything for you: there's a Bowie earworm that will hopefully dislodge Kasabian's dad-rock desecration of 'Heroes', which has been caterwauling all month over the ITV titles.)

HALF TIME: Germany 0–0 Italy. Lippi saunters off down the tunnel in search of crisps and cola.

46 min: Italy begin the second half, kicking from right to left.

50 min: Buffon makes a vital save from Klose! Kehl played a sharp pass forward to Klose, in a bit of space in an inside-right position, and he set off on a powerful, direct run infield. He held off Gattuso just outside the box and then, once inside the area, dragged the ball between Cannavaro and Gattuso. Buffon burst from his line to smother the ball as Klose tried to poke it in. Replays suggest Cannavaro caught Klose, who could have gone down but was so determined to score that he stayed on his feet. Moments later, Pirlo's delicious pass put Grosso through on goal and Lehmann came out to make a fine block. It wouldn't have counted as Grosso had been given offside, although it was a very tight and possibly incorrect call.

56 min: Metzelder is booked for a tackle from behind on Toni.

59 min: The match continues to be weirdly and admirably open for a World Cup semi-final. It's not just defences who are naked; the camera cuts to a group of topless Italian fans in the crowd, one of whom is so spectacularly hairy that he makes Ryan Giggs look like one of the Moomins.

62 min: Ballack is sent flying by Materazzi but the referee plays the advantage and it leads to a chance for Germany. Schneider combines with Kehl on the right before playing a delicate, slow pass into Podolski at the corner of the six-yard box. He holds off Materazzi, spins around him with an excellent first touch then hammers a shot that is beaten away by Buffon. Friedrich crashes the rebound into orbit from 15 yards. Friedrich's might have been the better chance actually; Podolski's was from a tight angle and on the turn. Klinsmann bounces a water flask off the ground in disgust. You won't pull Carrie Bradshaw throwing that kind of tantrum.

65 min: The falling Grosso is accidentally kneed in the noggin by Klose. He's scratching his head furiously. That looks pretty painful. 'My brain hurts!' says Clive Tyldesley in a Kevin and Perry voice. At least we assume it was Tyldesley; it was hardly likely to be wise old owl David Pleat, was it?

73 min: The first substitution, with Bastian Schweinsteiger replacing Borowski on the left of the midfield.

74 min: And now Italy's first change: Alberto Gilardino for Toni, who has put in a selfless shift on his own up front.

78 min: Camoranesi is fouled by Ballack. The referee comes over to have a word and Camoranesi bounces back to his feet. As Tyldesley says on ITV, the generosity of spirit in this match has been pretty amazing: there's an innocent, may-the-best-team-win mood about the game.

81 min: Now, this is interesting. Cannavaro is penalized for a foul on Podolski just outside the box – which is wrong on both counts. It almost certainly wasn't a foul, but if it was a foul it was just inside the area and should have been a penalty. Schneider on the right floated a long pass towards Podolski; Cannavaro got above him to head clear, apparently cleanly, but then the referee penalized him for jumping on Podolski. There are no appeals for a penalty – Podolski simply applauds the decision – but it was definitely inside the area.

82 min: REDEMPTION FOR BALLACK? NO. Germany have a free-kick nonetheless, 19 yards from goal. Ballack looks set to take it. All that failure and heartbreak, not least when he was suspended from the World Cup final four years ago, could be left behind if he puts this in. Here he comes . . . and it's comfortably over the bar.

83 min: The jet-heeled substitute David Odonkor – who can do 100 metres in under 11 seconds – has come on for Schneider.

89 min: Perrotta, just past the halfway line, pings a bouncing ball over the top for Gilardino. For a moment it looks like he's clear on goal but Lahm comes round to intercept on the edge of the area. As good as this game has been, there haven't been many clear chances– a credit to the exceptionally high quality of the defending. It looks like they will have to do it for another 30 minutes.

90 min: Camoranesi is booked for a weary lunge at Kehl. 'This is one for the purists,' says David Pleat. 'One to keep and savour.'

FULL TIME: Italy 0–0 Germany. Italy bring on Vincenzo Iaquinta for Camoranesi.

91 min: GILARDINO HITS THE POST! Italy's substitute so nearly gives them the lead. The chance came out of nothing. Schweinsteiger tackled Iaquinta and in so doing sent the ball down the right wing towards his own goal. Metzelder got there first but then fell over under pressure from Gilardino, allowing Gilardino to rumble into the box on the right. He was off-balance after the challenge from Metzelder and almost ran the ball out of play. He then suddenly composed himself to move away from Ballack on the six-yard line and screw a shot that hit the inside of the near post and dribbled right across the face of goal! Lehmann's weight was going the other way and, although he threw his hand back to the left, he may not have had it covered.

92 min: NOW ZAMBROTTA HITS THE BAR! Where's that exclamation-mark button? Italy have twanged the metalwork twice in the first two minutes of extra time!!! They're not so keen on penalties, are they? Pirlo's underhit near-post corner was only half cleared by Friedrich. It came to Zambrotta, who touched it back into the area and then hit a fierce rising drive from the right of the box that rattled off the top of the crossbar with Lehmann beaten!

94 min: 'Viewers who are turning on expecting to see *Emmerdale* will get a double bill tomorrow at 9.30,' says Clive Tyldesley. I know Sade is about to tell Ashley the truth about Cain and Jasmine but can you really imagine wanting to pop down the Woolpack while this is on?

96 min: Tyldesley sounds like he is having a 120-minute epiphany. He is totally in love with this match, and with football, and with life. In a second he is going to talk about the beauty of watching a plastic bag blowing in the wind. But you can understand his attitude: it's been a brilliant and almost unimaginably refreshing football match.

99 min: The pace has slowed down for the first time all night. It's a surprise it took so long.

102 min: Cannavaro makes another classy interception, nipping in front of Podolski. He has been immense, like he's been computer programmed. He's barely put a foot wrong.

104 min: Italy make their final substitution, with Alessandro Del Piero replacing Perrotta. They have four attackers on the field now, even if Iaquinta and Del Piero are playing in wide positions. You probably wouldn't be laughed out of the boozer if you opined that they are not playing for penalties.

105+1 min: PODOLSKI MISSES A SITTER! Germany should be in front. Totti went down on the edge of the area, the referee waved play on for the 893,232,109th time tonight and Germany set off on a leisurely counter-attack. Schweinsteiger and Ballack moved the ball to Odonkor, who ran at Grosso and then noticed Podolski in a scandalous amount of space ten yards in the box. Odonkor's near-post cross was almost perfect; Podolski's header was less so, planted comfortably wide of the near post on the run. That's the last act of the first period of extra time in this wonderful match.

EXTRA TIME, HALF TIME: Germany 0–0 Italy. Yet in a sense Germany lead by 0.5 goals to nil because only one team will want this to go to penalties: Germany have won five out of six shoot-outs at major tournaments, Italy have lost four out of five, including in all three World Cups in the 1990s. You've got more chance against the Grim Reaper than you have against Germany at penalties. But Italy deserve to win.

108 min: When a Germany corner is half cleared, Iaquinta blocks Odonkor's attempted cross to spark a three-on-three break. Iaquinta gets the ball back from Totti and gallops into the box on the left, cutting back inside Friedrich before Odonkor concedes a corner. He ran 70 yards to make up for his earlier mistake.

110 min: Almost always at this level, a game of this nature drifts to penalties. Bodies are shattered, minds even more tired, and in such circumstances it is human nature to postpone the moment of performance and seek comfort in the perceived 50/50 chance of penalties. Not here. Italy in particular are desperate to end this in 120 minutes.

111 min: The veteran Oliver Neuville – who took a penalty against Argentina on Friday – comes on for Klose. As soon as he jogs on to the field, another old substitute has a chance to win it. Pirlo's chip forward is headed on dangerously into the area by Totti. The offside-looking Del Piero gets to it first, eight yards out, but Friedrich and Lehmann just about manage to crowd him out. He eventually gets away from Friedrich and tries to wriggle round Lehmann, who dives to get a slight touch on the ball. Del Piero stabs it off to Iaquinta, who has a clearer but tight shooting angle. He hammers it goalwards and it hits Lahm.

112 min: Germany break from that Del Piero chance and Podolski forces a fine save from Buffon! This is breathless stuff. Germany played their way out of trouble from the left corner flag, with Lahm and Schweinsteiger combining. Then it went through Kehl and Odonkor and back to Kehl, who played a penetrative angled pass to Podolski in space on the left side of the box. He controlled the ball and whipped a fierce shot that was dramatically tipped over the bar by the right hand of Buffon, leaping almost backwards. It's a save he would expect to make but at this stage of a World Cup semi-final all bets are off and that was a vital stop. 'Wonderful, wonderful football match,' weeps Clive Tyldesley, threatening to break into a paean to the capital of Denmark.

114 min: You know a football match or goal is special when a commentator simply starts screaming. John Motson during France v Portugal in 1984, Martin Tyler during Inter v Sampdoria in 1991, Barry Davies when Dennis Bergkamp scored against Argentina in 1998 – and now Clive Tyldesley here. Totti curves a pass over the top to Iaquinta. He's on the right edge of the box, facing away from goal and covered by a defender, but Lehmann comes needlessly into no-man's-land before back-pedalling desperately. Iaquinta backheels it to Gilardino on the edge of the area, he lays it off to Del Piero – or 'DEL PIEARGHAIEEEEE!' as Tyldesley puts it – and he drags his shot well wide of the far post. By then Lehmann was just about in position, so it was probably not much more than a half-chance.

116 min: Some of the players can barely move now. There are pieces of their soul all over the pitch. It looks like penalties.

118 min: The wonderful Pirlo – who has played with almost crazy serenity given the stakes – almost wins it at the death, only to be denied by the equally wonderful Jens Lehmann. Pirlo took an awkward ball from Iaquinta and strolled away from Kehl. He ran to within 25 yards and decided to have one last blast, a rising left-footed drive that was palmed around the post by Lehmann, diving to his left.

119 min: GOAL! Germany 0–1 Italy (Grosso). ITALY ARE IN THE WORLD CUP FINAL!!! The left-back Grosso has won the match with a stunning goal. It all came from the corner following Pirlo's shot. Del Piero's outswinger was headed away by Friedrich to Pirlo in the D. He controlled the ball and, as three defenders closed in, sashayed across the line of the box, somehow keeping his cool, waiting for an angle for a pass. Eventually he found it with a gentle reverse pass, played between Metzelder and Schweinsteiger to Grosso. He still had so much to do – he was the right side of the box, with little pace on the ball and a group of bodies between him and the goal – but he used Ballack as a screen and swept a wonderful curling shot across Lehmann and into the far corner. Grosso is going doolally, shaking his head all over the place in an unconscious homage to Marco Tardelli's celebration in the 1982 World Cup final. He looks on the cusp of tears. So does Lippi. Perhaps he's run out of Pringles. Eventually Grosso is lovingly manhandled to the floor and takes his place at the bottom of the most joyous bundle you will ever see. Even Buffon is in the bundle. What a finish! And what a pass from Pirlo!

120 min: It's not over yet. Odonkor's cross is headed away by Cannavaro to Ballack, who hammers a half-volley well wide of the far post from the edge of the box.

120+1 min: GOAL! Germany 0–2 Italy (Del Piero). Del Piero finishes it off for Italy! It's another outstanding goal. Ballack's left-wing cross was headed away by the immense Cannavaro, who then roared from his own box to win the ball again off Podolski. He gave it to Totti, who swept it left to Gilardino. He ran to the edge of the box, teasing Metzelder, before playing the cutest of reverse passes to Del Piero, who had charged 90 yards – 90 yards! – in support. Del Piero, ten yards from goal, ran round the ball and placed a delicious curling shot into the far top corner. 'FAN-TAS-TIC!' screams Clive Tyldesley, a guttural and fittingly spine-tingling piece of commentary for one of the most sensational finishes to any World Cup match ever. Italy are going ballistic. You dream your whole life about reaching a World Cup final but you don't even dare fantasize about reaching one like this. Lippi straightens his collar and his pass, the coolest man in the stadium. In fact, that is the final kick of the match! The final whistle has gone during the Italian celebration.

EXTRA TIME, FULL TIME: Germany 0–2 Italy. It's been eight years since the last classic World Cup match. This undoubtedly meets that description. It was a played with an almost incongruous innocence and was eventually won – just – by the better side. You could pick about 25 men of the match, with the referee, Andrea Pirlo, Fabio Cannavaro and Clive Tyldesley at the top of the list. Klinsmann hugs Mertesacker, who is in on his knees almost in tears. Gattuso is on his back, also almost in tears. Italian fans are in tears, German fans are in tears. This has been an epic. A tear-jerker, if you will. Italy will play France or Portugal in Berlin on Sunday. Something weird, bordering on surreal, will have to go down at the Olympiastadion if the final's to live longer in the memory than this.

Italy v France

Final, Olympiastadion, Berlin, Germany,
Sunday, 9 July 2006

Whisper it quietly, because we all love our World Cup, but there hasn't been a good final since 1986. We've used a simple metric to measure that statement out: that was the last time both sides managed to get on the scoresheet. We could do with a little spirit of '86 this evening, a bit of to and fro, a smidgen of unpredictability – it's not too much to ask.

Italy have already done their bit in the nearest a World Cup has got to a stone-cold classic for a while, their Homeric struggle against hosts Germany in the semis. France, on the other hand, were laughably useless in the group stage, qualifying for the knockout stages more by default than anything else. But their run to the final has been nothing short of astonishing, with Zinedine Zidane, set to retire after this match, enjoying the latest and balmiest of Indian summers. First *les bleus* saw off an up-and-coming Spanish side. Then they did for tournament favourites Brazil. And in the semis they did enough to give Portugal a Cristiano Ronaldoesque bodyswerve. Both teams are peaking at the right time.

Time for the best final in a generation, then? Well, Italy have only conceded one goal in the tournament so far, while France have let in a mammoth two. Still, it's been 20 years now, so why the hell not? Kick-off's at 8 p.m. in front of a modest full house of 69,000. No Maracanã this, but what gorgeous asymmetrical architecture. Look at that staircase sweeping up to the Olympic cauldron! That'll be handy if anyone needs to make a quick exit.

Kick-off: 8 p.m. local time, 7 p.m. English time.

Referee: Horacio Elizondo (Argentina).

Italy: Gianluigi Buffon, Gianluca Zambrotta, Marco Materazzi, Fabio Cannavaro, Fabio Grosso, Andrea Pirlo, Gennaro Gattuso, Mauro Camoranesi, Francesco Totti, Simone Perrotta, Luca Toni.

France: Fabien Barthez, Willy Sagnol, Lilian Thuram, William Gallas, Eric Abidal, Patrick Vieira, Claude Makélélé, Franck Ribéry, Zinedine Zidane, Florent Malouda, Thierry Henry.

And we're off! And within 35 seconds, Henry is spark out on the floor, having clattered into Cannavaro while looking the other way. He'll not be getting the Green Cross Code gig any time soon.

4 min: After lugging on the salts, Henry is back on, though he doesn't half look queasy.

5 min: The first meaningful attack of the match sees Grosso tear down the left and loop a cross into the area for Toni and Perrotta. It's cleared to the edge of the box, where Vieira's scythed down by Zambrotta. He's practically cut off his legs! That'll be a booking.

6 min: PENALTY TO FRANCE! Henry's feeling a whole load better now. He wins a long ball down the left touchline, heading back inside into the path of Malouda, who is haring towards the area down the channel. He reaches the box before Cannavaro on his left and Materazzi on his right. The Italian captain Cannavaro is too clever to dangle out a leg. Materazzi, not so much. A no-brainer for the referee.

7 min: GOAL!!! Italy 0–1 France (Zidane pen). Zinedine Zidane is outrageous, outré, out there. Facing the most expensive goalkeeper in football history, he takes three short steps and Panenkas a chip straight down the middle. He's beaten Buffon, who dives to his right, the side Zidane put the winning penalty in the semi against Portugal. But he so nearly overcooks the chip, the ball bouncing off the underside of the bar, then over the line. But only just! It spins back out and Zidane looks over his shoulder at the linesman, fearing for a split second that he's been a wee bit too clever for his own good. It stands, though. He's pushed taking the piss right to the limit. You can't go any further than that, philosophically or physically. A quick reminder: this is *the World Cup final.*

9 min: Sagnol curves a cross towards the Italian area from the right. Materazzi appears to be playing for France. He intercepts the cross, backheading it at some pace towards the top-right corner of his own goal! It's probably going just wide but Buffon can take no chances. Corner to France. Corner *mauvais.*

14 min: Pirlo swings a free-kick into the area from the right. Thuram, diving, sends a header flashing wide of his own near post. That's not quite in the Materazzi class in terms of hapless-ness but it's something for Italy at least, who are rocking in the wake of France's hot start.

19 min: GOAL!!! Italy 1–1 France (Materazzi), Camoranesi wins a corner off Abidal down the right. Pirlo sends a high out-swinger to the far post, where Materazzi rises above Vieira on the edge of the six-yard area and absolutely thumps a header into the top left. Nobody was stopping that. Lovely finish, but what a delivery from Pirlo, and how about that for instant redemption for the big galoot? He points to the skies in dedication to a lost loved one or greater power. Hm, let's hope this schmaltzy non-sense doesn't catch on in professional sport.

26 min: The first flash of the Henry Arsenal fans love. He turns on the Special Boots and jets past Totti down the inside right. He then slides in Ribéry but his low cross – reminiscent of nobody so much as Henry's old pal Marc Overmars – is hacked away for a corner that leads to naught.

28 min: There's no keeping Materazzi down. Now he's sent another header fizzing goalwards but this one is kicked away by Thuram, and the big Italian's been a-foulin' anyway.

36 min: Totti, breaking into the area from the right, glances a ball down the channel for Toni, whose attempt to find the bottom right is blocked by Thuram. From the corner, another outswinging Pirlo delivery, Toni crashes a header off the top of the crossbar from six yards. He holds his mouth with both hands and looks around in despair, full in the knowledge that his place in the history books has gone begging. He should have scored.

HALF TIME: Italy 1–1 France. It's not been the classic we were hoping for but it's not been awful either, and at least both teams have scored this time. Who will be the Marco Tardelli or Zinedine Zidane *de nos jours*? Admittedly one side has a more obvious candidate than the other.

46 min: Malouda goes down on the left and doesn't get up. Henry goes on a romp down the left channel, breaking past three half-arsed challenges and reaching the area, before sidefooting weakly at Buffon. Italy seem to think Henry should have put the ball out for his stricken colleague and go ballistic. Play to the whistle, people.

50 min: Henry embarks on a glorious skitter down the right, almost running on top of the ball as he freewheels past three challenges and crosses low and hard into the six-yard box. Zambrotta clears his lines.

53 min: Ribéry scorches the right wing before rolling the ball infield to Zidane, who shuttles it further left to Malouda. The winger is bundled to the floor by Zambrotta, who comes in from the right to throw a leg across him. That's a penalty kick all day long but the referee isn't having it. Zidane is performing an ersatz tribute to Nobby Stiles, but this is a jig of anger.

58 min: A Zidane volley is blocked on the edge of the area by Pirlo. This is all France. Italy are an embarrassing shambles at the moment.

62 min: ITALY HAVE A GOAL DISALLOWED! From near the left touchline by the centre circle, Pirlo swings a free-kick towards the edge of the French area. Toni is all alone in the centre and helps the ball on with his head into the right-hand side of the goal! He races away in jubilation but is soon pulled back. The flag's gone up for offside, which is just about right. *Mon dieu*, what was the French defence doing there, though? They were all grouped to the right of the area. Had Toni timed that run correctly, he'd be on the scoresheet. It doesn't appear to be his day.

63 min: Again, this isn't a classic by any means but it's better than anything we've had for many a year. Henry battles with Cannavaro down the inside right, chasing a Makélélé pass. He gets a yard on the defender, but only that. His low shot from just inside the area – all the defender will allow – is parried by Buffon.

71 min: Zidane's free-kick is flapped away a little unconvincingly by Buffon, then Cannavaro comically shanks an attempted clearance.

76 min: After a long period of relative inactivity, which had arguably seen France in slight territorial ascendancy (how's that for trying to jazz up nothing?), Diarra, who's replaced Viera, claps his hand into Toni's coupon as the pair contest a high ball. He's booked and that's a free-kick to Italy, slap bang in the middle of the park, 30 yards out. Pirlo steps up and magic wands a shot towards the bottom-left corner. It curls just wide of the post. It really is debatable whether Barthez would have got across to that.

85 min: Henry wheechs past Zambrotta down the left and pulls back a peach from the byline. Zidane is rushing in but the ball is blootered away by Materazzi, who has done enough now for us to forget about those earlier aberrations.

FULL TIME: Italy 1–1 France. And so, after a final half hour where it was clear both teams were more obsessed with not conceding than scoring themselves, we move to extra time.

99 min: It's been all France in the opening stage of extra time and they should have just gone a goal up. Ribéry sashays in from the left, all hips and shoulders, one-twoing with Malouda then carving open a gap in the heart of the Italian defence. He looks to prod a violent finish into the bottom right and Buffon wouldn't have got there, but the ball flies just wide.

104 min: ZIDANE NEARLY WRITES THE FAIRYTALE ENDING! From a central position, 30 yards out, he slips the ball wide to Sagnol, who dispatches an immediate cross into the area. Zidane had continued his run and meets the ball with a thumping header. It's creeping under the bar but his old Juventus buddy Buffon bends backwards to tip the ball over with a strong right hand. What a glorious finish to a stellar career that would have been!

EXTRA TIME, HALF TIME: Italy 1–1 France. Italy are just clinging on for penalties.

109 min: ZIDANE: THE NIGHTMARE DENOUEMENT! Del Piero, on for Camoranesi, skitters down the inside-left channel. He slides to the turf and handles the ball. Before Wiltord, who has just entered the fray in place of Henry, can take the free-kick, the referee stops play as Materazzi's lying on the turf deep inside his own half. What's gone on here? Cannavaro is livid. The referee doesn't quite know what's going on. Zidane is fiddling nervously with his captain's armband. It's almost as though he knows he'll be taking it off very soon. The atmosphere in the Olympiastadion is very strange. And sure enough, he's given his marching orders! He took two steps towards Materazzi and planted a vicious headbutt straight in the middle of the Italian's breastplate! Materazzi sprung backwards and clattered to the floor. On the touchline, France manager Raymond Domenech is sarcastically applauding the official, a mime accompanied by several other Gallic handflaps, but he clearly can't have seen that. There goes Zizou! What a way to end a career!

111 min: It's almost impossible to pick the bones out of that. Materazzi and Zidane were both running back upfield. It looked like Materazzi put his left arm round Zidane and tweaked his left nipple from behind, like the Monty Python animation of a radio being tuned in using the breast of Botticelli's Venus. But that didn't spark it because they both took a few more steps upfield, whereupon Zidane suddenly exploded and made his fateful lurch forward! Was something said? Bet heavily that we'll never find out the true story about this. That's a JFK moment with added ABH.

115 min: Italy, with the extra man, are suddenly on the front foot. But having been on the defensive for so long, can't get anything serious going.

120 min: One last chance for France, who on balance of play deserve to win this match. Malouda sends Wiltord into space down the inside right, but he welts an awful shot miles over the bar and finishes with a flourish by sliding around on his arse with a confused look on his face.

IT'S PENALTIES! Italy 1–1 France. Well, whither a Hans Christian Andersen for the 21st century? They don't write fairy stories any more, do they?

PIRLO SCORES! Italy 1–0 France. Pirlo chips gorgeously down the middle.

WILTORD SCORES! Italy 1–1 France. Wiltord bangs one to Buffon's left.

MATERAZZI SCORES! Italy 2–1 France. Materazzi completes the most eventful of nights by hitting low and firm into the bottom left.

TREZEGUET MISSES! Italy 2–1 France. Substitute Trezeguet's fierce effort hits the underside of the bar and, unlike Zidane's penalty, bounces out and away. A World Cup, four years of work, could be decided by so small a margin.

DE ROSSI SCORES! Italy 3–1 France. A fantastic, unsaveable penalty hit by the Italian sub into the top-left corner.

ABIDAL SCORES! Italy 3–2 France. Calmly done by Abidal, who places it left as Buffon dives the other way.

DEL PIERO SCORES! Italy 4–2 France. Italy are on the brink of glory. Del Piero scores, high to his left, although Barthez would have had a decent chance had he gone the right way.

SAGNOL SCORES! Italy 4–3 France. Sagnol gives France a stay of execution with a violent penalty.

GROSSO SCORES AND ITALY ARE WORLD CHAMPIONS FOR THE FIRST TIME IN 24 YEARS!!! Italy 1–1 France (4–3 pens). Grosso – the hero of the semi – steps up to ram home the decisive spotkick. Italy scamper around like toddlers who have accidentally gotten into the cupboard where Mum and Dad keep the Red Bull. This is unfortunate on France, who were the better side on the night, and a personal tragedy for Zidane, who really has been a daft bugger. But Italy have been the best side in the tournament overall. Get your money on Italy as runners-up in 2018, because this continues a strange 12-year cycle: losing finalists in 1970, winners in 1982, losing finalist in 1994, winners in 2006. Not a classic, but dramatic as hell, and after the snoozefests of 1994, 1998 and 2002, we'll take this every time.

Spain v Holland

Final, Soccer City, Johannesburg, South Africa,
Sunday, 11 July 2010

Only three countries have held the world title and their continental pot at the same time. West Germany were the first to manage it, adding the 1974 World Cup to their Euro 72 title. France were next up, their win at Euro 2000 arguably the highpoint in qualitative terms of an imperial phase that also saw them lift the 1998 World Cup. Then Brazil became the first South American side to manage it, landing the 2004 Copa America a couple of years after their World Cup win in South Korea and Japan.

It's not easy. No, it's not easy. Which explains why Spain – a side with genuine claims to being one of the greatest teams of all time, having won Euro 2008 with swashbuckling ease, then made it ten victories out of ten in World Cup qualification – haven't quite set the 2010 World Cup alight in the manner we'd all hoped. They somehow managed to lose their opening game against Switzerland, edged past Honduras and made rather a meal of dispatching ten-man Chile to guarantee their passage into the next round. Since when it's been undistinguished 1–0s all the way, against Portugal, Paraguay and Germany.

Mind you, this is setting the bar as high as it goes. Spain have, after all, reached their first-ever World Cup final and won't be caring too much how they got there. The neutral fancies seeing a bit of the old Spain, though, and hopes for a sunshine splash from the Iberian aesthetes on the biggest stage of all.

And who better to tease it out of them than Holland? They're chock-full of attacking talent and yes, we do include the underrated Dirk Kuyt in there. They knocked out Brazil and Uruguay in two of the tournament's most colourful games. And they're doubtless desperate not to become the only country in World Cup history to make it to three finals and lose them all. A classic could be on the cards here.

Kick-off: 8.30 p.m. locally, 7.30 p.m. in England.

Referee: It's Howard Webb from England! Now, three British referees have taken charge of a World Cup final before: George Reader in 1950, Bill Ling in 1954 and Jack Taylor in 1974. Two of them have presided over almighty balls-ups. Ling controversially disallowed what looked like a good Ferenc Puskás goal, while Taylor awarded a penalty that probably wasn't, missed one that definitely was, and didn't even spot the corner flags were missing until seconds before kick-off. Webb doesn't have a high bar to clear, though this doesn't augur well.

Holland become the first team in World Cup history to name squad members 1 to 11 in the final: Maarten Stekelenburg, Gregory van der Wiel, John Heitinga, Joris Mathijsen, Giovanni van Bronckhorst, Mark van Bommel, Nigel de Jong, Wesley Sneijder, Arjen Robben, Dirk Kuyt, Robin van Persie.

Spain: Iker Casillas, Sergio Ramos, Gerard Piqué, Carles Puyol, Joan Capdevila, Sergio Busquets, Xabi Alonso, Xavi, Andrés Iniesta, Pedro, David Villa.

The kits: Holland are in all *oranje*, while Spain are in their away strip of blue.

Pre-match niceties: The 2006 winning captain, Fabio Cannavaro, comes out and holds aloft the trophy that'll be the property of Italy for another 120 minutes at most. Webb leads the teams out and plucks the Kick-off Ball from the Kick-off Ball Plinth. Football's come a long way since 1930, although not always in the totally correct direction.

The Dutch get into a huddle, the Spanish loll around trying to kid on they don't care – and Holland set the Kick-off Ball rolling by, well, kicking off. Kuyt is sent scampering down the left after a long pass, which sails out of play. Nine seconds was the sum total of Kick-off Ball's moment in the sun. Andy Warhol would be shocked at the transient nature of modern celebrity.

2 min: Van Persie rakes his shoe down Pedro's shin. Webb makes the decision to let this one go, something the Dutch striker had probably incorporated into his working.

5 min: Van Bronckhorst clatters into Xavi down the right. That was no-nonsense and probably no-fair too. Ramos gets on the end of the resulting free-kick, sending a header towards the bottom left, but Stekelenburg parries well.

Uruguay 1–1 Ghana (2010, quarter-final)

Uruguay are hoping to reach their first semi since 1970, while Ghana look to become the first African team to make the last four. Injury time in extra time approaches. Heartbreak and defeat in the penalty shoot-out await, though the route to the shoot-out is unconventional to say the least.

120 min: RED CARD AND PENALTY! Dominic Adiyiah trips over his own feet going down the right wing but the referee penalizes Jorge Fucile for a foul. Ghana load the box – there's no time left for Uruguay to break upfield so they throw the dice. Pantsil swings a setpiece into the mix. Kevin-Prince Boateng flicks on. Fernando Muslera comes off his line and flaps. John Mensah, at the far post, unselfishly heads into the middle for Stephen Appiah, whose shot is spectacularly stopped on the line by the knee of Luis Suárez. But the ball balloons up to Adiyiah, who sends a vicious header goalwards from six yards. Suárez clears again – but only by parrying clear with both hands. He's sent packing, and though Ghana have been denied a goal, they're one penalty kick away from the semis!

120+2 min: GYAN MISSES! Oh, this is heartbreaking for Ghana, as their big striker blooters a dreadful penalty off the top of the crossbar and into orbit. And that's . . .

FULL TIME: Uruguay 1–1 Ghana. It's still going to be settled from the spot, but now Uruguay are in with a chance thanks to their saucy striker. Can you blame him? There's a debate that'll rage, we'll be bound.

11 min: Ramos ghosts past Kuyt down the right and wins a corner. Alonso hits the setpiece long. Villa lashes a volley into the side-netting. This is a strong start by the Spanish.

14 min: Spain stroke it around the back awhile in the slightly sterile tiki-taka style, just because they can. The vuvuzelas are in full voice, all discordant drone and strange modulations. It's like listening to My Bloody Valentine through a cheap transistor radio full of bees.

15 min: We've had Kick-off Ball, now it's time for Kick-off Whistle and Kick-off Cards, as van Persie nearly starts a free-for-all with a ludicrously high challenge on Capdevila. He sees yellow.

17 min: And out comes the yellow again, this time for Puyol, who comes straight through Robben's right foot as he hoofs clear. Sneijder hits the free-kick, from 25 yards out on the right, straight at Casillas.

22 min: Van Bommel is booked, like this is news. He's very late sliding in on Xavi. Holland are meeting tiki-taka with a little bit of kicky-hacka.

24 min: Oh for goodness sake, what are these clowns up to? This is getting ridiculous now: Ramos is booked for upending Kuyt as he ambles down the left. We're just over a quarter of the way through the biggest match in football and already there are four names in the book. Two of those could easily have picked up another card, too.

26 min: Busquets and Sneijder tussle in the middle. Webb is beginning to panic. He could let play go on here, grown adults and all, but opts to nip things in the bud before they get any further out of hand. Let's see how this develops, eh.

28 min: Another yellow card. This is getting very tedious. Especially as this should probably have been a red, de Jong planting his studs in Alonso's chest! It should be noted that Alonso was standing bolt upright at the time, so hats off to de Jong's yoga and martial arts teachers. His anger management guru needs to look in the mirror, though. Spain were three on one down the right, too, so Holland really have got away with that one. Holland, as David Lacey of the *Guardian* once said, seem determined to remind us that 'as well as inventing Total Football, they also invented the clog'.

33 min: In the midst of all this nonsense, some sportsmanship! Puyol requires treatment so Casillas puts the ball out. The Dutch deliver it back once Puyol's patched up – but the ball rears up on the turf, forcing Casillas to tip the viciously arcing ball out for a corner! That was a misjudgement right up there with Gianluca Pagliuca allowing an easy catch to spin out of his hands and on to a post in the 1994 final! Holland take the corner and roll the ball back to Casillas, taking great care this time.

37 min: Robben wins a corner down the right and rolls the ball to van Bommel on the right-hand edge of the area. Mathijsen's heading in from the left. The ball's rolled out to him, but though he's presented with a clear shot at goal, he lets the ball slide under his foot and the chance is gone. That would have been the cleverest goal in World Cup final history.

42 min: Sneijder's studs meet Busquets's thigh. Presumably Webb's yellow card is literally too hot to handle, pocket friction and all that, as the referee doesn't yank it out this time.

HALF TIME: Holland 0–0 Spain. Robben fires a low shot towards the bottom right but Casillas tips round and the corner is wasted. And that, fans of disciplinary measures, is that.

48 min: For Mathijsen earlier, read Capdevila now. He wafts a foot at a Puyol flick-on from a right-hand corner and misses, six yards out.

53 min: All these people from the lands of tiki-taka and Total Football, and everyone's given up, it would seem.

55 min: This is van Bronckhorst's final game as a professional footballer and he's 50 per cent of the way to bowing out like Zinedine Zidane. He picks up a yellow for a blatant block on Ramos.

56 min: Now Heitinga is booked for a late clip on Villa, who probably ensured the yellow card was coming for a fairly inconsequential challenge by playing dead for a few seconds.

58 min: Iniesta is late on Robben and should be booked if the Heitinga foul is anything to go by. Which it is, but Howard Webb appears to be on a mission to fuse the laws of association football with freeform jazz. Holland don't seem particularly happy about this.

60 min: Pedro is replaced by Navas.

62 min: WHAT A MISS!!! The Dutch should be homing in on their first world title! But they're not. Not yet, at any rate.

Sneijder takes down a long goal-kick and slips an instant pass straight down the middle for Robben. He's clear, onside and making good for the area with only Casillas to beat. He waits until the keeper commits – all well and good so far – but chokes as he tries to dink the ball over him and into the unguarded net. No elevation, no goal. Casillas sticks out a leg to deflect the shot over. From the resulting corner, Robben skies a frustrated shot miles over the bar for three rugby points.

67 min: Van Persie breaks down the right. Capdevila breaks van Persie. Yellow.

70 min: ANOTHER TERRIBLE MISS!!! Navas fires a low cross through the Dutch six-yard area from the right. Heitinga ties his legs up in knots as he misses the ball and falls over. Villa is coming in from the left and will meet the cross two yards out with most of the goal gaping but his effort is deflected over the bar by a spectacular reaction save from Stekelenburg, who spreads himself as best he can. For sheer nanosecond-defying ludicrousness, that was up there with Jerzy Dudek's preposterous late palm from Andriy Shevchenko in the 2005 Champions League final. Villa, mind, like Shevchenko before him, needs to have a long hard think about that.

72 min: Kuyt off, Elia on.

77 min: MISS III!!! Villa one-twos with Xavi down the inside left, his deflected shot winning a corner. From which Ramos manages to spam a header over the bar from six yards. This has been an awful final as a spectacle and yet how much more excited we'd be if these three chances had all gone in, which they should have. Who'd be a critic?

83 min: Robben is booked for losing the place at the referee. He's arguing that Puyol had been grappling with him as the pair chased a ball through the middle. Robben nearly managed to poke the ball round Casillas, but under pressure he allowed the keeper to get there first.

86 min: Alonso is replaced by Fàbregas.

89 min: Van Persie rounds Casillas on the right then hits the left-hand post, but this isn't a Rensenbrink '78 moment; he'd been caught miles offside but played on anyway.

FULL TIME: Holland 0–0 Spain. It wasn't much, but that's that.

And so extra time begins. Spain get things moving.

95 min: Another poor miss, though not up there with what's gone before. Fàbregas is sent clear down the centre but his attempt to stroke it into the bottom-right corner is smothered by Stekelenburg.

96 min: Robben wins a corner down the right. The setpiece falls to Mathijsen, six yards out, after the increasingly hapless Fàbregas accidentally blocks his own keeper. The Dutch defender sends the header sailing over. This is ineptitude on a grand scale. Cruyff, Rep and Neeskens must be spitting feathers. As must Torres, still sitting on the bench.

100 min: Van der Vaart replaces de Jong.

101 min: Navas races down the inside-right channel, cuts inside and hits a low shot towards the near post. The ball clanks off van Bronckhorst, who breathes again as it billows the side-netting. The corner is a waste of time.

EXTRA TIME HALF TIME: Holland 0–0 Spain. Van Bronckhorst was replaced by Braafheid before the first period of extra time came to a close. During the turnaround, Torres finally comes on for Villa.

106 min: Braafheid quickly gets up to speed with the silent-movie slapstick stylings, Xavi's cross from the left hitting the back of his head and twanging with perfect comic timing back into the arms of Stekelenburg.

109 min: RED CARD! It had to happen. Heitinga, already booked, is shown a second yellow after dragging Xavi down as the Spanish midfielder made hay down the inside left. He's the fifth player to be dismissed in a World Cup final, after Pedro Monzón and Gustavo Dezotti for Argentina in 1990, Marcel Desailly in 1998 and Zidane last time round.

112 min: Holland don't care now. Van der Wiel is booked for Heitinga-ing Iniesta down the left. Netherlands, word puzzle fans may have noted, is a mere letter A away from being an anagram of Neanderthals.

114 min: Robben should be shown a second yellow for pelting the ball into the Spanish net long after the offside flag had been raised and acknowledged.

115 min: Robben hits a free-kick from 30 yards off the Spanish wall and out on the left for a corner. A goal-kick's given. And what a decision that turns out to be because, with the Dutch going into nuclear meltdown, the play goes up the other end, whereupon . . .

116 min: GOAL!!! Holland 0–1 Spain (Iniesta). Torres guides the ball into the centre from the left. By the D, Fàbregas shuttles it right to Iniesta, who takes one touch and, just as the ball dinks up off the turf a little, creams it into the bottom left! What a glorious finish, totally out of keeping with the rest of the match! He raises his shirt to display a touching tribute to his pal Antonio Puerta, the tragic Sevilla star who died after suffering an on-pitch heart attack back in 2007.

118 min: Mathijsen is booked for crumping the ball into the turf while discussing matters with the linesman, the 14th yellow card of the match. That's adding insult to injury. You can't blame the Dutch for being upset, even though the incorrect award of the goal-kick wasn't in itself the eventual cause of the goal.

120+1 min: As Holland desperately fling crosses into the area, Spain hoick it upfield. Torres chases – and his hamstring snaps! Oh my. Still, he'll be unlikely to feel the pain too much, because . . .

FULL TIME!!! Holland 0–1 Spain. The Spanish have won their first World Cup! On balance they just about deserve that. As Spain change into their trademark red shirts to mount the Full Time Podium for their trophy, van Bommel and Sneijder engage in a steam-powered debate with the officials, a fitting end to this bad-tempered affair. It hasn't quite been up there with the Battle of Santiago, modern football being an altogether softer affair, but it was scrappy enough. The Skirmish of Sun City? So much for the arty classic we were after!

Acknowledgements

We would like to thank: Hugh Barker, Tim Bradford, Becca Allen, Clive Hebard, André Piza, Celso Unzelte, Cassiano Gobbet, Jonathan Wilson, Cris Freddi, Ed Wilson, Mike Gibbons, Jay Jennings, Nicola Barr, Wendy Mitchell, Margaret Murray, Philip Cornwall and James Dart.